MISCELLANEOUS CABELL COUNTY, [WEST] VIRGINIA RECORDS

Order Book
Overseers of the Poor, 1814–1861

Fee Book, 1826–1839

1857–1859 (Rule Book)

Cabell Land for Tax Purposes, 1861–1865

Carrie Eldridge

HERITAGE BOOKS
2015

HERITAGE BOOKS
AN IMPRINT OF HERITAGE BOOKS, INC.

Books, CDs, and more—Worldwide

For our listing of thousands of titles see our website
at
www.HeritageBooks.com

Published 2015 by
HERITAGE BOOKS, INC.
Publishing Division
5810 Ruatan Street
Berwyn Heights, Md. 20740

Heritage Books by the author:

Cabell County's Empire for Freedom

Minute Books: Cabell County, [West] Virginia Minute Book 1, 1809–1815

Miscellaneous Cabell County, West Virginia Records: Order Book Overseers of the Poor, 1814–1861; Fee Book, 1826–1839; 1857–1859 (Rule Book); Cabell Land for Tax Purposes, 1861–1865

Nicholas County, Kentucky Property Tax Lists, 1800–1811 with Indexes to Deed Books A & B (2), and C

Nicholas County, Kentucky Records: Stray Book 1, 1805–1811; Stray Book 2, 1813–1819; Stray Book 3, 1820–1870; and Execution Book A, 1801–1878

Torn Apart: How Cabell Countians Fought the Civil War

International Standard Book Numbers
Paperbound: 978-1-58549-658-7
Clothbound: 978-0-7884-6088-3

TABLE OF CONTENTS

CABELL COUNTY, VA/WV

ORDER BOOK

OVERSEERS OF THE POOR

1814-1861

The Overseers of the Poor were gentlemen and property owners selected by the county court to protect the poor and indigent of the county. They were responsible for setting the Poor Rate and seeing that it was collected. From that Rate, they received a payment for their services and allotted monies to assist persons in need.

This order book covers most of the first fifty years of Cabell County's existence. (the period under Virginia control) This book had not been microfilmed. Since it one of the few "small books" still remaining in the court house basement, I have taken this opportunity to abstract its valuable information.

Carrie Eldridge

1824 CABELL COUNTY

SETTLED AREAS

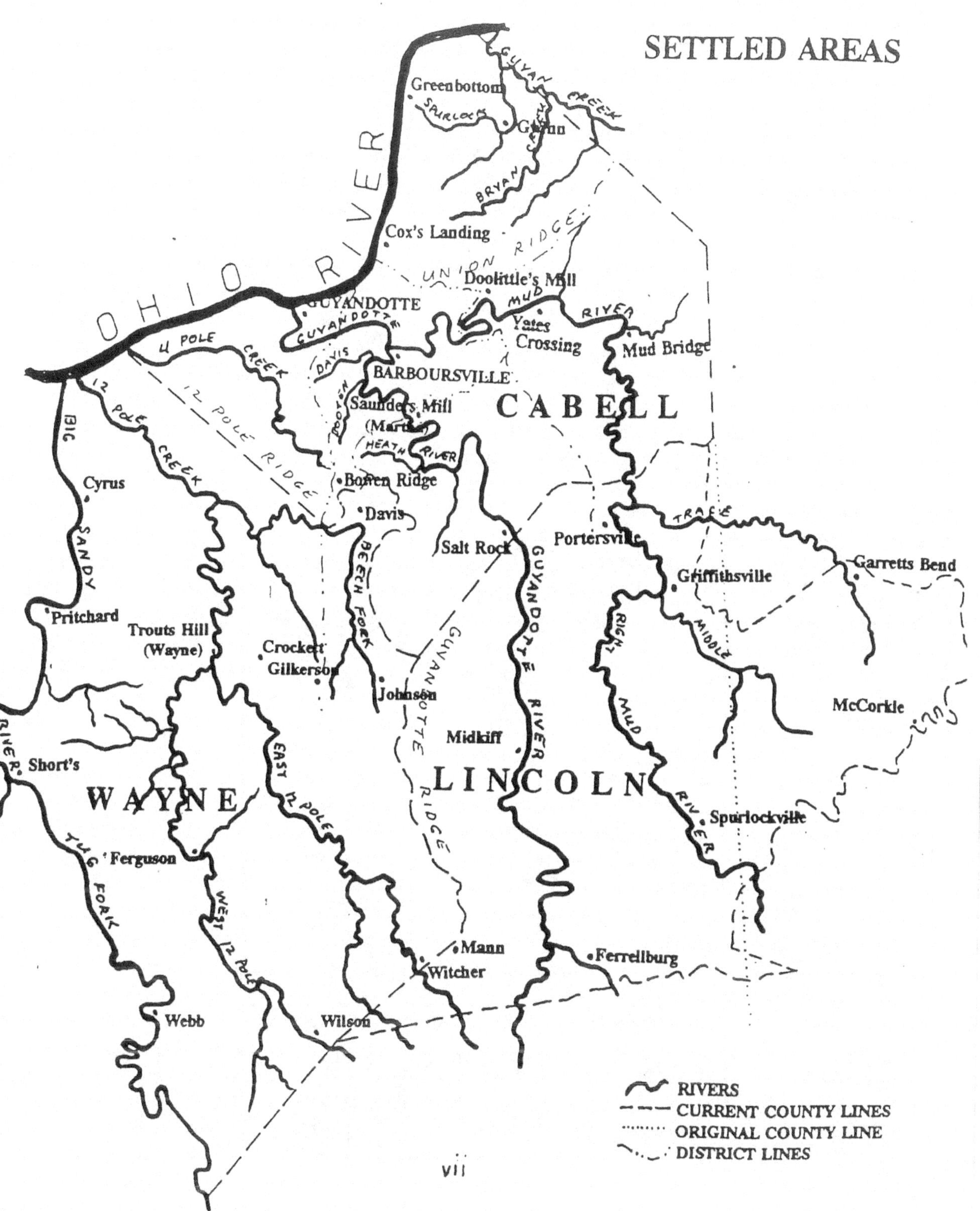

S 55° E 50p 4 feet 6 inches

STREET 60 feet wide

LOT No. 1 MELCHOR STROOP
LOT No. 2 CHARLES CUMMINGS
LOT No. 3 ZACHARIAH ESTILL
LOT No. 4 ESTILL
LOT No. 5 ESTILL
LOT No. 6 ADAM BLACK
LOT No. 7 ADAM BLACK

Alley one Pole wide

S 55° E 18p
JAIL
PUBLIC SQUARE
COURT HOUSE
S 35° W 18p

LOT No. 9 WILLIAM MERRITT
LOT No. 8 JOHN IRWIN
LOT No. 10 JOHN GREEN
LOT No. 11 THOMAS WARD
LOT No. 13 MOSES BRADSHAW
LOT No. 12 JOHN EVERRET

WATER STREET 60 feet wide

CENTER STREET - 60 feet wide

N 35° E 70 poles 1 foot 6 inches

MAIN STREET 60 feet wide

LOT No. 20 SANDERS WITCHER
LOT No. 19 JOHN WARD
LOT No. 18 THOMAS MORRIS
LOT No. 17 WILLIAM MERRITT 6p by 10
LOT No. 16 WILLIAM MERRITT
LOT No. 15 JOHN MORRIS JR.
LOT No. 14

ALLEY ONE POLE WIDE

LOT No. 21 WILLIAM MERRITT
LOT No. 22 WILLIAM MERRITT
LOT No. 27 CUFF CAULWELL
LOT No. 23 BENJAMIN GARRETT 5p by 12
LOT No. 24 JOHN EVERETT
LOT No. 26 JACOB STALEY
LOT No. 25 CUFF CAULWELL

ALLEY ONE POLE WIDE

LOT No. 28 WILLIAM COLLINS
LOT No. 29 PHILIP BAUMGARDNER
LOT No. 34 JOHN IRWIN
LOT No. 30 BEN MAXEY
LOT No. 31 JOSEPH McGONAGLE
LOT No. 33
LOT No. 32 JOSEPH McGONAGLE

LOT No. 35 12p by 3of
LOT No. 36 6p by 3of
LOT No. 37
LOT No. 38

N 55° W 50 poles 4 feet 6 inches

PLAN of TOWN of BARBOURSVILLE

By William Buffington, County Surveyor

LAID out FOR WILLIAM MERRITT

1814

FIRST PROPERTY OWNERS

FACSIMILE OF ORIGINAL MAP

CARRIE ELDRIDGE

CABELL COUNTY, VA/WV

ORDER BOOK, OVERSEERS OF THE POOR 1814-1861

(Punctuation added for clarity- original spelling retained.)

inside front cover "Idiot a fool of nature." 1814
Book No. 1 Overseers of Poor

page 1 - Record Book for the Overseers of Cabell County paid $1.50
(page 1 & 2 have been torn from the book and are in poor condition.)

At a meeting of the Overseers of the Poor at the house of Joseph McGonigal in the county of Cabell on the first Monday of June 1814. Gentlemen present: Jesse Spurlock, Benjamin Brown, Edmund McGinnis, Samuel Smiley who then proceed to examine the exhibited claims which are as followeth:

Ordered that Nathaniel Scales be allowed the sum of $80 for keeping William & Nancy Coxe from the 7th of June 1813 until June 1814.

Also we do order and direct that Richard Brown be allowed $14.21 for making one coffin and other services done for said Nancy Coxe together with other services rendered as one of the former overseers of the poor for the said county which claim is discharged in full by a credit given him to that amount off of a sum of money deposited in his hands as Treasurer to the former Overseers of the Poor.

Ordered that Nancy Lambert be allowed a sum of $5 for keeping and (torn)
(aliane) William Coxe one month.

page 2

Ordered George Spurlock allowed $5 services as former Overseer of the Poor.

Ordered John Russell allowed $2 services as former Overseer of the Poor.

Ordered that Jesse Spurlock, Benjamin Brown $4 each for Tuesday's attendance heretofore as Overseers of the Poor. It is to be understood that the (—) of this order is (clearly) to Confirm a Supplement order made 7th day of June 1813 signed Benjamin Brown.

Ordered that Dr. Benjamin Brown be allowed $35 for administering medicine to Nancy Coxe, deceased, in her last illness.

Ordered $40 for keeping Jamima Roberts one year to 1st Monday June 1815.

Ordered $50 be allowed for keeping and supporting William Coxe from the 1st Monday in June 1815 until the 1st Monday in June 1815

Ordered that Edmund McGinnis Overseer of ---torn---

page 3

Coxe place of residence & keeping for the above time.

Ordered that members of the Board be allowed for their services rendered this meeting the following sums towit: (Jesse) Spurlock, President $2, Samuel Smiley $3, Cadwalder Chapman $2, Edmund McGinnis $1.

Ordered that a contingency of $40 be allowed this present year to be applied by the board of Overseers as they may ( ) direct and necessity require.

Ordered that Jesse Spurlock be appointed Treasurer for the Overseers of the Poor and to receive of the Collector of the Poor Rates for the Year 1814 and to pay such money to such persons until (March).

Ordered that Hugha Bowen be & is hereby appointed Collector of the Poor Rates in the County of Cabell and that he shall immediately proceed to collect off of each Tithable in said County the sum of 33 cents and shall account with the Overseers of the Poor for the (same) and pay the full amount when collected to Jesse Spurlock, President if not otherwise directed and for the full discharge of such duties the said H. Bowen shall enter into bond with the approved security in the ( ) of $500 payable to the said President of the Board aforesaid in behalf of the Overseers of the Poor of the said Court.

E. McGinnis in the name of the whole

page 4

At a Court held in Barboursville by the Overseers of the Poor 17th of October 1814. Present: Jesse Spurlock, President, Edmund McGinnis, Samuel Smiley & Benjamin Brown.

Ordered the clerk of the Overseers of the Poor issue certificates to each claimant. For these respective claims ordered as heretofore which shall be a sufficient voucher for the Collection of the Poor Rates with Overseers of the Poor.

- = ordered

- Edmund McGinnis be allowed $1.75 providing house for William Coxe.

page 5

- Edmund McGinnis $2 for services as clerk protem for Benjamin Brown.
- Benjamin Brown allowed $2 for acting as clerk.
- Jesse Spurlock $1 for superintending the election of the Overseers of Poor.
- Edmund McGinnis $1 for attendance on (Mr. Forst Morre) in October. 1814
- Jesse Spurlock, Edmund McGinnis & Benjamin Brown $1 each for attending general board meeting. Ordered Board be adjourned until 1st Monday in June unless called by the president. Jesse Spurlock, Edmund McGinnis, Samuel Smiley, Benjamin Brown.

page 6

At a meeting of the Overseers of the Poor of Cabell County at the Court House of said County June 5th 1815. Gentlemen present: Jesse Spurlock, Edmund McGinnis, Samuel Smiley, Cadwalder Chapman and Benjamin Brown to examine the exhibited claims.

Ordered Samuel McGinnis be allowed $60 for keeping, victualing and clothing William Coxe from 5th June 1815 until the first Monday 1816. Note: Jesse Spurlock did provide one month for said Coxe and Samuel McGinnis allowed only until May and the rate be $65 per year.

- Benjamin Brown allowed $5 for medical services to William Coxe.

- Samuel Smiley allowed $50 for furnishing Jamima Roberts with meat, drink & clothing and other necessaries of life.
- $20 be allowed for keeping victuals & clothing John Short from 1st Monday in June 1815 until 1st Monday in June 1816.

page 7 - blank

page 8

Ordered that John Hiza be allowed $15 for keeping his daughter from 1st Monday in June 1815 until 1st Monday in June 1816. {Highsey}
- Edmund McGinnis $3.50 for services rendered as member of the Board.
- Samuel Smiley $3 for services rendered.
- Jesse Spurlock & Cadwalder Chapman $2 each for services rendered.
- Collector of the Poor rates collect 25 cents from each County tithable and return such to Jesse Spurlock, President.
- Sheriff of Cabell county be appointed Collector of the Poor Rates.

page 9

Adjournment called: Jesse Spurlock, Benjamin Brown, Samuel Smiley, Cadwalder Chapman, Edmund McGinnis.
- Edmund McGinnis be appointed Clerk of the Board of Overseers of Poor.

Jesse Spurlock, President.

At a meeting of Overseers of the Poor 1st Monday in June 1816. Gentlemen present: Jesse Spurlock, P., Cadwalder Chapman, Edmund McGinnis.

Ordered Edmund McGinnis allowed $6 services rendered.
- Jesse Spurlock allowed $8 services rendered for last year.
- Cadwalder Chapman allowed $3 services rendered.

page 10 1817
- $65 support of William Coxe from this day until the 1st Monday in June 1817.
- $50 be allowed for keeping & support of Jamima Roberts from this day until 1st Monday in June 1817 and that said $50 be paid from the Poor Rates unto Jamima's mother, the wife of Robert Webb.
- that $20 be allowed for keeping John Short from this day until June 1817.

Ordered - a part of the page of the original Record which would shew the meeting held for the year 1817, the clerk was not furnished with as the President took the papers & proceedings of the board previous to the year 1817 and is supposed that he either lost or mislaid that part of the proceedings that ought to be recorded on this page.

page 11

- $20 be allowed for keeping & support of John Short, pauper, from this day until the 1st Monday in June 1818 and the $20 should be paid to his mother Widow Short.
- $15 be allowed and paid to Rudolph Hoozer for keeping his sister, an idiot, from this day until 1st Monday June 1818. {The name was Van Hoose.}

- John Hiza be allowed $15 for keeping his daughter, Bets, until June 1818.
- Jesse Spurlock and Cadwalder Chapman $3 each, services rendered.
- Edmund McGinnis $6 services rendered.
- Acheles Morris allowed $5 for taking care of Hanah Paul.
- 25 cents be collected from each tithable in Cabell County.

page 12

- Board be adjourned until 1st day of October Court. Jesse Spurlock, Cadwalder Chapman, Edmund McGinnis.

At a meeting of the Overseers of the Poor for Cabell County held at the Court House on the 1st Monday in June 1818. Gentlemen Present: Jesse Spurlock, Cadwalder Chapman and Edmund McGinnis.

Ordered Samuel McGinnis be allowed $65 for keeping William Coxe from this day until the 1st Monday of June 1819.

- $50 be allowed for keeping Jamima Roberts until 1st Monday of June 1819.
- $15 for support of Rudolph Hoozers sister until 1st Monday of June 1819.
- $15 for support of John Hiza's daughter. until 1st Monday June 1819.

page 13

- Dr. Thomas Collens $3 for medicine for the relief of William Coxe, a pauper.
- that 21 cents be collected from each tithable in Cabell County.
- Jesse Spurlock $4, services rendered.
- Cadwalder Chapman $5, services rendered. 1818
- Edmund McGinnis $6, services rendered.

Adjourned until November Court. J. Spurlock, C. Chapman, E. McGinnis. 1st June 1819.

page 14

At a meeting of the Overseers of the Poor 1st Monday in June 1819. Gentlemen present: Jesse Spurlock, Cadwalder Chapman, Joseph Barrett and Edmund McGinnis.

Ordered $50 for the support of Jamima Roberts until 1st Monday in June 1820.

- $70 for Keeping William Coxe until 1st Monday in June 1820 to be paid by the Collector of Poor Rates to Samuel McGinnis.
- $15 for support of Rudolph Hooze's sister - June 1820.
- $15 for keeping Betsy Hiza - June 1820
- Jesse Spurlock $8, services rendered for 1818.

page 15

- Cadwalder $3, services rendered for 1818.
- Joseph Barrett & E. McGinnis $6 each, services rendered for 1818.
- Sheriff of Cabell County collect Poor Rate of 25 cents of each tithable.
- $20 for the support of an anonymous foundling from 1th of last March until 1st Monday in June 1820 to be paid by Joseph Barrett as Overseer of the Poor.

- Jesse Spurlock, President of the Board of the Overseers of the Poor, calls a meeting of the several Sheriffs & collectors of the Poor as far back as 1816 to render proper vouchers.

page 16

- David Patten allowed $5 for keeping aforesaid annonomous child.
- Adjourned until 1st Monday of June 1820. Edmund McGinnis, clerk.

At a meeting of the Overseers of the Poor on the 1st Monday of June 1820. Gentlemen present: Cadwalder Chapman, Joseph Barrett, John Wellman, Edmund McGinnis proceeded to adjust the Poor Rates.

Ordered that $50 be allowed to keep Jamima Roberts until the 1st Monday in June 1821 and that Collector is to turn over said sum to John Wellman who is to divide the sum into four parts and pay out quarterly to a person who undertakes to keep said pauper upon the best terms.

- $15 allowed for keeping Rindolpp Hoozer's sister until 1st Monday on June 1821 and sum is to be paid to John Wellman or keeper of said pauper in one amount.

page 17

Ordered $70 allowed for keeping William Coxe, pauper until 1st Monday of June 1821 to be paid to the person who will keep on best terms.

- $15 allowed for keeping Betsy Hizer until 1st Monday June 1821, etc. 1820
- $10 allowed Mrs. Clark who is sorely afflicted with cataracts on both eyes.
- $12 allowed for support of Thomas Sanders Ward until 1st Monday in June 1821 and that sum be taken from Poor Rates and paid to Milly Ward, mother of pauper.
- Edmund McGinnis $10, services rendered as clerk.
- John Wellman, Cadwalder Chapman & Joseph Barrett $4 each, for attendance as Overseers of the Poor in 1819.

page 18

- Edmund McGinnis selected as President of the Board of Overseers of the Poor.
- Sheriff to collect Poor Rate of 18 cents of each County tithable.
- President to meet with Collector of Rates to settle all accounts for 1816.
- Adjourned until 1st Monday in June 1821. Edmund McGinnis, Clerk.

page 19

At a meeting of the Overseers of the Poor held at the Court House on the 4th of June 1821. Present: Cadwalder Chapman, Joseph Barrett, John Wellman and Edmund McGinnis. Proceed to examine claims in relation to the poor of Cabell County.

- James Gray be allowed $26 for keeping & clothing a woman named Ferguson.
- Samuel McGinnis $70 for keeping William Coxe until 1st Monday in June 1822.
- $50 allowed for supporting Jamima Roberts to 1st Monday in June 1822.
- $10 allowed Reoodolph Hoger for keeping his sister until 1st Monday June 1822.
- John Hiza allowed $10 for keeping his daughter until 1st Monday in June 1822.
- John Brown allowed $25 to support his mother until 1st Monday in June 1822.

page 20

- $5 is allowed Martin (Busad) to support his family.
- $25 allowed Martin (Busad) to keep his mother until 1st Monday in June 1822.
- Joseph Barrett $7, services rendered 1820.

- John Wellman $6, services rendered 1820.
- Cadwalder Chapman $4, services rendered 1820.
- Edmund McGinnis $10, services as clerk for 1820.
- Sheriff to collect Poor Rate of 25 cents.
- Adjourned until 1st Monday in June 1822. Edmund McGinnis, Clerk.

page 21

At a Meeting of the Board of the Overseers of the Poor at the Court House on the 1st Monday in June 1822. Present: John Wellman, Cadwalder Chapman, Joseph Barrett and Edmund McGinnis who examined claims exhibited.

- $75 allowed for support of William Coxe until 1st Monday in June 1823.
- Rudolph Hoozer $15 to support his sister until 1st Monday in June 1823. 1822
- John Everett Jr. allowed $5 which he paid to Rudolph Hoozer for 1821.

page 22

- John Hiza allowed $10 to keep his daughter, Betsy, to 1st Monday in June 1823.
- Martin Busard allowed $20 for keeping his mother, the same as last year.
- John Brown allowed $25 to support his mother until 1st Monday in June 1823.
- $20 allowed to keep David Withrow until 1st Monday in June 1823.
- John Wellman allowed $35 for attending Randolph Marcum for 16 days and burying him in a Christian like manner.
- Josiah Marcum allowed $15 for attending his son Randolph Marcum, sum to be paid by Collector to John Wellman and by him as necessary.
- $10 be refunded Hugha Bowen for the Widow Short's claim of 1817.
- Joseph Barrett and John Wellman $6 for services rendered 1821.

page 23

- Cadwalder Chapman $4, services rendered 1821.
- Edmund McGinnis $10 services rendered and as clerk, Overseers of Poor 1821.
- Sheriff to collect Poor rates for 1822.
- 25 cents to be collected of each tithable.
- Adjourned until 1st Monday in June 1823. Edmund McGinnis for all.

page 24

At a meeting of the Overseers of the Poor at the Court House on the 1st Monday in June 1823. Present: John Wellman, William Spurlock, William Brumfield, Cadwalder Chapman and Edmund McGinnis.

- Edmund McGinnis is chosen as clerk.
- Edmund McGinnis is also chosen President of the Board.
- Stephen Marcum allowed $7 for his service to Randolph Marcum before his decease and Jacob Marcum allowed $13.50 for services to Randolph during his last illness.
- Dr. Spangler allowed $40 for medicine and visits to Andrew Cooper during his illness at Joseph Garrett's and also while at Robert Cooper's in 1822.
- Robert Cooper allowed $40 for lodging and attending Andrew Cooper at his own house for eleven weeks during his illness in 1822 which same is for the comfort of A. (Holderby).

page 25

- William Wassons allowed $14 for keeping Molly Adkins from the 19th of February until the present.
- $50 allowed for the support of Molly Adkins until the 1st Monday in June 1824.
- $10 allowed for sister to Roodolph Hoozer, an idiot and pauper, until 1st Monday in June 1824.
- $10 allowed for support of Elisabeth Hozer until 1st of June 1824.
- $20 allowed for support of David Withrough until 1st Monday in June 1824.
- Richard O. Everett $1.69 for attending James Dunlap on behalf of Overseers of Poor.
- $75 allowed for keeping William Coxe until 1st Monday in June 1824.
- Joseph Barrett $7, services rendered in 1822.

page 26

- Frances Stowers allowed $20 for keeping infant child of Sarah Blankenship from November 1822 until 1st Monday in June 1824.
- Cadwalder Chapman $4, services rendered 1822.
- William Spurlock $2.25 for a winding sheet for the body of a dead man in 1818- (at end of line) Buckels
- William Spurlock $4, attendance as Overseer of Poor.
- William Brumfield $2, for attendance.
- John Wellman, $7, services rendered 1822.
- $20 allowed Edmund McGinnis, for services 1822 and as clerk 1824.
- Sheriff charged to collect Poor Rate of 37 1/2 cents.

page 27

- Edmund McGinnis allowed $1.50 for record book. { This book.}

- Ordered that the former records of the Overseers of the Poor from the year 1814 to the present be recorded in the new book and that the old records be kept safely by the Clerk of the Board.

- Adjourned until 1st Monday in June 1824. Edmund McGinnis, Pres., Cadw. Chapman, William Spurlock, Wm. Brumfield.

At a meeting of the Overseers of the Poor at the house of Joseph Garden in the town of Barboursville on the 1st Monday in June 1824. Gentlemen present: John Wellman, William Spurlock, William Brumfield, Cadwalder Chapman and Edmund McGinnis.

page 28

- $10 allowed Davis for keeping Abraham Millard & his wife Susanah.
- Floyd Turley allowed $50 for his support until the first Monday in June 1825 which sum shall be paid to Turley or his creditors in 3 different payments by William Brumfield.
- Polly Adkins allowed $50 support until the 1st Monday in June 1825 provided she lives to that period and in the event of her death an amount as needed.
- $10 allowed Reudolph Hoozer to support of his sister to 1st Monday June 1825.

- John Hiza allowed $10 to support his daughter, Elizabeth, June 1825. 1824
- $20 allowed David Withrow until 1st Monday in June 1825.
- $75 allowed for keeping William Coxe until 1st Monday in June 1825 to be paid to Margaret McGinnis if she takes care of the pauper.
- $10 allowed for support of Susannah (torn --ager) , an old crippled woman to be laid out at her request by John Wellman. {Frazier}

page 29

- Cadwalder Chapman $6, services rendered 1823.
- William Spurlock $8, services rendered 1823.
- John Wellman $20, services 1823.
- William Brumfield $14, services rendered 1823.
- $24 allowed Edmund McGinnis services rendered 1823 and as clerk 1824.
- 37 1/2 cents to be collected for the Poor Rate by Sheriff.
- Adjourned until 1st Monday in June next. Edmund McGinnis, John Wellman, William Spurlock, Cadwd. Chapman, Wm. Brumfield. {actual signatures}

page 30

At a meeting of the Overseers of the Poor on the 1st Monday in June 1825 at the Court House. Present: John Wellman, William Brumfield, William Spurlock, Thomas McCallister and Edmd. McGinnis.

- Charles W. Drechsler allowed $2.81 1/4 cents and 9 mills for furnishing clothing to a poor boy named Daniel(s).
- $55 allowed to Floyd Turley for his support until 1st Monday of June 1826 to be paid in 3 installments. $11.14 paid to Turley.
- $10 to Rudolph Hoozer to support his sister until 1st Monday in June 1826.
- $10 allowed John Hiza to support his daughter, Betsy an idiot, until 1st Monday in June 1826.

page 31

- Jeremiah Lambert is allowed $20 for supporting David Withrow until 1st Monday in June 1826 and we, the board members of the Overseers of the Poor pledge that Lambert shall have the said pauper for 1826 & 1827 at $15 support per year.
- Susana Frazer allowed $10 for her support until 1st Monday in June 1826.
- $15 allowed for support of Nancy Clark until 1st Monday in June 1826.
- $20 allowed for support of an aged woman by the name of Blue, the mother-in-law of Iseral Heath until 1st Monday in June 1826.
- $20 to support William Patterson & wife until 1st Monday in June 1826.
- John Thompson allowed $7 for boarding a boy named Daniel Bogus for 14 days from the 1st to the 14th of March 1825.

page 32

- Claim of John Thompson for boarding William Henry be registered.
- The account of Dr. Louis Spangler of $7 for administrating medicine to William

Coxe, a pauper in the management of Margaret McGinnis be registered.

- John Ward allowed $15 for supporting Polly Knite & child from 20th December 1824 until 6 June 1825.
- $5 allowed for support of Polly Knite until the 1st Monday in June 1826.
- $25 allowed Dr. Spangular for medical administration to Daniel Bogus.
- Richard O. Everett $10 for interning the body of Richard Vernon in 1824.
- Edmund McGinnis $6, services rendered 1824.
- Edmund McGinnis $20 for services as clerk of Board 1825.

page 33

- $10 allowed William Brumfield for keeping 2 children of Betsy (Snap- Sneff ?) for 5 months in 1824. {Snell}
- William Brumfield allowed $22 for 11 days services rendered 1824.
- John Wellman $20 for 10 days services rendered 1824.
- William Spurlock $10 for 5 days services rendered 1824.
- $4 allowed Thomas McCallister for attending meetings.
- Sheriff to collect Poor Rate of 25 cents from each tithable.
- Adjourned until 1st Monday in June 1826 unless called. Edmd. McGinnis, John Wellman, Wm. Brumfield, William Spurlock, Thomas McCallister.

page 34

At a meeting of the Overseers of the Poor for Cabell County at the Court House on the 1st Monday in June 1826. Present: John Wellman, William Brumfield, Patrick Keenan, John Ferguson and Edmund McGinnis.

-Rudolph Hoozer allowed $20 to keep his sister, an idiot and a pauper of this county, until the 1st Monday in June 1827.

-$10 allowed John Hiza to support his daughter, an idiot and a pauper of this county, until the 1st Monday in June 1827.

- Floyd Turley allowed $50 for his support until 1st Monday in June 1827.
- Jeremiah Lambert allowed $15 to keep David Withrow, a blind white pauper, until 1st Monday in June 1827.

page 35 This page shews cost & expense of Paupers from year 1813 to year 1825 inclusive.

1813-1825		total $923.70	
1815	Jamima Roberts for 8 years	390.00	
1815	Nancy Coxe for 1 year		59.21
1814	John Short for 4 years		80.00
1820	Thomas S. Ward for 1 year		12.00
1821	Mrs. — Ferguson for 1 year	26.00	
1822	John Brown's mother for 1 year		25.00
1823	Randle Marcum for 1 year		35.00
1823	Molly Adkins for 2 years		102.00

page 36 - blank

page 37

- $15 allowed for the support of Nancy Clark until 1st Monday of June 1827, in consideration of catteracts on both eyes.

-William Patterson allowed $5 to buy necessaries of life until June 1827, subject to the orders of (Col.) Thomas McCallister.

- $20 allowed Milly Ward to defray necessary expenses until June 1827, sum will be handed over to any person that will convey her to her Brothers and friends in Pyttsilvania County.

- $15 allowed for support of --- Blue, Mother-in-law of (Iearcle) Heath until 1st Monday in June 1827. {Israel}

- $20 allowed for support of Thomas Loe until 1st Monday in June 1827.

page 38

- John Wellman allowed $10 to pay Moses Dameral for expenses he had keeping Thomas Loe since December 1825.

- Edmund Ausbern allowed $30 for supporting his mother, a blind woman of about 90 years old until 1st Monday in June 1827. {Osburn}

$10 allowed for support of Catherine King, daughter of Jesse (McCoin)until 1st Monday in June 1827 and that sum be paid to Jesse McComas for his to purchase necessaries required.

- Thomas McCallister, $4.50 services rendered.

- $10 allowed John Ward, keeping Polly Knit's child for one year ending today.

- Exhibit from Robert Holderby: Alexander Catlett allowed $10 for supporting James Johnson(a sick man off a steam boat) for one month August 13th 1825.

page 39

- $15 allowed Dr. James S. Hepburn, it being part of his account of $29.50 for medical rendered James Johnson, a sick man off a steam boat on 13th of August 1825.

- President of the Board is to meet with the several sheriffs and former presidents and settle all claims and vouchers of the Overseers of the Poor.

- John Hiza to be paid $10 for claim of 1822 which was unpaid.

- Edmund McGinnis be paid $20 for services as clerk in 1826.

page 40

- Edmund McGinnis $10 for services rendered 1825.

- William Brumfield $14, services rendered 1825.

- John Wellman $20, services rendered 1825.

- William Spurlock $18, services rendered 1825.

- Patrick Keenan $4, services rendered.

- John Ferguson $10, services rendered.

- Sheriff to collect Poor Rate of .374 cents.

page 41

- Board adjourned until 1st Monday in June 1827. John Wellman, Wm. Brumfield, John Ferguson, P. Keenan, Edmd. McGinnis

- 37 1/4 cents be collected of each tithable for the poor Rate.

- Board adjourned until the 1st Monday in June 1827. John Wellman, Wm. Brumfield,

John Ferguson, P. Keenan, Edmd. McGinnis.

At a meeting of the Overseers for the Poor at the Court House 1st Monday in June 1827. Present: Patrick Keenan, William Brumfield, John Wellman, John Ferguson, Edmund McGinnis and William Spurlock.

- Rudolph Hoozer allowed $30 for keeping his sister, an idiot, until 1st Monday in June 1828.
- $15 allowed John Hizes for keeping his daughter, Elizabeth, until June 1828.

page 42

- $50 allowed Floyd Turley for his support until June 1828.
- $15 allowed Jeremiah Lambert for keeping David Withrow until June 1828.
- Nancy Clark allowed $15 support until June 1828.
- William Patterson allowed $5 for his use until June 1828.
- $20 allowed Widow Blue for her support until June 1828.
- $30 allowed for support of Thomas Loe until June 1828.
- $50 to Edmund (Ausbern) for keeping his mother & daughter until June 1828.
- $14 to Dr. James S. Hepburn for medical services rendered Jane Woods in 1826, for the benefit of Solomon Thornburg.

page 43

- Nathaniel Scales $10 for attending and interning body of Robert Lewis a poor man of this county having no property of his own.
- E. Wellington $5 for making coffin for Robert Lewis who departed this life in the month of April 1827.
- Joseph Turner $8 for keeping Robert Lewis for 2 months.
- $20 allowed John (Morego) for supporting Mr. Broom for 14 days and interning his body at his decease.
- $9 to Paul Davis for keeping a young child for 3 months from March 1827.
- Dr. Edward Jones $4.87 for attending a sick child.

page 44

- Frances Stowers $6 for boarding a poor old man March last past.
- George W. Gardner $3 for apprehending Hugh Bowen and Greenville Rigs by virtue of a warrant from the Justices of the Peace on instance of Overseers. [Men were sheriff & deputy]
- $10 allowed for support of Susan Frazer until June 1828, order/John Wellman.
- $20 allowed William Cox for his support until June 1828, order/John Wellman.
- $30 for support of Robert Forth to be paid to (Abiah Kin/Kerr) for use of Forth.

page 45

- $10 to Edmund McGinnis for services as 1 of Overseers of Poor 1826.
- $20 to Edmund McGinnis as clerk of Board.
- $4 to Patrick Keenan as 1 of Overseers of Poor.
- $16 to William Spurlock for services as Overseer of Poor.
- $20 to John Wellman for services as Overseer of Poor.

- John Ferguson $12 for his services to the Poor.
- William Brumfield $10 for his services for the Poor.

page 46

- 31 1/4 cents to be collected as the Poor Rate for 1827.
- Board adjourned until 1st Monday in June 1828. Edmd. McGinnis, clk.
  P. Keenan, John Wellman, Wm. Brumfield, John Ferguson, William Spurlock.

At a meeting of the Overseers of the Poor of Cabell County on the 1st Monday in June 1828. Present: William Buffington, John Wellman, John Ferguson, Patrick Keenan, William Spurlock, William Brumfield.

- William Buffington appointed President of the Board.
- Patrick Keenan appointed clerk in place of Edmund McGinnis who has removed from this Commonwealth.

page 47

- Daniel Gallidahe $7.50 for the benefit of Persevill Smith for keeping a base born infant for 6 months.
- Joshua Willis $10 for keeping a base born child named Joseph Gates, 5 months.
- James Snodgrass allowed $15 for keeping Sally Snell, a base born child, 10 months last past.
- Rudolph Hoozer allowed $30 for keeping his sister, an idiot, until June 1829.
- John Hizer $10 for support of his daughter Elizabeth until June 1829.
- Floyd Turley allowed $50 for support until 1st Monday in June 1829.
- Nancy Clark allowed $7.50 support until June 1829.

page 48

- William Patterson allowed $7.50 for his use until June 1829.
- Widow Blue allowed $20 support until June 1829.
- Edmund Ausburn allowed $50 for keeping his mother & daughter to June 1829.
- Susannah Frazer allowed $10 fro support until June 1829, subject to control of John Wellman.
- William Clark allowed $15 support until June 1829.
- Martin Hollenback & wife allowed $30 for support until June 1829.
- Dr. John Talbot $25 for medical services in care of Harvey Lusher, an infant.

page 49

- Joseph Fulkerson $8 for superintending an election of the Overseers of the Poor in the South West District with Hugh Bowen deputy (sheriff).
- Sheriff allowed $15.37, the amount he paid out over what was collected in 1827.
- Rudolph Hoozer allowed $30 for keeping his sister in 1827 as there was not funds to pay him at that time.
- John Furgeson $21 for his expenditures as one of Overseers.
- xx John Wellman $13 for his expenditures. xx
- William Brumfield allowed $6 for his expenditures.

page 50

- William Buffington $2 for his expenditures as an Overseer.
- William Spurlock $6 for his expenditures.
- Patrick Keenan $6 for his expenditures.
- Collector of Poor Rates to collect 34 3/4 cents of each of the taxables in the County for Poor Rate for 1828.
- P. Keenan, clerk of the Board, to certify a true copy of this days preceding within thirty days with a list of expenditures to the Clerk of the County Court.

page 51

- P. Keenan $20 for services as Clerk of Board for 1828.
- Board adjourned. P. Keenan, John Ferguson, Wm. Brumfield, William Spurlock, John Wellman, Wm. Buffington.

page 52 - blank

page 53

At a meeting of the Overseers of the Poor for Cabell County in the Courthouse on the 1st Monday in June 1829. Present: John Samuels, John Spurlock, William Brumfield, James Galliher, Abia Reace, Littleberry Adkins.

- John Samuels appointed President of the Board.
- Floyd Turley allowed $30 for his support until 1st Monday in June next, subject to control of John Samuels.
- Edmund Ausbourn $25 for support of his Mother until June 1830.
- Martin Hollenback & wife allowed $30 support until June 1830.
- James Snodgrass $5.25 for keeping Sally Snell, a base born child, for 3/12 months.
- James Pinnell $1.89 for executing warrant to summon 6 witnesses for Overseers.
- Joshua Willis $21.25 for keeping a child named Joseph Gates 34 weeks, 2 days.

page 54

- Dr. John Talbott $13.37 1/2 for attending Samuel Butcher in his last illness.
- Paul Davis $6.87 1/2 for keeping an infant child of Elizabeth Davis for 11 weeks.
- Sheriff allowed $12.76 for Levy last year.
- Each member of the Board allowed $1 for attendance this day.
- P. Keenan $5 for making out report under the Law of 1829.
- P. Keenan $6 for services as clerk.
- (Previous 2 orders transferred to Joseph Gardner.)
- Poor Rate of 14 cents in specie to be collected of each tithable in 1829.
- Board adjourned until 1st Monday in June next.

page 55

John Samuels, Jas. Gallaher, Abia Rece, Wm. Brumfield, Little Berry Adkins, John Spurlock. {actual signatures}

At a meeting of the Overseers of the Poor of Cabell County at the Courthouse on Monday the 7th day of June 1830. Present: John Samuels Pres., Wm. Brumfield, Littleberry Adkins, James Gallaher, Abia Rece, John Spurlock.

- P. Keenan being necessarily absent from this meeting, John Samuels is appointed clerk protem.

- $40 for support of Floyd Turley until June next, subject to control to John Samuels.
- Edmund Ausburn allowed $50 for support of his mother & daughter, part of which money is to get necessary bedding for the paupers

page 56

- Catherine Hollenback allowed $20 for her support until June 1831.
- $20 allowed for support of Dinah Hoozer, subject to control of John Spurlock.
- Nancy Ann Clark allowed $15 support until June 1831.
- John Highsey $10 for support of his daughter Elizabeth until June next.
- $30 allowed for support of Thomas Noe, under control of Littleberry Adkins, Sr. who is furnish him a home.
- Susannah Frazier allowed $15 support until June next, subject to control of Littleberry Adkins Sr.
- Samuel Webb allowed $15 for supporting Levina Frazier & her youngest child until the 7th of December next.

page 57

- $15 support for Polly Walker, John Samuels is to get her a home until next June.
- $20 allowed for support of Polly Thacker & her child, control Wm. Brumfield.
- $20 to support (Jane) Forth until June next, should said Jane be (remarried) before the expiration of time residue of support to return, control to Abia Rece.
- Samuel Griffiths $6 for keeping Jane Forth for 2 months.
- James Gallaher $9.41 for expenses for last year.
- Dr. Archibald McLewskey for his attendance on St Clair & Brummell $35.
- To Ch. W. Smith for keeping same $22.
- Isaac Bloss $3.08 expenses.
- John Samuels $1.34 costs against Overseers.
- John Russell $30.12 1/2 for keeping sundry paupers and for coffin shroud & gown & grave clothes.

page 58

- Dr. Jas. H. Hereford $10 for attending James Halsey in his last illness.
- $1 to each of the Overseers for attendance.
- Wm. Fullerton, sheriff of Cabell, allowed $2.50 for deficiency of levy last year.
- Clerk of Board $6 for services.
- 37 1/2 cents to be collected of each tithable to defray cost of Parish Levy.
- Board adjourned. John Samuels, Abia Rece, James Gallaher, John Spurlock, William Brumfield, Littleberry Adkins.

page 59

At a meeting of the Overseers of the Poor of Cabell County at the house of A. Holderby on Monday 6th of June 1831. Present: John Spurlock, Wm. Brumfield, Littleberry Adkins, James Galleher.

- Floyd Turley allowed $40 for support until next June, order to John Samuels.
- Edmund Ausborn allowed $25 for support of his daughter until next June.

- Catherine Hollenback allowed $20 support until next June.
- Jane Ann Clark allowed $15 support until next June 1832.
- John Hiza allowed $10 support for his daughter Elizabeth until next June.
- Littleberry Adkins allowed $50 for supporting Thomas Noe until June 1832.

page 60

- Susannah Frazier allowed $15 support until next June, order to John Welman.
- William Clark, Sr. allowed $15 until June 1832.
- Roda Vincent $7 for expense & trouble for burying orphan child last April.
- $50 allowed to Mrs. Rachel Donnathan for keeping 2 young men for the last eleven months, one a cripple and one subject to fits.
- Rachel Donnathan allowed $40 to keep the same young men until next June.
- Joseph Robertson $6.50 for keeping Sabby Cox, a cripple, 31 days.
- Elizabeth Tally allowed $25 support for herself and children until next June.

page 61

- Harvey Garrett $2.25 for burying clothes for (overwritten) (H-S--iah) Harris.
- John Ward allowed $8.75 for expense of burying Polly Night, to go to the benefit of Rowling Byas, Jr.
- John Merritt $7.50 for making 3 coffins for poor persons.
- $50 allowed for support of Jane Fourth until next June, order to Abiah Reace.
- James Pinnell $2.75 for hauling and burying boddy of ----Hart.
- Samuel Short $15 for keeping poor man for 3 months.
- Elizabeth Frasure allowed $17 for keeping Levina Frazure for 4 months.

page 62

- Each of the overseers of the Poor allowed $1 for today's attendance.
- Poor Rate of 31 1/4 to be collected of each tithable for Parish Levy.
- P. Keenan $6 for services as clerk.
- John Samuels appointed commissioner to settle with sheriff.
- Board adjourned until 1st Monday in June next. John Samuels, Wm. Brumfield, John Spurlock, Abia Rece, Littleberry Adkins.

page 63

At a meeting of the Overseers of the Poor for Cabell County at the house of John Merritt in the town of Barboursville on Monday the 4th of June 1832. Present: John Samuels, Stephen Spurlock, Jesse Toney.

- Stephen Spurlock appointed president of the board.
- Floyd Turley allowed $40 until next June.
- Edmund Ausburn allowed $20 to support his daughter until next June.
- Catherine Hollenback allowed $20 support until next June.
- Jane Ann Clark allowed $20 support until next June.
- Littleberry Adkins allowed $60 to support Thomas Noe until next June.

page 64

- Micager Frazieur & wife allowed $30 support until next June.

- William Clark, Sr. allowed $20 support until next June.
- Rachal Donnathan allowed $40 to support Harben & Marmaduke Wells.
- Elizabeth Tally allowed $25 to support herself & children until next June.
- $50 allowed to keep Jane Forth until next June.
- Elizabeth Sexton allowed $20 to support her son James.
- Old Mrs. Cooper allowed $15 support until next June.

page 65

- James Johnston $1.50 for burying infant child.
- Each of the Overseers of the Poor $1 for today's attendance.
- P. Keenan $6 as clerk. (Benefit of order to S. Thornburg)
- Sheriff to collect 31 1/4 of each tithable for benefit of the poor.
- John Samuels appointed to settle with sheriff.
- Board adjourned until 1st Monday in June next. Stephen Spurlock, John Samuels, Jesse Toney.

page 66 blank

page 67

At a meeting of the Overseer of the Poor for Cabell County at the Clerk's Office on Monday the 3rd of June 1833. Present: John Samuels, Stephen Spurlock, Allen McGinnis, Daniel Love, Jesse Toney.

- Floyd Turley allowed $40 support until next June.
- Edmund Ausburn allowed $25 to keep his daughter, Hulda, until next June.
- Littleberry Adkins allowed $66 to keep Thomas Noe until June 1834.
- Catherine Hollenback allowed $20 support until June 1834.
- Jane Ann Clark allowed $20 support until June 1834.
- Micajer Frasure & wife allowed $30 support until June 1834.

page 68

- William Clark allowed $30 support until June 1834.
- Moses Wells allowed $40 to support his 2 sons until June 1834.
- Elizabeth Tally allowed $25 to keep her 2 infant children until June 1834.
- Samuel Griffith allowed $66 to keep Jane Forth until next June.
- Elizabeth Saxton allowed $20 to support her son James until next June.
- Mrs. Cooper allowed $20 support until next June.
- Samuel Griffith allowed an additional $10 for keeping Jane Forth in 1830 and $16 for 1832.

page 69

- Asher Crocket allowed $12 for keeping an infant child 11 months.
- Jesse Low allowed $20 support until June 1834.
- Paul Davis allowed $25 for keeping Mrs. Gilkison-Grisham)(overwritten) for 8 months last past.
- Windon Emmons $4 for making coffin for Joseph Huller.
- Each of the Overseers $1 for attending annual meeting.
- Clerk $10 for present year.

- Poor Rate of 37 1/2 cents be collected to defray cost of publick levy.

- Sheriff to pay from the collected levy to Stephen Spurlock(one of the Overseers of the Poor) $181 to pay parish claims of Edmund Osburn, Littleberry Adkins, Micajah Frazier & wife, Moses Wells, Jesse Low & his own claim of $1.

page 70

- Sheriff to pay Jesse Toney $133 for claims of Catherine Hollenback, William Clark, Elizabeth Talley, Mrs. Cooper, Asher Crockett, Paul Davis & his claim of $1.
- Sheriff to pay Daniel Love $113 to pay claims of Samuel Griffiths, Elizabeth Sexton & his claim of $1.
- Sheriff to pay Allen McGinnis $75 to pay claims of Floyd Turley, Jane Ann Clark, Windon Emmons, Patrick Keenan & his claim of $1.
- Sheriff to pay John Samuels $1.

page 71

- John Samuels appointed to settle with the sheriff or sheriffs who may be in arrear & have failed to settle with the Overseers for the last 2 or 3 years.
- Board adjourn until 1st Monday in June 1834. Stephen Spurlock, Daniel Love, Jesse Toney, John Samuels, Allen A. McGinnis.

page 72

At a meeting of the Overseer of the Poor for Cabell County called by the President this 28th day of October 1833. Present: Stephen Spurlock, Jesse Toney, Allen McGinnis.

- Patrick Keenan, the former clerk of the Board, has removed from this county and it is ordered that John Samuels be appointed clerk of this Board. {Samuels was also the Cabell County clerk.}

- Stephen Spurlock to make favorable contract with some person to keep 3 children named Porter until next annual meeting.
- Jesse Toney to make contract with someone to keep Betsey Highsey, an idiot, until next annual meeting.

page 73

- Board adjourned. Stephen Spurlock, Jesse Toney, Allen McGinnis, John Samuels.

At a meeting of the Overseers of the Poor on Monday 2nd day of June 1834. Present: Stephen Spurlock President, Jesse Toney, Daniel Love, Abraham Syrus, Allen McGinnis, John Samuels.

- $40 allowed for support of Arthur Floyd Turley & his family, order to John Samuels, funds are not to be paid on Turley's debts.
- Edmund Osturn $25 for keeping his daughter Hulda until next June.
- Jane Ann Clark allowed $25 for support until next June.
- Micajah Frazier & wife allowed $30 support until next June.

page 74

- William Clark allowed $30 support until next June.
- $40 allowed to support 2 sons of Moses Wells until next June.

- Elizabeth Sexton allowed $20 to support her son James until next June.
- $25 allowed for support of Sally Cooper until next June.
- $30 allowed for support of Jesse Low until next June.
- Henry Miller allowed $18 for keeping Betsey Highsey, an idiot, from 1st of December until today.
- Henry Miller allowed $35 to keep Betsey Highsey until next June.
- Samuel Hunter allowed $40 for keeping John & William Porter, 2 infant children, from 1st of September last until today.
- $40 allowed to keep John & William Porter until next June or until time taken away if before that time.

page 75

- Jesse Adkins allowed $10 for keeping Peggy Eplin, an infant, 6 months last past.
- $20 to keep Peggy Eplin until next June or at that rate until it shall be taken away.
- Joshua Henwood allowed $20 to aid in supporting him & his family until next June.
- Catherine Donathan allowed $25 for keeping and infant child named Alderson Wells for the last 6 months.
- $30 allowed to keep Alderson Wells until next June.
- $10 allowed toward support of Lewis Conrad until next June.
- $25 allowed for keeping Rebecca West until next June.
- $15 allowed for support of Samuel Stuck, control to Jesse Toney.
- Susannah Webb allowed $25 support until next June.
- xx Jesse Toney $9.82. xx

page 76

- Settlement of the Overseers of the Poor, they have all paid out funds in their hands to persons entitled except Stephen Spurlock , who owing to the death of one of the paupers retains $22.53 which he paid over to the Board. From that sum $9.83 paid to Jesse Toney and to Daniel Love $3.19 and $4.44 to Allen McGinnis as commissioners leaving a balance of $6.92.

- John Samuels $10 as clerk.
- Each of the Overseers $1 for today's services.
- Sheriff to collect 40 1/4 cents of each tithable.
- Thomas Killgore, late sheriff, to pay over $38.04 the amount of the settlement for 1832 and 1833.

page 77

- Sheriff to pay Stephen Spurlock, Overseer, $331 to pay claims of paupers: Osburn, Frazier & wife, Wells, J. Low, Infant Porters, Infant Eplin, Alderson Wells, R. West, S. Webb & his claim of $1, less $6.92 which Spurlock has in his hands.

- Sheriff to pay Allen McGinnis $46 to pay claims of J.A. Clark, Joshua Henwood and his claim of $1.
- Sheriff to pay Daniel Love $31 to pay claims of Sexton & Conrad & his $1.
- Sheriff to pay Jesse Toney (   ) to pay claims of Wm. Clark, Sally Cooper, Betsey Highsey, Stuck & his $1.

- Sheriff to pay John Samuels $40 to pay claims of Turley & his own $10.
- Sheriff to pay Abraham Syrus $1.
- Board adjourned. Stephen Spurlock, Daniel Love, Abraham Sires, Jesse Toney, A. McGinnis, John Samuels.

page 78

At a meeting of the Overseers 22nd of December 1834.

- Sheriff to pay each of the Overseers 6% upon the amount each Overseer must pay for the paupers placed under his care, from the amount now in the sheriff's hands.
- Board adjourned. S. Spurlock, Daniel Love, Jesse Toney, Allen McGinnis, John Samuels.

page 79

At a meeting of the Overseers for Cabell County 1st Monday in June 1835. Present: Andrew Barrett President, Daniel Love, John Plymale, Joseph Fulkerson, John Samuels, Jesse Toney.

- Edmund Osburn allowed $25 for support of his daughter Hulda until next June.
- $25 allowed for support of Jane Ann Clark until next June.
- William Clark allowed $30 until next June.
- Elizabeth Sexton allowed $20 for support of her son James.
- $15 allowed for support of Sally Cooper until next June.
- $30 allowed for support of Jesse Low until next June.
- Henry Miller allowed $25 to keep Betsey Highsey until next June.
- $15 allowed for support of Alderson Wells, an infant child, until next June.

page 80

- $25 allowed for support of Rebecca West until next June.
- $25 allowed for support of Susannah Webb until next June.
- James Plymale $2 for making coffin for Old Mrs. Cooper.
- Martha Blankenship allowed $6.25 for keeping Martha Porter, an infant, for 4/12 months.
- John Laidley $10 fee for case of Overseer against Cremeans & Merritt.
- James Pinnell $1.26 for serving 2 warrants on John Kyle & Thomas Dundas.
- $25 allowed for support of Joshua Henwood, the application of this money is subject to the control of the Overseers of the Poor until next June.
- Andrew Barrett, Daniel Love, Jesse Toney, John Plymale, Joseph Fulkerson each allowed $1 for today's service.

page 81

- John Samuels $10 as clerk.
- Upon settlement with sheriff there is a balance of $1.16 which is to be applied to new levy.
- Carr Low allowed $30 for keeping Mrs. Wells . $20 for last year, $10 for this.
- Sheriff pay Joseph Fulkerson $136 for claims of Osburn, Low, Donathan, Webb, Carr Low and his $1.

- Sheriff pay John Plymale $77.75 for claims of Wm. Clark, S. Cooper, R. West, Martha Blankenship & his $1.
- Sheriff pay Daniel Love $47.76 for claims of Sexton, Pinnell, Henwood and his $1.
- Sheriff pay Jesse Toney $63 for claims of Nancy Clark, Henry Miller, Jas. Plymale & John Laidley & his $1.
- 28 1/2 cents to be collected of each tithable for parish levy for 1835.

page 82

- John Samuels, clerk, is to take bond from John W. Ferguson together with his security Hugha Bowen in penalty of $1000 conditioned for keeping all the paupers with board, clothing, washing and lodging for one year. Overseers having liberty to examine monthly.
- Board adjourned until 1st Monday in June next. Andrew Barrett, Daniel Love, J. Fulkerson, John Plymale, John Samuels, Jesse Toney.

page 83

At a meeting of the Overseers of the Poor for Cabell county at the clerk's Office on Monday the 6th of June 1836. Present: Andrew Barrett, Daniel Love, John Plymale, John Samuels.

- $40 allowed Dr. Joseph Shallcross for 20 days attendance and medicine for James Murry who was badly wounded.
- James Martin (partner of Gardner & Everett) allowed $8.75 for attendance on James Murry.
- Robert Ashby(for the use of Tiernan & Gardner) $6 for boarding James Murry.
- Carter C. Dotson $10.50 for 7 days attendance on James Murry.
- John McGinnis, coroner, $10 for 2 inquests.
- Asher Crockett $15 for keeping Martha Porter, an infant, 9 months.
- John Plymale $3 for keeping Martha Porter, an infant, 2 months.
- Thomas Joy $2 for making coffin for Joshua Henwood.
- Hugha Bowen $6 for keeping Nancy Clark's child for 7 months.

page 84

- Pellington Merritt allowed $47 for keeping Levi Jenkins 5 months & 9 days.
- xx $50 for William Clark, $30 for Nancy Clark & child, $15 for Martha Porter, $75 for Levi Jenkins, $30 for Jesse Low, $25 for Old Mrs. Short, $20 for Mrs. Wells, $25 for Rebecca West until next June. xx
- Andrew Barrett, Daniel Love & John Plymale $1 each for today's service.
- John Samuels $10 as clerk.
- Sheriff to pay each of the Overseers of the Poor, except John Samuels, $2.32 1/2.
- $20 allowed William (Brumley) for keeping Mary Short until next June.
- Eldridge Smith $20 for keeping Rebecca West until next June.
- Hugha Bowen $24 for keeping Nancy Clark & child until next June.
- Wm. Low allowed $24 for keeping Jesse Low until next June.

page 85

- Larkin Bias (and in case of his refusal Rowland Bias) allowed $60 for keeping Levi Jenkins until next June.
- William Thompson allowed $16 for keeping Thankfull Wells until next June.
- Hugha Bowen allowed $40 for keeping William Clark until next June.
- $15 allowed for keeping Martha Porter, an infant, until next June.
- Upon settlement with sheriff it is found that $132.30 from last years levy remains in the hands of the sheriff. Ordered that Hugha Bowen, deputy to Levi McCormick, pay over to the present sheriff to defray cost of present levy.
- Parish Levy of 18 3/4 cents to be collected of each tithable.
- Should any of the paupers die within the year, a proportion of their claim to be paid for their care.
- $25 for support of Harben Wells, order to Joseph Fulkerson by John Plymale.
- Board adjourned. Andrew Barrett, Daniel Love, John Plymale, John Samuels.

page 86

At a meeting of the Overseers of the poor for Cabell County at the Clerk's Office on Monday the 5th of June 1837. Present: Andrew Barrett President, Daniel love, John Plymale, John Samuels.

- $15 allowed for support of Martha Porter, an infant, for one year and if she be bound out, a proportion of that sum.
- Hugha Bowen allowed $35 for Keeping Nancy Clark & child until next June.
- William (Brumley) allowed $20 for keeping Mary Short until next June.
- Eldridge Smith allowed $20 for keeping Rebecca West until next June.
- William Low allowed $20 for keeping Jesse Low until next June.
- xx George Hatfield xx allowed xx$60xx $70 for keeping Levi Jenkins until next June, order to A. Barrett.
- $35 allowed for keeping Thankful Wells until next June, order to Jos. Fulkerson.

page 87

- $25 allowed for support of Harben Wells until next June, order to Joseph Fulkerson.
- $50 allowed for keeping William Clark until next June, order to John Plymale.
- Epps Johnson $1.50 for making coffin for Mary Humphrey, an infant.
- James Russell $3.06 1/4 for articles furnished William Clark.
- $40 for supporting 6 small children of Wm. Campbell, order to John Plymale.
- Andrew Miller allowed $6 for keeping and clothing Ida Adkins.

$30 allowed for support of an orphan child of Sherrod Adkins, decd., order to Andrew Barrett.

- $40 allowed for support of A. Floyd Turley's family, order to John Samuels.
- Richard Brown allowed $50 for keeping Thomas Clap until next June.
- Dr. John Seachols $8.25 for medicine for Jenkins.

page 88

- Dr. John Seachols $44.50 for attendance on Elias Humphrey, Mary Humphrey, Francis Humphrey and for examination of Tabitha Russell & her infant.
- John Samuels $6.50 for amount he paid Alex. Newman & Mrs. Partlow for attending

Elias Humphrey family.

- James Pinnell $9 for keeping Francis Humphrey 3 weeks in his illness.
- James Pinnell $11.28 for summoning a jury and holding inquest over Tabitha Russell's child, washing, lying out and burying said child.
- John Newman $30 for keeping Francis Humphrey, an infant, for 10 months.
- John Newman allowed $25 for keeping Francis Humphrey until next June.
- William Sheff allowed $40 for keeping 2 of Elias Humphrey's infant children.

$20 allowed for keeping John Humphrey, an infant child, until next June, order to John Samuels.

- $50 allowed for keeping Thomas Walker until next June, order to John Plymale.

page 89

- Andrew Barrett, Daniel Love, John Plymale each $1 for services.
- Charles L. Roffe $3.75 money paid Atta Newman for attending Elias Humphrey.
- Sheriff allowed $39.10 to defray cost of levy.
- John Samuels $10 for services as clerk.
- $15 allowed for keeping Alderson Wells, an infant, until next June.
- 54 1/4 cents to be collected for the Parish Levy this year.
- If any of the paupers provided for should die before the 1st Monday in June next, then a proportion of their claim to be paid.
- Board adjourned. Andrew Barrett, Daniel Love, John Plymale, John Samuels.

page 90

- At a meeting of the Overseers of the Overseers of Cabell County at the Clerk's Office on the Monday the 4th of June 1838. Present: Andrew Barrett Prest. , Daniel Love, John Plymale, Joseph Fulkerson, John Samuels.

- Andrw. Barrett, Daniel Love and John Plymale be allowed 6% of $269 equally divided amount them and to be disbursed to the paupers .
- $15 allowed for support of Martha Porter, an infant, order to John Plymale.
- $35 allowed for keeping Nancy Clark & her child until next June.
- William (Brumley) allowed $30 to support Mary Short until next June.

page 91

- Eldridge Smith allowed $20 to support Rebecca West until next June, order to John Plymale.
- $20 allowed for support of Levi Jenkins, order to Andrew Barrett.
- $35 for keeping Thankfull Wells until next June, order to Joseph Fulkerson.
- $25 allowed for support of Harben Wells, order to Joseph Fulkerson.
- $50 allowed for support of William Clark, order to John Plymale.
- $40 to Mrs. Campbell to support of her 6 small children, order to John Plymale.
- William McComas allowed $20 for keeping Ida & Malvina Adkins, infants, for the past 6 months.
- William McComas allowed $40 to keep Ida & Malvina Adkins, 2 infant children, until next June.

page 92

- Andrew Barrett $2 for keeping Sally Adkins, an infant, for 4 weeks.
- $40 allowed support of Arthur Floyd Turley's family, order to John Samuels.
- $20 to be paid to John Newman for supporting Francis Humphrey, an infant, until June 1838.
- William Sheff allowed $20 for keeping John Humphrey, an infant, until next June, order to John Samuels.
- $15 allowed for keeping Alderson Wells, an infant, order to John Plymale.
- Dr. John Seashols $9.27 for medical services to Levi Jenkins.
- John Everett Jr. $1.10 for articles furnished James Murry.
- John Hammrick $3 for keeping John Toney, an infant of James Toney, decd.

page 93

- Andrew Barrett, John Plymale, Joseph Fulkerson & Daniel Love allowed 6% of the levy money to disburse.
- Henry Miller allowed $20 for keeping Elizabeth Highsey for 10 months.
- Andrew Barrett, Daniel Love, John Plymale & Joseph Fulkerson each $1.
- John Samuels clerk $10.
- Joseph Fulkerson allowed $9 for keeping Thomas Walker 6 weeks.
- Sheriff to pay over $22.86 to defray cost of levy.
- Parish levy to be collected, 31 1/4 cents.
- $5 to be paid Daniel Love, $5.57 to Andrew Barrett and John Plymale for paupers who died this last year with a sum remaining for their care.

page 94

- If any paupers should die before 1st Monday of June next then a proportion of their care only be paid.
- Board adjourned. Andrew Barrett, J. Fulkerson, Daniel Love, John Plymale, John Samuels.

page 95

At a meeting of the Overseers of the Poor of Cabell County at the clerk's office 3rd day of June 1839. Present: Daniel Love President, John Plymale, John Samuels.

- Sheriff to pay $3 to Daniel Love & $3.40 each to John Plymale, Andrew Barrett & Joseph Fulkerson as commission on funds disbursed.
- Philip Bumgardner to receive $15 extra compensation for keeping Nancy Clark & child last year.
- $10 allowed support for Martha Porter, an infant, order to John Plymale,
- $50 allowed support for Nancy Clark & child, order to John Plymale.
- $30 allowed support for Mary Short, order to Joseph Fulkerson.
- $40 allowed support for Rebecca West, order to John Plymale.
- $130 allowed for support of Thankfull Wells & Harben Wells for ensuing year, order to John Plymale.
- $60 allowed support of William Clark, order to John Plymale.

page 96

-$30 allowed aid to Mrs Campbell to raise her 6 children, order John Plymale.
- $40 allowed support for Ida & Malvina Adkins, order to Andrew Barrett.
- $50 for support of Arthur F. Turley until next June, order John Samuels.
- $15 allowed support of Alderson Wells, an infant, order to John Plymale.
- $20 allowed support of James Sexton until next June, order Daniel Love.
- $15 allowed Elisha Barbour for keeping Lewis (Porter/Barter), an infant, from 15 September last, order to John Plymale.
- $10 allowed support for Josiah W. Floyd, order John Plymale.
- $25 allowed support for Hulda Osburn, order to John Plymale.
- Dr. John Seashols $7.50 for attending Gromey, order John Samuels.
- Dr. John Seashols $7 for setting Francis Humphrey's leg which was broke, order John Samuels.

page 97

- Philip Bumgardner $9.50 for attending to Gormey who was sick 19 days at his house, order John Samuels.
- John Newman $4 for attending to Francis Humphrey with his broken leg, order to Daniel Love.
- $15 allowed for Fereba Workman & $15 for her child, order to John Plymale.
- $15 allowed for support of Thomas Crabtree, order John Vaughan.
- John Plymale $3 for binding out Thomas Adkins, Nathaniel Adkins & David Dick by indentures.
- John Plymale & Daniel Love $1 each for services.
- Overseers of the Poor , except John Samuels, allowed 5% to disburse.
- Sheriff to pay Daniel Love for the use of Lee Jordan $5.
- John Samuels $10 as clerk.
- 37 1/2 cents to be collected as Parish Levy this year.
- Board adjourned. Daniel Love, John Plymale, John Samuels.

page 98

At a meeting of the Overseers of the Poor of Cabell held at the clerk's office on Monday the 1st day of June 1840. Present: Daniel Love President, Andrew Barrett, John Plymale John Samuels.

- $5 allowed for support of Martha Porter, an infant, order to John Plymale.
- $50 allowed for support of Nancy Clark & her child, order to John Plymale.
- $15 allowed for support of Mary Short, order Joseph Fulkerson.
- $40 allowed for support of Rebecca West , order to John Plymale.
- $130 allowed for support of Thankfull Wells and her son Harbin Wells, order to John Plymale.
- $60 allowed for support of William Clark ensuing year, order to John Plymale.
- $30 for support of Ida & Malvina Adkins, 2 infants, order Andrew Barrett.

page 99

- $25 allowed for support of Arthur F. Turley, order to John Samuels.

- $15 allowed for support of Alderson Wills, an infant, order to John Plymale.
- $20 allowed for support of James Sexton until June 1841, order to Daniel Love.
- $10 allowed for support of Josiah W. Floyd, order to John Plymale.
- $15 allowed for support of Hulda Osburn, order to John Plymale.
- $25 allowed for support of Fereby Workman & child, order to John Plymale.
- $25 allowed for support of Thomas Crabtree until next June, order to Plymale.
- $25 for the support of John Shelton until next June, order to Andrew Barrett.
- $10 to Rebecca Toppins to support her infant children, order John Plymale.

page 100

- $25 allowed for support of Richard Johnson, order to Andrew Barrett.
- Allen A. McGinnis allowed $50 for keeping Mrs. Plank & her son from January to June 1840, boarding & clothing.
- $100 allowed for keeping Mrs. Plank & her son, Christopher Plank.
- $20 allowed for support of Mary Curtis, order to Andrew Barrett.
- $18 allowed Benjamin Stephenson for keeping, attending and furnishing coffin & shroud for Betheny Stephenson in her last sickness, order to John Plymale.
- Dr. John Seashols $4.10 medical services rendered Frances Humphrey & Nancy Clark.
- John Plymale $4 for binding out Preston Toppins, Eleanor Adkins, Sally Adams and John Wells by proper indentures.
- Andrew Barrett, Daniel Love & John Plymale $1 each for services today.
- John Samuels $10 as clerk.

page 101

- Sheriff to pay Daniel Love $10 and Andrew Barrett and John Plymale $12.50 each for commission on money disbursed.
- Sheriff to collect 50 cents of each tithable for Parish Levy.
- Board adjourned. Daniel Love, John Plymale, Andrew Barrett, John Samuels.

At a meeting of the Overseers of the Poor of Cabell County at the clerk's office on Monday the 7th of June 1841. Present: Daniel Love President, John Plymale, John Samuels, Andrew Barrett.

- $45 allowed for support of Nancy Clark & child, order to John Plymale,
- $40 allowed for support of Rebecca West, order to John Plymale.

page 102

- $130 allowed for Thankfull Wells & her son Harben, order to John Plymale.
- $75 allowed for support of William Clark, order to John Plymale.
- $15 allowed for support of Alderson Wells, order to John Plymale.
- $20 allowed for support of James Sexton, order to Daniel Love.
- $10 allowed for support of Josiah W. Floyd, order to John Plymale.
- $30 allowed for support of Hulda Osburn, order to John Plymale.
- $20 allowed for support of Farely Workman & her child, order to John Plymale.
- $20 allowed for support of Thomas Crabtree, order to John Plymale.

- $25 allowed for support of John Shelton, order to John Samuels.

page 103

- $25 allowed for support of Richard Johnson, order to Andrew Barrett.
- $75 allowed for support of Mrs. Plank & her son, order to John Samuels.
- $15 allowed for Mary Curtis, order Andrew Barrett.
- Henry (Bostal) $4 for making coffin for Mrs. Elizabeth Riley.
- Dingess Henderson $4 for coffin and burying Henry Adkins.
- John Hannan $30.62 for keeping, attending, furnishing coffin and grave clothes for (George Farrow.)
- Absolum Holderby & William C. Miller $5.18 for shrouds for Henry Adkins & Elizabeth Riley & grave clothes.
- $20 allowed for support of Susanna Webb, order to John Plymale.
- Frederick Moore $20 for sundry articles furnished Susanna Webb last year.
- Dr. John Seashols $15.50 for medical aid to Nancy Clark & Mrs. Plank

page 104

- $25 allowed for support of Nancy for ensuing year & further ordered upon settlement of estate of James Cox, decd. if there is any estate remaining then it shall be applied to reimbursing the county. {slave}
- $25 allowed for support of Phil, a slave belonging to James Kinsolving, and that John Samuels, clerk, do give notice to said Kinsolving that a motion will be made in the county court for a judgement against him for the $25 levied to support his Negro slave Phil, and costs.
- Andrew Barrett $5.80 for provisions furnished Martha Roach.
- $20 allowed for support of Mrs. Esther Bullman, order to Andrew Barrett.
- $20 allowed for support of Rebecca Holten, order to Andrew Barrett.
- John Plymale, Daniel Love and Andrew Barrett each allowed 5% for disbursing the sums levied today.
- John Samuels $10 services as clerk.

page 105

- $1 each to Daniel Love, Andrew Barrett and John Plymale for service today.
- John Plymale $1 for binding out Nelson Wiley to Hugh Bowen by indenture.
- Sheriff to pay $8 to Daniel Love and $8.95 each to Andrew Barrett & John Plymale for disbursing county levy.
- Sheriff to collect 42 cents for the Parish Levy of each tithable and to make settlement with John Samuels of last years levy.
- Board adjourned. Daniel Love, Andrew Barrett, John Plymale, John Samuels.

page 106

At a meeting of the Overseers of the Poor of Cabell County on Monday the 7th day of June 1842. Present: Andrew Barrett President, Daniel Love, John Samuels.

- John Plymale allowed $20 for money paid by him to remove William Clark from this county, with interest from 1st of March 1842 until 1st day of November next.
- $20 allowed for support of James Saxton, order to Daniel Love.

- $20 allowed for support of Richard Johnson, order to Olly Johnson, his mother.
-$55 allowed for support of Mrs. Plank & Christopher Plank, her son, for ensuing year, order to John Samuels.
- $7.50 allowed for support of Mary Curtis, order to Andrew Barrett.
- $20 allowed for support of Nancy, a slave of the estate of James Cox decd., order to Daniel Love.
- Sugar Johnson allowed $23 for support of Phil, order to Andrew Barrett.

page 107

- $20 allowed for support of Rebecca Holten, order to Andrew Barrett.
- $20 allowed for support of James Adkins, son of William Adkins of 4 Mile Creek, order to Andrew Barrett.
- $20 allowed for support of Mrs. Green from 1st of October 1841 until this day, order to Greenville Newman.
- $30 allowed John Collins for his support.
- Dr. J. Seashols $1 for medicine for Phil, a pauper.
- Dr. John Seashols $9.25 for medical aid to Widow Shoemaker.
  {1850 Census Nancy L Shoemaker aged 87}
- Frances Howell $9 for keeping a daughter of John (McDilda) for 7 weeks.
- William Merritt $5 for coffin, winding sheet and burying a man found dead in the Ohio River.
- Charles T. Love $20.25 articles furnished Old Mrs. Shoemaker & her family.
- $25 for support of Old Mrs. Shoemaker for ensuing year, order to Daniel Love.

page 108

- $5.08 to William Jordan for coffin, winding sheet & grave clothes and burying William Lane.
- Andrew Barrett to apply the residue of the money levied for Esther Bullman, $6.25, for the relief of Martha Roach and her children.
- xx An indenture from Andrew Barrett to Thomas McComas binding Elizabeth Adkins until 18 years of age. xx
- Andrew Barrett $3 for binding out Hulda Snell, Steven Bragg & Elizabeth Adkins.
- John Samuels $10 for services as clerk.
- Sheriff to pay Daniel Love, Andrew Barrett & John Plymale $11 each as commission on levies disbursed last year.
- Daniel Love, Andrew Barrett, John Plymale, $1 for service today.
- Sheriff to collect 31 1/4 cents for Parish Levy.
- Board adjourned. Andrew Barrett, Daniel Love, John Samuels.

page 109

At a meeting of the Overseers of the Poor of Cabell Count 5th day of June 1843 at the clerk's office. Present: Andrew Barrett President, Daniel Love, John Samuels.

- $20 allowed for support of James Sexton, order to Daniel Love.
- Olla Johnson allowed $10 for support of her son Richard for ensuing year, order to A. Barrett.

- Achillis Davis allowed $17 for keeping Polly Dick for 8 months last past.
- Joseph Stailey $20 for support of Elizabeth Highsey ensuing year. {wife's sister}
- William Adkins $20 for support of his son James Adkins, order Andrew Barrett.
- Jacob Stuck allowed $20 for support of his son, an idiot.

page 110

- Sugar Johnson allowed $140 for support for Mrs. Plank and her son, Nancy a Negro, Phil a Negro, Old Mrs. Shoemaker, Polly Dick, Nancy Clark & her child, subject to order of Andrew Barrett.
- Andrew Barrett $10 for keeping Lucinda Adkins, an orphan who was confined with sickness to his home for 3 months.
- Dr. R. G. (Deviner) $10 as physician to Lucinda Adkins, an orphan child confined at Andrew Barrett's.
- $20 allowed for support of John Collins, ensuing year.
- Charles T. Love $8.46 for articles furnished Mrs. Shoemaker.
- $10 allowed for removing for Mrs. Rose & 4 children from this county to Ohio among her friends.
- $17.50 allowed for support of Jonas Nisely, order to Daniel Love.
- Upon settlement with sheriff a balance of $4.22 remains unaccounted for.
- Daniel Love $5 commission and Andrew Barrett $5.52 for disbursing levy.

page 111

- Daniel Love & Andrew Barrett $1 each for service today.
- John Samuels $10 as clerk.
- 37 1/2 cents to be collected for parish Levy this year.
- Sheriff to apply $4.22 towards defraying cost of levy.
- Andrew Barrett $1 for binding Stephen Bragg, an orphan, to Robt. G. (Doviner). {?doctor see page 110}
- Board adjourned. Andrew Barrett, Daniel Love, John Samuels.

page 112

At a meeting of the Overseers of the Poor of Cabell County held at the clerk's office on the 17th day of June 1844. Present: Andrew Barrett President, Daniel Love, John Samuels.

- $20 allowed for support of James Sexton, order to Daniel Love.
- Olla Johnson allowed $18 support for her son Richard, order to A. Barrett.
- Joseph Stailey $30 to support Elizabeth Highsey, an idiot, order John Samuels.
- William Adkins $20 to support his son James Adkins, order to A. Barrett.
- Jacob Stuck $20 to support his son, order to John Samuels.
- $17.50 allowed for support of Nancy, a Negro lately belonging to Jas. Cox decd., order to John Samuels.

page 113

- $17.50 allowed for support of Phil, a Negro, order to Andrew Barrett.
- $17.50 allowed for support of Old Mistress Shoemaker, order to Daniel Love.
- $35 allowed for support of Polly Dick, order to Andrew Barrett.
- Ruel Porter $6 to support Nancy Clark & her child ensuing year, order D. Love.

- Burwell Johnson $12.87 1/2 for support of Mrs. Plank ensuing year, D. Love.
- $17.50 allowed aid to Jonas Nisely, order to Daniel Love.
- Harry Barrett $2.10 for apprehending Harden Johnson for the Overseers.
- Anderson Roberts allowed $8 for keeping George Jordan, an infant, for 10 weeks & 3 days.
- Andrew Barrett $25 for keeping Ida Butcher, 20th of August 1843 until today.

page 114

- $6.50 allowed for support of Ida Butcher until next June, order Andrew Barrett.
- Charles Holten $7.50 for keeping Rebecca Holten from 29th of March 1844 until 17th of June 1844.
- Charles Holten allowed $25 to support Rebecca Holten ensuing year.
- Sugar Johnson allowed $4 for keeping Old Mrs. Plank and Phil for 2 weeks from June 3rd until June 17th this year.
- Charles Holten $6.50 for keeping Ida Butcher, an infant child, 2 months & 25 days last year.
- Benjamin Davis $10 for support of Polly Dick last year.
- $25 for aid to Solomon and Polly Harris ensuing year, order to John Samuels.

page 115

- $25 allowed for support of Arthur F. Turley, order to Andrew Barrett.
- Dr. John Seashols $9 for services for Floyd Turley in 1844, order J. Samuels.
- Andrew Barrett & Daniel Love $1 each for service today.
- John Samuels $10 as clerk.
-Upon settlement with sheriff there remain $94.54 in his hands, to be paid over to the Overseers.
- Parish Levy this year to be 34 1/2 cents.
- Sheriff pay Andrew Barrett & Daniel Love $5.80 for disbursing levy last year.
- Adjourned until June next. Andrew Barrett, Daniel Love, John Samuels.

page 116

At a Board of the overseers of the Poor 2nd day of June 1845. Present Andrew Barrett President, Daniel Love, John Samuels.

- $20 allowed to support James Sexton, order to Daniel Love.
- Olla Johnson allowed $18 to support her son Richard, order to Daniel Love.
- Joseph Stailey $30 to support Elizabeth Highsey, an idiot, order John Samuels.
- William Adkins allowed $20 to support his son James Adkins, order A. Barrett.
- Jacob Stuck $20 to support his son, order to John Samuels.
- $20 allowed for support of Nancy, a Negro woman lately belonging to James Cox, decd., order to Daniel Love.
- $20 allowed for support of Phil, a Negro man, order to Andrew Barrett.

page 117

- $20 allowed to support Old Mrs. Shoemaker, order to Daniel Love.
- Benjamin Davis $35 to support Polly Dick, order to Andrew Barrett.
- Ruel Porter $6 to keep Nancy Clark ensuing year, order to Daniel Love.

- $15 allowed to support Old Mrs. Plank, order to John Samuels.
- $30 allowed support for Rebecca Holten, order to Andrew Barrett.
- $25 allowed to support Mother & brother of Solomon & Polly Harris, order to John Samuels.
- xx $25 allowed for support of Arthur F. Turley, order Andrew Barrett. xx
- Drs. Seashols & Maupin $3 medical services to Christopher Plank last year.
- Drs. Seashols & Maupin $27 for attending Arthur Turley for uclers of the thigh.

page 118

- $6 to Samuel A. Childers for making coffins for Nisely & Tophouse's child and for burying child.
- Dr. William Paine $14.38 for medical attention and burying John Boughman.
- Dr. S. J. Yates $15 for a post mortem examination of Nathan Holten, decd.
- Willis Mays $10.50 for support of George Jordan, an infant, for 10 1/2 months.
- William Gunnow allowed $10 for support of Jacob Bragg.
- Armstead B. Howell allowed $17 for keeping James Butcher the last 5 months and for the ensuing year, order to John Samuels.
- $25 allowed for support of Old Mrs. Carmeans, order to Daniel Love. {1850 Census 222-227 Sarah Cremeans aged 67}
- William Fielder $10 for keeping Christopher Plank 3 months last winter.

page 119

- John Collins allowed $20 aid for ensuing year, order to Andrew Barrett.
- $20 allowed for support of John Shelton, order to Andrew Barrett.
- Andrew Barrett & Daniel Love each $1 for service today.
- John Samuels $10 for services of clerk.
- Sheriff to pay Andrew Barrett $8.21 and Daniel Love $7 for disbursing levy.
- Holderby & Miller $6.08 for goods furnished Parraleus Clark, Floyd Turley and Plank.
- Upon settlement with the sheriff Overseers find $137.54 remaining in the sheriff's hands from previous levies, amount to be paid by last sheriff to present sheriff.
- Sheriff to collect Parish levy of 43 3/4 cents of each tithable.

page 120

- Board adjourned. Andrew Barrett, Daniel Love, John Samuels.

At a Board of the Overseers of the Poor for Cabell County on the 1st Monday in June 1846. Present: Daniel Love President, James T. Carrell, John Samuels.

(NOTE: clerk Samuels writes Carrell, name is signed Carroll.)

- Daniel Love appointed President.
- $20 allowed for support of James Saxton, order to Daniel Love.
- Alta Johnson allowed $18 to support her son Richard, order to Daniel Love.
- Joseph Stailey allowed $30 to support Elizabeth Highsey, an idiot, for ensuing year, order to John Samuels.
- William Adkins $20 for support of his son, James Adkins, order to James T. Carrell.

- $20 allowed for support of Phil, a Negro man, order to James T. Carrell.
- $20 allowed for support of Old Mrs. Shoemaker, order to Daniel Love.
- $50 allowed for support of Polly Dick, order to John Samuels.
- xx Ruel Porter xx $10 for support of Nancy Clark, order to James T. Carrell.
- $25 allowed for support of Mrs. Plank, order to John Samuels.
- $30 allowed for support of Rebecca Holten, order to James T. Carrell.

page 122

- $25 allowed for support of Mother & Brother of Solomon & Polly Harris, order to John Samuels.
- Armstead B. Howell $12 to support James Butcher, an infant, order Samuels.
- $25 allowed for support of Old Mrs. Carmeans, order to Daniel Love.
- $20 allowed for support of John Collins, order to James T. Carrell.
- $20 allowed for support of John Shelton, order to James T. Carrell.
- $2.87 1/2 to Charles L. Roffe for furnishing burial clothes for Mrs. Elkins.

page 123

- Samuel M. Johnson $10.06 1/4 for flour & meal for Mrs. Henry for last 7 (months).
- $30 allowed support for Arthur Floyd Turley, order to James T. Carrell.
- $30 allowed for support of Old Mrs. Rider, order to Daniel Love.
- Isaac Mines $5 for keeping Old Mrs. Rider for 2 months last past.
- Charles Holten allowed $12 to support 2 orphans, children of Nathan Holten, decd. until they shall be bound out to him.
- $20 allowed Old Mr. John Adkins & wife for ensuing year. order to J.T. Carrell.
- John Hibbons $5 for making 2 coffins for Mrs. Elkins and Old Negro Nancy.
- Edmund Rece $3 for making coffin for Morris Hudson.

page 124

- $20 allowed for support of Violet Warner, an infant, order to James T. Carrell.
- John Collins allowed $15 for keeping Violet Warner, an infant, last year.
- Edmund McGinnis $10 for services rendered Jane Taylor & burying her child.
- Absolum Bias $7.50 for keeping Mary Curtis 5 months last year.
- $25 allowed for support of Mary Curtis ensuing year, order to James T. Carrell.
- Drs. Seashol & Maupin $5 medical services rendered Christopher Plank , 1845.
- Dr. Hy Maupin $18.75 for medical services to Catherine Cannon in 1845 & 46.
- Drs. Maupin & McCullough 75 cents for medicine for mister John Shelton.
- James T. Carrell & Daniel Love each $1 for today's service.

page 125

- John Samuels $10 for services of clerk.
- Sheriff to pay Daniel Love & Andrew Barrett's Adm. $9.
- Daniel Love & John Samuels to settle with late sheriff.
- Sheriff to collect 50 cents for parish levy.
- The late sheriff of the county having failed to settle with the Overseers, Board is adjourned until next June when such settlement will be made. Daniel Love, James T. Carroll, John Samuels.

page 126

At a Board of the Overseers of the Poor at the clerk's office of Cabell County on the 1st Monday in July 1846. Present: James T. Carrell President, Daniel Love, John Samuels.

- The board allows the sheriff a credit of 92 tithes and his commission for collecting $605.91 3/4. In addition $192.60 3/4 remains in the hands of John Hannan late sheriff, after paying the levy for 1845 to bring the sum to $490.56. Add to that the sum remaining for the support of Nancy, Old Mrs. Shoemaker, Mrs. Cremeans and the cost for George W. Shelton for removing Parallee Clark to Stauton Institution for the Blind (not having yet been paid his expenses), amount of expenses allowed to remain in his hands {sheriff's ?}.

- Board adjourned until 1st Monday in June next. James T. Carroll, Daniel Love, John Samuels.

page 127

At a Board of the Overseers of the Poor on Monday the 7th of June 1847 at Cabell Court House, Virginia. Present: James T. Carrell President, Daniel Love, John Samuels.

- $20 allowed for support of James Sexton for ensuing year, order to Daniel Love.
- Olla Johnson allowed $18 to support her son Richard, order to Daniel Love.
- Joseph Stailey $30 to support Elizabeth Highsey, order to John Samuels.
- Williams Adkins $20 to support his son James Adkins, order James T. Carrell.
- $20 allowed for support of Phil, a Negro man, order to James T. Carrell.
- $25 allowed for support of Old Mrs. Shoemaker, order to Daniel Love.
- $50 allowed for support of Polly Dick, order to John Samuels.

page 128

- $10 allowed for support of Nancy Clark, order to James T. Carrell.
- $25 allowed for support of Old Mrs. Plank, order to John Samuels.
- $25 allowed for support of Christopher Plank, order to John Samuels.
- $25 allowed for support of Solomon & Polly Harris, order to John Samuels.
- $25 allowed for support of Old Mrs. Carmeans, order to Daniel Love.
- $10 aid allowed John Collins to support himself, order to James T. Carrell.

page 129

- $50 allowed for support of Arthur F. Turley, order to James T. Carrell.
- $25 allowed for Old Mr. John Adkins & his wife, order to James T. Carrell.
- $20 allowed to support Violet Warner, an infant, order to James T. Carrell.
- $10 allowed to support Mary Curtis, order to James T. Carrell.
- $25 allowed for support of Phebe Chapman, an idiot, order to Daniel Love.
- Charles Holten $8 for funeral expenses & keeping Joseph Runion 4 days last summer.
- Dr. Henry B. Maupin $8 medical services rendered Catherine Conner & Christopher Plank up to April 9th 1847.

page 130

- J & S Miller $4.45 for provisions furnished the Planks last year.

- Jeremiah Flint $1.50 for a coffin for Sa—— King's child. (ink spot)
- Drs. P. McCullough & H.B. Maupin $24 for medical services rendered Mrs. Plank, the child of Rachel Carter, the pauper child at Howel's, Christopher Plank and Old Mr. Powell last year.
- Daniel Love $2 for indentures of Thomas Galaspie & (Linanda) Elkin last year.
- John Samuels $10 as clerk.
- John Merritt $4 for provisions to Old Mrs. Henry in 1846.
- $15 allowed for support of Mrs. Chapman, late Mrs. Shoemaker's child.
- $7.75 to James Syrus for services to Mrs Plank & her son Christopher in 1846.
- William C. Miller & Co. $32 necessaries to Mrs. Plank & her son Christopher.

page 131

- $20 allowed for the 2 youngest children of Widow Roach, order to J.T. Carrell.
- Daniel Love & James T. Carrell $1 each for services today.
- Sheriff to pay Daniel Love & James T. Carrell each $1.20 for disbursements.
- Sheriff to collect Parish Levy of 50 cents of each tithable.

- Upon settlement with sheriff for last year, there is a remainder of $52.41 allowing sheriff credit of 136 tithables & his commission on $705, said sum to be paid to the Overseer to purchase a Poor House for this county.

Board adjourned until 1st Monday in June 1848, Daniel Love, James T. Carroll, John Samuels.

page 132

At a meeting of the Board of the Overseers of the Poor on the 9th day of November 1847. Present: Daniel Love, John Samuels.

- Sheriff to pay Dr. Alexander M. McCorkle $8.25 for services rendered Powell out of money now in his hands.
- Same order to Dr. G.C. Rickets $10 for same services.
- Same order to Absolum Chapman $15 for boarding Powell in his last illness.
- Board adjourned. Daniel Love.

page 133

At a meeting of the Board of the Overseers of the Poor of Cabell county at he clerk's office on Monday the 5th of June 1848. Present: James T. Carrell President,
Daniel Love, John Samuels.

- $20 allowed for support of James Sexton, order to Daniel Love.
- Olla Johnson allowed $18 to support her son Richard, order to Daniel Love.
- $30 allowed for support of Elizabeth Highsey, order to John Samuels.
- $20 allowed for support of James Adkins by his father, order James T. Carrell.
- Westley Johnson $9.75 for keeping Phil, order to Daniel Love. (xx $25-$13-$10x)
- $17.87 1/2 allowed for support of Polly Dick, order to John Samuels. (xx $24 xx)

page 134

- $8 allowed for support of Nancy Clark, order to James T. Carrell.
- $12 allowed for support of Old Mrs. Plank, order to John Samuels.

- $16 allowed for support of Old Mrs. Carmeans & her daughter, order D. Love.
- $50 allowed for support of Arthur F. Turley & his wife, order James T. Carrell.
- $10 allowed for support of Violet Warner, an infant, order to James T. Carrell.
- $6 allowed support for Mary Curtis, order to James T. Carrell.
- $25 allowed for support of Phebe Chapman, order to Daniel Love.

page 135

$9.50 allowed to support Nancy J. Shoemaker, order to Daniel Love.
- Dr. Henry B. Maupin $21 for medical services to Polly Harris & James Butcher & Betsey Dotson in 1847 & 1848.
- Dr. Alexander M. McCorkle $10.50 medical services to Johnston in 1847.
- Dr. P. H. McCullough $10 for medical services to Elizabeth Dotson in 1848.
- $15 allowed for support of Old Mrs. Cook, order to James T. Carrell.
- Daniel Love ($-) for indenture made for Charles Shoemaker.
- James T. Carrell $4 for indentures of Roach's and H. Holten.
- Daniel Love $11 for disbursing levy.
- James T. Carrell $11.35 for disbursing levy.
- James T. Carrell & Daniel Love $1 each for today.

page 136

- Upon settlement with Benjamin Brown, sheriff, there remains in his hands for 1846 & 1847 a sum of $76.72 which is ordered paid to Benjamin Brown, sheriff less sum of $22.34 to Love & Carrell for disbursing levy makes $99.07 left in the hands of the sheriff after paying levy for last year.
- John Samuels $10 for services of clerk.
- Sheriff to collect 31 cents to pay off the parish levy.
- Board adjourned until the 1st Monday in June next. James T. Carroll, Daniel Love, John Samuels.

page 137

At a meeting of the Overseers of the Poor of Cabell County on the 1st Monday June 4th 1849. Present: James T. Carrell President, Daniel Love, John Samuels.
- $20 Allowed for support of James Sexton, order to Daniel Love.
- $25 allowed for support of Richard Johnson, order to James T. Carrell.
- $30 allowed for support of Elizabeth Highsey, an idiot, order to John Samuels.
- $20 allowed for support of James Adkins by his father.
- $25 allowed for support of Phil, a Negro, order to James T. Carrell.
- $35 allowed Benjamin Davis to support Polly Dick, order to John Samuels.

page 138

- $20 allowed for support of Nancy Clark, order James T. Carrell.
- $20 allowed support for Old Mrs. Plank, order to John Samuels. ($12.30 assigned to Dietz.)
- $16 allowed support for Old Mrs. Cremeans & her daughter, order to Daniel Love.
- $50 allowed for support of Arthur F. Turley & wife, order to James T. Carrell.
- $10 support allowed for Violet Warner, an infant child, order James T. Carrell.

- $10 support allowed Mary Curtis, order to James T. Carrell.
- $25 support allowed Phebe Chapman, order to Daniel Love.

page 139

- Dr. Henry B. Maupin $23.50 for medical services rendered Mrs. (Henry), Catherine Conner, L. Richey & H. Johnson in 1848 & 1849.
- Dr. P. H. McCullough $12 medical services to Mrs. Dotson & her grandchild.
- xx Dr. John Seashol $10 medical service to Thomas Burns in 1848 & 49. xx
- William C. Miller & Co. $2.60 for aid to Miss Moore.
- Dr. Joseph Sidebottom $10.50 medical service rendered Miss Moore xx Eliza Adkins xx in 1848 & 49.
- Adolphus A. Nuley $5 for keeping Mrs. Adkins & her children for 5 weeks.
- James Garrett $18.78 for provisions to Thomas Burns in 1848 & 49.
- xx Dr. Sidebottom $10 medical services to Nancy Clark. xx
- Elizabeth Dotson allowed $20 to support her grandchild for the last part of present year, order to John Samuels.

page 140

- Rufus Batzel $2.50 for making coffin for Old Mr. Powell in 1847.
- $20 allowed to support Sarah Moore, order to James T. Carrell.
- Samuel Childers $2.50 for making coffin for Miriam (Cornerll).
- $7.12 1/2 paid in addition to the $18.87 1/2 allowed last year for support of Polly Dick. Sum to be paid to Benjamin Davis.
- $25 allowed for support Old Mrs. Shoemaker, order to Daniel Love.
- John Duke allowed $20 for keeping Mavel Elkins in his last sickness for 3 weeks, for the benefit of Charles L. Roffe.
- Thomas Merritt $6.18 for provisions for Mrs. Henry in 1849.
- Charles L. Roffe $2.87 1/2 for burying clothes for Miriam (Conwell) decd.

page 141

- Armistead Howell $10 for keeping Old Mrs. Henry 6 or 8 weeks in 1848.
- Daniel Love $2.25 for 4 1/2 bushels of meal furnished Old Mrs. Henry in 1849.
- David Porter $6.25 for keeping Elizabeth Adkins 5 weeks in 1848.
- $20 allowed for support of Old Mrs Mowman, order to James T. Carrell.
- Nelson B. Heath $6.33 1/3 for keeping Old Mrs. Mowman the last 4 months.
- James T. Carrell $5 for indentures of Mary F. Adkins, Clarinda Adkins, Jonas Adkins, Sarah G. Adkins and Eliza Carpenter.
- Daniel Love $5 for support he paid for Old Mrs. Shoemaker last year.
- James T. Carrell and Daniel Love $6.92 each for disbursing the levy.
- Same persons allowed $1 each for today's service.

page 142

- John Samuels $10 as clerk.
- Upon settlement with sheriff as balance was found of $73.67 1/2, said sum to be paid over to present sheriff by late sheriff.
- 41 cents to be collected as parish levy for the year.

- Board adjourned until 1st Monday in June next. James T. Carroll, Daniel Love, John Samuels.

page 143

At a Board of the Overseers of the Poor held on the 3rd day of August 1850.
Present: James T. Carrell President, Daniel Love, John Samuels.

- $20 allowed support for James Sexton, order to Daniel Love.
- $25 allowed support for Richard Johnson, order to James T. Carrell.
- $35 support allowed for Elizabeth Highsey, an idiot, order to John Samuels.
- $20 allowed for support of James Adkins by his father, order to John Samuels.
- $24 allowed for support of Phil, a Negro, order to James T. Carrell.
- $35 allowed for support of Polly Dick, order to John Samuels.
- $20 allowed for support of Nancy Clark, order to John Samuels.
- $16 allowed to support Old Mrs. Cremeans & her daughter, order Daniel Love.

page 144

- $50 allowed for support of Arthur F. Turley & wife, order to James T. Carrell.
- $10 allowed for support of Violet Warner, an infant child, order J.T. Carrell.
- $25 allowed for support of Phebe Chapman, order to Daniel Love.
- $20 support allowed Sarah Moore for ensuing year, order to James T. Carrell.
- $25 allowed for support of Old Mrs. Shoemaker, order to Daniel Love.
- Charles L. Roffe $2.50 for burial clothes for Burwell Dodd.
- Laven Swan $3 for coffin furnished Burwell Dodd, decd.
- Jacob Miller $6 for making 2 coffins for Mavel Elkins & Levi Rowland.
- Edward Nixon $1.50 for burial sheet for Rowland.

page 145

- Eli H. Walton $1.65 for shroud for John Adkins.
- James A. Holley $18 for keeping John Adkins & wife 1 month & 24 days.
- Samuel Smith $50 for keeping John Adkins & wife 4 months & 6 days last year.
- Dr. Milton McCoy $5.75 medical services to Mrs. Rhodes in 1850.
- Mary Pillow $5 for attention to Mrs. Rhodes in her illness in 1850.
- $20 allowed for support of Jefferson H.C. Bowen, an infant, order Daniel Love.
- John G. & C. S. Miller $2.48 for necessaries furnished Old Mrs. Henry.
- Dr. Henry B. Maupin $9 for medical services for C. Cannon, Mrs. Harris, & Old Mrs. Henry up to this day.
- Drs. Maupin & McComas $7.75 medical services to Old Mrs. (Mathews) 1849.
- Dr. P.H. McCullough $8.87 1/2 for medical services to Old Mrs. Henry & al in 1848 & 1849.
- John M. Rece $1.08 for bacon furnished J. Hinkley.
- Daniel Love $6 for meal furnished Old Mrs. Henry at 50 cents a bushel.

page 146

- William M. Williams $2.05 for a coffin & shroud for Clarissa Reins' child.
- $25 allowed Mrs. Dodd to support her children, order to John Samuels.
- John M. Rece $5 for necessaries furnished Mrs. Mathews.

- James T. Carrell $1 for indenture written to bind (Sinate Hudlin) to Adolphus Newley.
- James T. Carrell & Daniel Love $1 each for today's service.
- John Samuels $10 as clerk.
- Upon settlement with sheriff a balance remains of $17.79 after allowing him 162 delinquent tithes and deducting his commission out of $536.80 now in hands of Dr. B. Brown to be turned over to present sheriff.
- James T. Carrell & Daniel Love $9.90 each for disbursing the levy.
- Sheriff to collect parish levy of 40 cents.

page 147

- Board adjourned. James T. Carroll, Daniel Love, John Samuels.

At a Board of the Overseers of the Poor for Cabell County 3rd of June 1851. Present: James T. Carrell, Daniel Love, John Samuels.

(In this section each amount allotted has been crossed and a smaller amount used.)

(Until these entries, all support was from June 1st until June 1st. Q whole page has a large X drawn across it.)

xx- ($20) $15 allowed for support of James Sexton until 1st of March next.
- ($25) $18.75 allowed for support of Richard Johnson until 1st March 1852.
- ($30) $22.50 allowed for support of Elizabeth Highsey until 1st March 1852.
- ($20) $15 allowed for support of James Adkins until 1st March 1852.
- $18 allowed for support of Phil, a man of color. xx

page 148

At a meeting of the Board of the Overseers of the Poor for Cabell County held at the Court House 3rd of Jun 1851. Present: James T. Carrell, Daniel Love, John Samuels.

- $16.65 allowed for support of James Sexton until the 31st of March next.
- $20.80 allowed for support of Richard Johnson until 31st of March 1852.
- $25 allowed for support of Elizabeth Highsey until 31st March 1852.
- $15.65 allowed for support of James Adkins until 31st March 1852.
  {1850 Cabell Census #127-131 father William, son James aged 29, idiot)
- $20 allowed to support Phil, a Negro, for same time.
- $29.10 allowed for support of Polly Dick, same time.
- $16.65 allowed for support of Nancy Clark, same time.
- $13.33 allowed for support of Old Mrs. Carmeans & daughter, same item.
- $41.66 allowed for support of Arthur Turley & wife, same time.
- $10 allowed for support of Violet Warner, same time.
- $20.80 allowed for support of Phebe Chapman, same time.

page 149

- $16.65 allowed for support of Sarah Moore, same time.
- $20.80 allowed for support of Old Mrs. Shoemaker until 31st March next.
- $16.65 allowed for support of Jefferson H.C. Bowen for same time.
- $20.80 allowed for support of Mrs. Dodd's children, same time

- $15 allowed for support of James Holdridge, same time.
- $40 allowed for support of David Parsons, same time.
- Same for his support for last 11 months to be paid to xx Rebecca Lucas, widow of Calvin Lucas xx (inserted "the state").
- $15 allowed for support of James H. Adkins until 31st March 1852.
- $15 paid to Harrison McComas for keeping same child last year.
- Drs. Maupin & McCorkle $9.50 for medical services for Mrs. Dodd & her family in 1850.
- John Porter $25 for keeping Old Mrs. Mowman last year.
  {1850 Census # 109-113 Sarah Mooman aged 56)
- $25 allowed for support of Old Mrs. Mowman until 31st March next.
- C.L. Roffe $19.83 for necessaries furnished John Thompson's family in 1851.
- $10 allowed for support of Mary Curtis until 31st March 1852.
- Mrs. John Bias $1 for nursing Mary Curtis.

page 150

- Absolum Bias allowed $10 for keeping Mary Curtis & child last year.
- James Ballard $4 for keeping Alexander Ruggles 3 days and for hawling him to Charles Holten's.
- Charles Holten $10 for 8 days attendance on Alexander Ruggles in his sickness and for funeral expenses.
- John T. Hibbons $2.50 for making coffin for Mrs. Dodd's child.
- Edmund C. Rece $3.50 for making coffin for Hezekiah Hudson.
- John M. Rece. $2.37 for burial clothes for Hezekiah Hudson, decd.
- Benjamin L. Perry $3 for making coffin for Old Mrs. Plank last year.
- James T. Carrell $4 for his services in attending Alexander Ruggles and for getting him a place to stay in his last illness and for indenture for Manual Adkins.
- William C. Miller & Co. $20 being the sum agreed to be paid to Augustus Colins for keeping Old Mrs. Plank.
- James T. Carrell & Daniel Love and John Samuels $1 each as overseers.
- Upon settlement with sheriff there remained $22.32 over & above the levy.
- Drs. McKorkle & Maupin $30 for attending paupers for the ensuing year.

page 151

- $20 allowed for support for Old Mrs. Plank for 1848.
- Adjourned. James T. Carrell President.

At a board or meeting of the Overseers of the Poor of Cabell County met at the Court House on Wednesday 31st day of March 1852. Present: James T. Carrell, Daniel Love, John Samuels.

- $20 allowed for support of James Sexton until March 31st, 1853.
- $25 allowed for support of Richard Johnson until March 1853.
- $30 allowed for support of Elizabeth Highsey until March 1853.
- $20 allowed for support of James Adkins until March 1853.
- $35 allowed for support of Polly Dick until March 1853.

- $20 allowed for support of Nancy Clark until March 1853.
- Mrs. Turley allowed $20 support until March 1853.
- $12 allowed for support of Violet Warner until March 1853.

page 152

- $25 allowed for support of Phebe Chapman until 31st of March 1853.
- $20 allowed for support of Sarah Moore until March 1853.
- Mrs. Shoemaker allowed $25 support until March 1853.
- $25 allowed for support of Jefferson H. C. Bowen until March 1853.
- $25 allowed for support of Mrs. Dodd's children.
- $18 allowed for support of James Holdride until 31st March 1853.
  {1850 Cabell Census #78-80 James aged 60 living with John W. Holdryed}
- $15 allowed for support of James H. Adkins up to 31st March 1853.
- $25 allowed for support of Old Mrs. Mowman up to 31st March 1853.
- $10 allowed for support of Mary Curtis.
- Drs. Maupin & McCorkle $30 for their service up to 31th March 1853.
- James T. Carrell & Daniel Love & John Samuels $1 each for their services.

page 153

- $7.50 allowed Andrew & Smoot Johnson for making coffin & burying Old Phil.
- William C. Miller & Co. $5.50 for fannell & money to remove Mrs. (Opauhuce-Opaussnce) from this county.
- James Adkins $7 for necessaries furnished by his store by Alexander Griffith to Samuel Moore, a pauper.
- $50 allowed to support Henry Miller family until March 1853.
- $20 allowed for support of Michael Lawler until 31st March 1853.
- $30 allowed to support —Keaton, a blind girl and a daughter of George Keaton for last year and $15 for the ensuing year until 31th March 1853.
- Doolittle & Howell $1 for meal furnished Mrs. Henry.
- Joseph Miller $5 for necessaries furnished William Chapman.
- Daniel Love $1 for meal furnished Mrs. Henry.

page 154

At a meeting of the Board of the Overseers of the Poor of Cabell at the Court House on Monday the 4th day of March 1853. Present: George Killgore, John L. Baker, John D. Holdryde, John S. Nicholas.

- On Motion by John S. Nicholas, George Killgore was appointed president.
- Motion by John S. Nicholas, Henry J. Samuels was appointed clerk of board.
- $20 for support of Nancy Clark for ensuing year, order to George Killgore.
- $15 allowed for support of Mrs. Dodd's children ensuing year, order Killgore.
- $35 allowed for support of Old Mrs. Shoemaker, order Killgore.
- $20 allowed for support of James H. Sexton, order to John D. Holdryde.
- $25 allowed for support of Phebe Chapman, order John S. Nicholas.
- $20 allowed for support of Sarah Moore, order Nicholas.
- $18 allowed for support of James Holdride, order to John D. Holdryde.

- $15 allowed for support of Old Mrs. Cook, order Killgore.
  {1850 Census #684-707 Sarah aged 60}

page 155

- $36 allowed for support of Daniel McMillon & wife, order to Holdryde.
- $10 allowed for support of Samuel Moore, order Nicholas.
- $20 allowed for support of Ewaletta Keyton, order Nicholas.
- $20 allowed for support of Susan Wysong, order Nicholas.
- Henry Vincent Adkins allowed $20 for his support, order John L. Baker.
- $25 allowed for support of William Jenkins, order to Killgore.
- $30 allowed for support of Richard Johnson, order to Baker
- $20 allowed for support to Patsy Turley, order to Killgore.
- $20 allowed for support of Michael Lawler, order to Baker.
- $15 allowed for support of James Adkins, order to John L. Baker.

page 156

- $15 allowed for support of James Edwards, order to John L. Baker.
- $15 allowed John Eplin to support his son Henry, order to George Killgore.
- $15 allowed for support of Old Mrs. Dolen, order Killgore.
  {1850 Census #675-698 Luckey aged 83}
- John M. Rece $16 for necessaries furnished Susan Wysong last year.
- Dr. Joseph Sidebottom $12 for medical services to Old Mr. Mathews and Susan Wysong last year, order to John S. Nicholas.
  {1850 Census #238-243 James Mathews aged 63}
- Dr. J.G. Harriman $12 for medical services to sundry paupers last year.
- $10 allowed for burial of Old Mrs. Henry, order George Killgore.
- William Jordan allowed $18.65 for taking care of Mrs. Shoemaker through a long illness, order to J.S. Nicholas.
- Allen McGinnis $9.50 for necessaries furnished D. McMillian last year, order John D. Holdryde.
- xx $7.30 allowed for necessaries for Old Mrs. Shoemaker, order Holdryde. xx
- John M. Rece $14 for necessaries furnished family of Daniel McMillian last year, order to John D. Holdryde.
- George W. Summers $1.50 for necessaries furnished D. Millian,

page 157

- Absolum Holderby $12.40 for necessaries furnished Old Man Teal & wife, Old Mrs. Cook & Nancy Clark last year, order to George Killgore.
- J. & S. Miller $13 for necessaries to Old Mrs. Dolen & Old Mrs. Henry.
- $5.25 to John L. Baker for burial expenses of Mrs. Beach.
- E. H. Walton $2.19 for shroud for A. F. Turley, order John L. Baker.
- $15.86 to V.D. Letulle for necessaries furnished sundry paupers, order Baker.
- John S. Nicholas & John L. Baker $3 for attendance here 3 days.
- George Killgore & John D. Holdryde $1 each.
- Thomas Kyle $8 for extra services rendered Nancy Clark.

- Board adjourned until 2nd day of May next. George Killgore, H.J. Samuels, clk.

page 158

At a meeting of the Board of the Overseers of the Poor at the Court House of Cabell County 2nd May 1853. Present: George Killgore, John S. Nichols, John D. Holdryde.

- Dr. W.W. McComas $3.75 for medical services to Old Man Jenkins last year.
- $25 allowed for support of J.H.C. Bowen, an idiot, payable to his mother, order J.D. Holdryde.
- W.C. Miller & Co. $2 for blankets furnished Old Mrs. Shoemaker.
- $12 allowed for support of Violet Warner, order to John S. Nicholas.
- $30 to William Smith for keeping Clarinda Adkins 3 years last past.
- $20 allowed for support of Old John Chapman & wife, order Nicholas. {1850 Census #292-301 John 79 & Molly 72.}
- Samuel Smith $71 for support of Elizabeth Adkins from June 1850 until today.

page 159

- $25 allowed for support of Elizabeth Adkins this year, order Nicholas.
- John Hannon $12 for keeping 2 men while sick, John & Dominique (Dwoato) (French) 16 days, order John D. Holdryde.
- $25 allowed for support of Old Mrs. Mowman, order John L. Baker.
- $35 allowed for support of Polly Dick, order Baker.
- Upon settlement with sheriff — (area left blank by clerk)
- John S. Nicholas $3 for 3 days service to Board.
- George Killgore & John D. Holdryde $1 each.
- H.J. Samuels $10 for services as clerk.
- Board adjourned until day of annual meeting prescribed by law. George Killgore, H.J. Samuels.

At a called meeting of the Overseers of the Poor on Saturday 31th of December 1853. Present: George Killgore President, P.C. Buffington, John D. Holdryde, John L. Baker, John S. Nicholas.

- H.H. Wood allowed $10 as assignee of William Stanley for keeping Clara Rains for 4 1/2 months while lying in and occasionally sick, order to George Killgore.
- Order made last spring to Absolum Holderby be corrected so that he receives $17.40.
- President of the Board to advertise in the *Guyandotte Herald* for proposals from persons to take the superintendency of the Poor House and Farm of this county. Propositions to be before the Board by the 1st Saturday in March next.

Board adjourned. George Killgore, H.J. Samuels, clk.

page 161

At an adjourned meeting of the Overseers of the Poor, Saturday 4th of March 1853. Present: George Killgore President, Peter C. Buffington, John D. Holdryde, John L. Baker, John S. Nicholas.

- J.D. Holdryde is appointed to make contact with someone to take the superintendency of the Poor House and the president of the board to make provision for supplies to the Poor House with necessary bedding and that they make a report at the annual meeting.

- Board adjourned until annul meeting. George Killgore, H.J. Samuels, clk.

page 162

At the Annual meeting of the Board of the Overseers of the Poor on Friday the 31st of March 1854. Present: George Killgore President, John L. Baker, John S. Nicholas, John D. Holdryde.

1854 Cabell County Deed Book 11, page 326
County Court purchased 243 acres on Trace Creek, McComas District
from Richard McKendree, the site is still called "The Poor Farm"

An article of agreement between the Overseers of the Poor & A. F. McKendree was presented to the board, approved and ordered recorded in the clerk's office of the Cabell County Court.

The following paupers are to be sent immediately to the Poor House:
Nancy C. Clark, Old Mrs. Shoemaker, Sarah Moore, Samuel Moore, William Jenkins, Daniel McMillon & wife, Patsy Turley, Michael Lawler, James Edwards, Violet Warner, Old Mrs. Mowman, Old Mrs. Cook.

- $20 allowed for support of James H. Sexton.(Margin - dead)
- $18 allowed to James Holdryde, order J.D. Holdryde.
- $20 allowed to E. Keaton, order Nicholas.
- $25 allowed for S. Wysong, order Nicholas.

page 163

- $35 for Elizabeth Highsey, order P.C. Buffington.
- $30 for James Adkins, order J.L. Baker.
- $15 for Hy Eplin, order to J.L. Baker.
- $15 for old Mrs. Dolen, order to George Killgore.
- $25 for J.H.C. Bowen, order Holdryde.
- xx $25 for Elizabeth Adkins xx.
- $20 for Benjamin Johnson, order Baker.
- $38 to J.L. Baker, $20 for keeping John Johnson, $16 for T. Carroll, $3 for Peter Smith & wife.
- W.C. Miller $14 for necessaries furnished Old John Kyle, burial clothes for Canton & clothes for Adkins, order Killgore.
- George Killgore: $15 for an extra allowance for Old Mr. Jenkins, $9.30 for burial expenses for Old Mrs. Teal, $8 to James (Lygs) & wife & $7.30 to A.W. Wingo for burying an Irish girl who burned to death, total $39.60.
- Griffin Reynolds $9 for keeping L. Chapman 6 days sick and burying said Chapman,

order J.S. Nicholas.

- $76 allowed to John S. Nicholas for necessaries furnished: $2 Mrs. Wallace, $20 Christina Johnson, $25 McComas' wife, $10 Lovejoy's boy & $1 for S. Wysong.

page 164

- $20 allowed for keeping old Mr. Teal, order to George Killgore.
- $35 allowed for support of Richard Johnson, order to J.L. Baker.
- Board adjourned. George Killgore.

At a called meeting of the Overseers of the Poor at the Court House, 15th May 1854. Present: George Killgore, John Nicholas, John D. Holdryde.

- $5.50 burial expenses for Old Mrs. Elizabeth Adkins of which $2.08 remained of her support for last year.
- Following sums allowed for conveying paupers to the Poor House: James L. Herndon $2 for Nancy Shoemaker, James Nicholas 50 cents for Richard Welch.

page 165

- County Court requested to levy $300 for keeping Poor House in supplies.
- $150 necessary to be levied to pay superintendent's salary for present year.
- $30 allowed superintendent for getting beds and furniture for Poor House.
- George Killgore $4 for 4 days attendance as overseer.
- J.D. Holdryde $5, John S. Nicholas $12, J.L. Baker $9 and P.C. Buffington $1.
- $10 allowed H.J. Samuels as clerk.
- Board adjourned. George Killgore, H.J. Samuels, clk.

page 166

At the annual meeting of the Board of the Overseers of the Poor at the Cabell County Court House 31th March 1855. Present: George Killgore, John D. Holdryde, John L. Baker.

- Upon settlement with superintendent of Poor House, there remains a surplus of $107.62 which was not needed to furnish clothes & bedding.
- Superintendents receipts of $222.38 shall be legal vouchers for him besides his annual salary.
- Following allowances made for supporting paupers at their present residence:
- $25 for John Chapman & his daughter Phebe.
  {1850 Cabell Census #292-301 John aged 79, Phebe 35 idiot}
- $20 for E. Keyton.
- $18 for James Holdryde, all on order to J. S. Nicholas.
- $30 for James Adkins, order to J.L. Baker.
- $15 for Old Mrs. Dolen, order to George Killgore.
- $25 for J.H.C. Bowen, order to J.D. Holdryde.
- For keeping Henry Vincent Adkins last year $25, order to J.L Baker.

page 167

- Broaddus Perry $2 making coffin for Martin Higgin, who died at Poor House.
- John W. Dick $2.50 for making coffin for Susan Thompson.

- George Killgore $3 for removing William Jenkins to Poor House, also $2 for Old Mrs. Mowman.
- J.L. Baker $2 for removing H.V. Adkins to Poor House.
- W.G. Davis allowed $7.81 for keeping Old Mr. Jenkins until removed to Poor House, order to George Killgore.
- $8 allowed for necessaries furnished Welch, a pauper, order to George Killgore.
- George Killgore $4.50 for necessaries furnished poor Irish family(Bramiger)
- (superseded by another order) Sarah Davis $85 for maintenance of Polly Dick, $35 for last year and $50 for present year, order to J.L. Baker.
- Thomas Holley $9 for keeping Elizabeth Jenkins in a spell of sickness, order to J.D. Holdryde.
- Dr. A. M. McCorkle $4.32 for attendance on Elizabeth Jenkins, J.D. Holdryde.
- $8.85 allowed for burial expenses and coffin for Mrs. Kyle, order Geo. Killgore. {1850 Census #70-72, Jane Kyle w/John approximate age 50}

page 168

- W.C. Miller & Co. $6 for necessaries to John Kyle's family, order Geo. Killgore.
- Drs. H.B. Maupin & Brother $99 for medical services last 2 years.
- $300 for maintaincy & expenses of Poor House & Farm for ensuing year and salary of superintendent.
- An article of agreement changing the salary of the superintendent to $15 per pauper per annum to be paid in proportion to the time the paupers are kept.
- $58.38 allowed on balance for building houses on the poor farm and sheriff to pay contractor $107.62, order George Killgore.
- John D. Holdryde $3 for 3 days attendance, J.L. Baker $9 for 3 days, J.S. Nicholas $2 for 2 days and clerk H.J. Samuels $10.
- Board adjourned George Killgore.

page 169

At a called meeting of the Board of Overseers of Poor for Cabell County at the Court House 26th of May 1855. Present: George Killgore, John L. Baker. John D. Holdryde, John S. Nicholas.

- Sarah Davis allowed $75 for keeping Polly Dick last year, order J.L. Baker.
- $100 allowed to Sarah Davis for keeping Polly Dick for ensuing year.
- John S. Nichols $11.75 for necessaries furnished Old Mrs. Wysong & Nancy Ellison and for removing Holten children to the Poor House.
- $500 levied for last payment on Poor House to Richard McCallister.
- Samuel Porter $15 for expenses and burial of Old Mrs. Mowman, order to J.L. Baker. Order given 30th Aug 1856 William E. Feazel.
- George Killgore $5 for 5 days attendance as overseer.

page 170

- J.D. Holdryde $2-2 days, John S. Nichols & John L. Baker $3-1 day - Court House.
- Thomas J. McComas $38 for building chimney at Poor House, order J.L. Baker.
- A.F. McKendree $18.75 for building houses and chimney at the Poor Farm.

- John Johnson $20 for keeping Benjamin Johnson, a pauper, order to J.L. Baker.
- Old Mr. Shawns $15 for keeping George W. Zirkle's children, order J.L. Baker.
- Board adjourned. George Killgore.

page 171

At a meeting of the Board of the Overseers of the Poor held at the Cabell County Court House 2nd September 1855. Present: George Killgore, John L. Baker, John S. Nicholas, John D. Holdryde.

- A. F. McKendree, superintendent of the Poor House allowed same terms as per agreement 31th March last.
- Mrs. A. F. McKendree $10 for attendance on Nancy Shoemaker, J.L. Baker.
- William F. Joy $13 for burial expenses for Samuel Kyle at Cincinnati, order to George Killgore, order given 11th of September William Feazel.
- J.M. Rece $10 for necessaries furnished Nancy Ellison, order J.S. Nichols.
- Perdue $2.50 for coffin for Mother Adkins, order Nichols.

page 172

- J.M. Rece $10.96 for necessaries furnished Welch, $3.96 and burial expenses for Mother Chapman $7, order to John S. Nicholas.
- $10 allowed T. J. McComas for balance of stone work, order J.L. Baker.
- Following sums allowed overseers and clerk: $1 J.D. Holdryde, George Killgore, $3 John S. Nicholas, John L. Baker and $1 James Kyle, clerk.
- Board adjourned, George Killgore.

page 173

At a regular meeting of the Overseers of the Poor held at the Court House 31th March 1856. Present: George Killgore president, John S. Nicholas, John D. Holdryde.

- Following allowances made to support paupers at their present residence:
- $35 John Chapman and daughter Phebe, order J.S. Nichols.
- $35 Susan Wysong and $18 James Holdryde, order J.S. Nichols.
- $30 for James Adkins, order to overseers of Falls District(issued to William Adkins November 9th 1857). - (margin-issued J.M. Rece - issued J. Davis)
- $25 for J.H.C. Bowen (issued J. Herndon 25 Aug 1856), order J.D. Holdryde.
- $100 for Polly Dick, order to overseer of Falls Dist.
- Upon settlement with superintendent $158.60 be paid him out of the $300 levy for last year leaving $141.34.
- W.C. Miller & Co. $58.82 for necessaries & clothing furnished paupers last year at the Poor House.

page 174

- That leaving a balance of $92.52 from the levy.
- $54.50 allowed Dr. H.B. Maupin for medical services last year, order George Killgore.
- John Peyton $25 for keeping Old Mr. Lunsford 5 weeks in his last sickness, order to George Killgore.
- W. C. Miller & Co. $7.26 for burial clothes for John Lunsford, order Killgore.

- John Dick $2.50 for coffin for John Lunsford, order to Killgore.
- Squire F. Workman $25 for keeping Wesly Webb for 6 weeks in his last illness, order to P.C. Buffington.
- John Ward $70 for keeping Robert Foy, an orphan child 1 year, and David Ward, a cripple 6 months, order George Killgore.

page 175

- Armstead Howell $5.50 for burial clothes for Susan Thompson, order Killgore.
- $8.62 to M. Thompson for furnishing H. Smith's family necessaries and Mrs. Dodd fuel, order George Killgore.
- $10 allowed Old Mrs. Williams for keeping Nancy Clark, order John S. Nichols.
- $10 allowed Elizabeth Toney for keeping her 2 grandsons 14 weeks, order to John S. Nicholas.
- Andrew Jorden allowed $33 for keeping John Statute, 11 weeks while sick, order to John S. Nicholas.
- $107.50 allowed for support of Poor Farm next year.
- Dr. John Peyton $18 for medical services to paupers. (Order given 2nd day of August 1856 Wm. E. Feazel.)
- Following sums allowed overseers and clerk:
- $1 George Killgore, John D. Holdryde, $3 John S. Nicholas, $10 H.J. Samuels.
- Board adjourned, George Killgore.

page 176

At a meeting of the Board of the Overseers of the Poor of Cabell County at the Poor House Saturday 12th day of July 1856. Present: Wm. E. Feazel, Martin Dillon, A.B. Roberts, James T. Herndon, Jefferson McComas. (The clerk has changed the spelling of Herndon overwriting d/t each time the name is used, the spelling today in Herndon.)

On motion of James T. Herndon, Wm. E. Feazel is appointed President.

On motion of Wm.E. Feazel, George W. Williams is appointed clerk.

- Wm. E. Feazel & James T. Herndon appointed to settle with sheriff.
- John S. Nicholas allowed $7 for services for ensuing year, order A.B. Roberts.
- $2 (tow) to James B. Byas for digging grave for Martin Higing at the Poor House, order to Jefferson McComas.

page 177

- $50 to (Dr.)H.B. Maupin & Brother for medical services for ensuing year.
- Board adjourned until Saturday 26th of July 1856. Wm. E. Feazel, president. George W. Williams, clk.

At a meeting of the Board of the Overseers of the Poor at the Poor House on Saturday 26th day of July 1856. Present: Wm. E. Feazel, Martin Dillon, Jefferson McComas, James T. Herndon, A.B. Roberts.

- Following sums allowed overseers for services: $4 for 4 days, Wm. E. Feazel, Jefferson McComas, James T. Herndon, A.B. Roberts, G.W. Williams, $6 for 6 days Martin Dillon.
- Clerk is have published in the *Unionist* and to make known to the citizens of Cabell

County that his Board has employed H.B. Maupin & Brother, fazisions, (physicians) to attend the paupours(paupers) of said county the ensuing year from July 12th 1856 and no other will be aloud(allowed) only is special cases. Wm. E. Feazel, Pr.

page 178

-Board Adjourned. Wm. E. Feazel, G.W. Williams clrk.

At a meeting of the Board of the Overseers of the Poor for Cabell county held at the Courthouse on 22nd day of Sept 1856. Present: Wm. E. Feazel President, Martin Dillon, James T. Herndon.

- Upon settlement with superintendent of the Poorhouse, it is ordered that he be allowed $99.43 after deducting $50 for half a years rent, fir necessaries and attention from 31th of March 1856 to 1st Oct 1856.
- Sheriff to pay A.F. McKendree $99.43 out of the levy for 1856.

page 179

- Henry Miller allowed $30 for keeping Elizabeth Highsey from 31st of March 1855 until 31st of March 1856, President's order.
- Allen Webb allowed $14 for keeping Wesley Webb for 14 weeks in 1855, a man that became a county charge formerly a resident of Kanawha County, VA.
- Agreement reached between Board and A.F. McKendree for keeping Poor House, ordered recorded in clerk's office.
- Wm. E. Feazel appointed to examine an report on repairs needed at Poor House, to be on file at annual meeting 1857.
- Overseers allowed as follows: J.T. Herndon & Wm.E. Feazel 2 days, $2, Martin Dillon 1 day $1.
- Board adjourned until 31th of March 1857. Wm.E. Feazel, President.

page 180

At a meeting of the Board of the Overseers of the Poor on 31st of March 1857. Present: Wm. E. Feazel President, James T. Herndon, Marlin Dillon, A. B. Roberts, Jefferson McComas.

- Sarah Davis allowed $40 for keeping Polly Dick last year, order Jeff McComas.
- Sarah Stone allowed $20 for her support ensuing year, order Wm. E. Feazel.
- Joseph R. (Jimiser) $7 for burial expenses for a pauper at the Poor House.
- John Ong $1 for digging grave for Catherine Jewel, order to Wm. E. Feazel.
- Mathew Thompson for (something) for Old Man Jenkins.
- Thomas J. Jenkins $10 for furnishing paupers --

page 181

- James T. Herndon $10 for furnishing James Gipson's family necessaries.
- Anderson Jenkins (Genkins) for taking care of Alex Cremeans in his last illness. (issued to Thomas Holley)
- J.B. Bowen $10.69 for necessaries furnished Hanner Jenkins.
- Jacob Bumgardner $10 for taking Thomas Edwards to the Poor House.
- Maklen Ayers $10 for taking care & burying David Craig.

- Henry Miller $30 for keeping Elizabeth Hyse in 1856.
- Wheeler & Wallace $10 for advertising.
- W. B. Pery $5 for making 2(tow) coffins for paupers.
- A. B. Rowsey $3.47 for schooling Elizabeth Crump, pauper of Cabell county.
- T.J. Hayslip $2.50 (Tow dollars and fifty cents) for making coffin for Webb, pauper of this county.

page 182

- William Merritt $1.50 for keeping William Heart, pauper.
- John T. Hatfield allowed $3 for Harshbarger to take William Heart to Poor House.
- George Killgore $4.50 for taking care of William Heart.
- James B. Byas $2 for digging grave for pauper.
- W.B. Perry $2.50 for making coffin for pauper.
- Anderson Johnson $2.50 for making coffin for Richard Johnson, pauper.
- Rolin S. Byas $3 for moving Mrs. McComas to Poor House, Wm.E. Feazel.
- John Ong $2 (tow) for digging grave for pauper. (issued to E.J. Blankenship.)

page 183

- Enoch Blankenship allowed $11.50 for furnishing Chas. (Kys-IEys or 19ys.)
- Sampson Hanley $10.50 for bacon furnished Mrs. McComas, pauper.
- Washington Angel $12 for keeping Elizabeth Jenkins confined.
- Alexander McCallister $11.50 for making & repairing fences on Poor Farm.
- A. M. Porter $52 (tow) for keeping Alexander Now last year.
- E. Wellington $6.50 for making coffins for paupers.
- Wm. C. Miller & Co. $76.72 (tow) for furnishing sundries to paupers. (margin - issued to E.J. Blankenship.)
- Jeroam Shelton $18 for keeping Old Mr. Lanler in 1855.(Jerome raised order.)
- David Harshbarger $5 for flower furnished Mrs. McComas.

page 184

- $8.90 allowed Neece Dillion by Dutchman for attendance to William Heart.
- Rezon Wheeler $15 for keeping Nancy Clark last year.
- Wm. Williams allowed $89.50 for repairs to kitchen at Poor House.
- A. F. McKendree $50.33 the remains of his allowance for 1856 to 31 March 1857.
- Zacharia Niceal $1.50 for boarding Wm. Heart for the benefit of A.F. McKendree.
- A.F. McKendree $15 for extra furnishing for paupers of Cabell County.
- A. F. McKendree $9 for Board of Overseers & fezision (physician?) last year.
- H.B. Maupin & Bro. $30 extra services to paupers, payable order of Wm.E. Feazel.

page 185

- (Dr.) S.C. Ricketts $32 for services to paupers.
- (Dr.) S.C. Ricketts $5 for services to David Craig.
- (Dr.) S.C. Ricketts $1.50 cost paid Wolcott for sundries for Row.
- Dr. Moss $10 for services to George Hagen.
- $12 allowed Wm. Curry for services rendered John Rough. (doctor?)
- Wm. Curry $6 for services rendered Armilda Byas during her illness.

- A.B. Roberts allowed $6.76 for taking care of John (Rough).
- A.B. Roberts allowed $7 for taking paupers to poor House.
- Following allowances to paupers for ensuing year:
- $25 for Henry Miller.
- Elizabeth McComas allowed $25 for keeping (Embessa) McComas ensuing year.

page 186

- Sarah Holdrhyde $24 for keeping James Holdrhyde.
- $30 to Mrs. Bowen for keeping James C. Bowen in 1856.
- $10 to Nancy Clark for 1857.
- (Susan) Wysong allowed $40 support.
- $12 for Clarinda Holt on order of A.B. Roberts.
- $300 allowed for support of Poor Farm the ensuing year.
- A.F. McKendree to buy clothes for paupers at Poor House.
- James T. Herndon allowed 3 days & $2 binding 2 boys for $5.
- A. B. Roberts allowed 6 days, $6.
- Martin Dillon allowed 3 days, $3.
- Jefferson McComas 5 days and binding boy, $6.
- Wm. E. Feazel 5 days & indenture of 1 child, $6.
- G.W. Williams 2 days as clerk, $2.
- Board adjourned until 3rd Friday in April next at the Poorhouse, this 31st of March 1857 (157) Wm. E. Feazel Pres. G.W. Williams clk.

page 187

At a meeting of the Overseers of the Poor at the Poor House of Cabell County on the 3rd Friday of April 1857. Present: Wm.E. Feazel President, Martin Dillon, A.B. Roberts, James T. Herndon.

- Benjamin Byas allowed $41.20 for keeping Thomas Gallaspie in his last illness.
- Sampson Hanley $5 for keeping Thomas Gallaspie while sick, order James T. Herndon.
- H.B. Maupin $13 for services rendered to Gallaspie during his illness.
- Wm.M. Williams $4 for lumber furnished Poor House.
- W.B. Perry $3 for making coffin for paupers at Poor House.

page 188

- James H. Roffe $47 for repairing barn at Poor Farm.
- President is ordered to notify A.F. McKendree 6 months before his contract is to expire and that contract is renewed until 1st March 1858
- Wm. E. Feazel is to bind Elizabeth Crump to some discreet person with permission of County Court.

page 189

- Also to bind out Elizabeth McComas and to have Court give permission to bind out any of the children at the Poor House.
- James T. Herndon, A.B. Roberts, Wm. E. Feazel each $2, Martin Dillon $3.
- G.W. Williams $2 as clerk.

- Board adjourned until 3rd Saturday in August 1857. Wm.E. Feazel.

page 190

At a cald meeting of the Overseers of the Poor of Cabell County head at the Court House Friday 28th of August 1857. Present: Wm.E. Feazel President, James T. Herndon, Martin Dillon, A.B. Roberts, Jefferson McComas, G.W. Williams clerk.

- Upon settlement with superintendent of Poor House, he is to be paid $80.23 the balance due him to 28th August 1857 and to be taken from the levy.
- Voted A.F. McKendree remain superintendent of Poor House and according to his former contract.

- President to inform County Court that the Poor House lands belonging to the Overseers as (mis------) and are in favor of same lands being sold and the proceeds appropriated to the county 28th Aug 1857.

- Board adjourned, Wm. E. Feazel. G.W. Williams

At a annual meeting of the Overseers of the Poor of Cabell County at the Poor House 31st March 1858. Present: W.E. Feazel, Jas. T. Herndon, A.B. Roberts, Jefferson McComas, Martin Dillon.

- Upon settlement with sheriff --- (section blank)----.
- A.F .McKendree $63.91 balance due him for services rendered to Poor House from 1857 to 31 March 1858.

page 192

- (Dr.) V.R. Moss $63.75 for services rendered to paupers.
- Alex McClary $8 for attending Mrs. (Mitchum), a sick woman.
- William J. Dillion $27.62 for keeping Sherwood Shelby while sick.
- (Dr.) H.B. Maupin $74.25 for medical services up to March 31st, 1858.
- William M. Williams Co. $9.00 for 3 coffins and carrying same to Poor House.
- John M. Rece $50.24 for merchandise furnished paupers.
- John Arthur $22 for keeping Willis (Hamblett).
- James O. Cox $2.86 for burial expenses.

page 193

- Edmund Reece $7.50 for coffins.
- Jewel Porter $11.25 for keeping Nancy Clark up to 31st March 1858.
- Dr. A.M. McCorkle $20.88 for medical services.
- (Fudiett-Indiett) Winn $24.50 for keeping William Webb.
- James T. Herndon $2.45 for necessaries furnished Willis Hamblette.
- Estate of J.D. Holdryde $1 for his services rendered.
- John G. Hibbins $21 for making 4 coffins and burying paupers.
- John Peyton $33 for keeping Eliza Rains and for taking Mary (Mitchm) to the Poor House.

page 194

- William Adams $1 for halling (hauling) Willis Hamblete to his grave.
- William G. Fielder $42 for keeping Patsey Turley and taking care of (Pary) & Bill &

Jo. (listed on 1860 Cabell Census #119-116.)
- Peyton Spears $15.75 for taking care of Sarah Adkins while sick.
- John Merritt & Co. $3.92 3/4 for flour & meal to John Kile.
- William Peyton $2.25 for a shroud for Eliza Raynes.
- H.H. Miller $3.35 for a shroud for David Craigh. (issued to W.K. Moore.)
- William F. Dusenberry $2 for flour furnished James Gipson.
- McKendree & Blume $1.65 for liquor for medical purposes furnished paupers.
- Jesse W. McComas $5 for making coffin & funeral expenses for Mrs. Selbee. (issued to John Franklin.)

page 195
- A.F. McKendree $4.50 for digging 3 graves at the Poor House.
- Miller Salmon & Miller $53.67 for merchandise, by order of Board.
- Wm. C. Miller & Co. $48.39 for merchandise.
- Dr. A.B. McGinnis $27 for medical services to Jackson Jefferson & others.
- John Porter 75 cents for corn furnished Minery Johnson. (issued by S.G. Miller)
- Board adjourned until tomorrow morning at 8 O'clock. Wm.E. Feazel.

April 1st, 1858
- A.B. Roberts $20.79 for necessaries furnished Parker Adkins & George Morrison & Clarinda Holt, paupers of Cabell County.
- Mical(Michael?) Rogers $9.75 for keeping John Rough.

page 196
- (Dr.) S.C. Ricketts $10 for medical services rendered William Webb & Mrs. Winns, order of the Board.
- Wm.E. Feazel $10 for benefit of Nancy Miller & Minerely(Minery) Johnson.
- $25 allowed for Henry Miller & family, order Jefferson McComas.
- Edward Vertigans $9.49 for conveying Sherwood Selby to Poor House.
- Robert Edwards $15 for keeping James Edwards in 1857.
- Mathew Thompson $30 for necessaries furnished Mrs. Dad (Dodd?) in year of setting of old Board - by a mistake by Board.
- Matilda Gipson allowed $45 for her support, order by Wm.E. Feazel. (over the line $12.50, $5.00, $3.00.)
- Henry Miller to be confined at the Poor House for the ensuing year.
- Jefferson McComas by permission of the County Court be allowed to bind out such children as may become a county charge in his district.

page 197
- $20 allowed (Pebey) Chapman, order A.B. Roberts.
- $40 allowed for support of Susan Wysange.
- $30 allowed for support of James C. Bowen.
- Sarah Holdryde allowed $30 for her support of James Holdryde.
- $350 be levied for support of Poor House.
- Following allowances be made to Board: $7 James T. Herndon, $15 A.B. Roberts, $10 Wm.E. Feazel President, $9 Martin Dillon, $9.50 Jefferson McComas,

$6 G.W. Williams clerk.

- President of Board to settle with superintendent and sheriff, Board adjourned.
  Wm.E. Feazel President, G.W. Williams, clerk.

page 198

At a called meeting of the Overseers of the Poor of Cabell County, VA at the Poor House on 20th Aug 1858. Present: J.T. Herndon, A.B. Roberts, Martin Dillon, Alex McClary.

- Motion by J.T. Herndon, Alexander McClary appointed President of the Board to fill the vacancy occasioned by the resignation of Wm.E. Feazel.
- J.W. Williams be discharged as clerk and Wm.E. Feazel appointed to fill that position.
- On settlement with A.F. McKendree, he be allowed $126.86 for keeping paupers from 31st of March 1858 until 20th of August 1858 and to be paid out of the Poor House Levy.
- Board adjourned until 31st of March 1858 {9?} Alx. McClary 20th Aug 1858.

page 199

At a called meeting of the Overseers of the Poor for Cabell County held at the poor house 4th of Sept 1858. Present: A. McClairy President, A.B. Roberts, James T. Herndon, Jefferson McComas.

- We the above named Board in agreement with the stewart of the Poor House, A.F. McKendree, give order to the sheriff of Cabell County that all money levied by the court and $111.56 for improving land, making fence and furnishing clover under a former lease with McKendree, which McKendree relinquishes said lease and gives peaceable privilege to sow wheat on any lands and on any land in corn as soon as corn can safely cut, he also give possession of all houses and farm at Christmas.

A.F. McKendree, A. McClary, J.T. Herndon, A.B. Roberts, Jefferson McComas.

page 200

- xx Indenture 4th day of Sept. 1858 between the Overseers of the Poor & A. McClary. Witness that the Overseers employ A. McClary as stewart of the Poor House commencing ---- May ----185--. That is to say that A. McClary agrees to take charge of the Poor Farm & all the paupers of the county and furnish 1 horse, 2 cows, 2 sows and pigs to be used to the benefit of farm & paupers for one year with diligence. Overseers agree upon his performance to pay said McClary $350 for his services and to return to him at the end of the year all the above stock except what he used for the benefit of the paupers. Hands & seal: 4th Day of Sept. 1858. A. McClary, James T. Herndon, A.B. Roberts, Jefferson McComas and A.F. McKendree, clerk protem. xx
- A.F. McKendree $17 owed.
- A.F. McKendree $53.14 balance of $350 from keeping Poor House 1857/58/59.

page 201 (blank)

page 202

At a meeting of the Overseers of the Poor of Cabell County at the Courthouse 31st of

March 1859. Present: James T. Herndon, Jefferson McComas, Alex. B. Roberts, Martin Dillon.

On motion of A.B. Roberts, James T. Herndon elected President to fill the vacancy of Alexander McClary removed.

- Morning Williams $25 for keeping Sally Holton's children.
- James B. Byas $1.50 sending for doctor for pauper at the Poor House in 1858.
- James N. Rowsey $6.50 for plowing the Poor Farm.
- Dr. Wm. E. Herndon medical attention on Mrs. Reynolds, a daughter of John Forth.
- Wolcott & Everett $15 for goods furnished on order of Martin Dillon. (Issued to More on order of G. Miller.)

page 203

- H.A. Fetter $9.50 for saddlery furnished stewart of Poor House.
- Miller Salmon & Miller $63.62 for goods furnished paupers in 1858 & 1859 until 31st of March.
- A.F. McKendree allowed $124 for services rendered by himself and wife while stewart at Poorhouse.
- Archibald Reynolds $2 for digging grave for William Jenkins at the Poor House in 1858. (issued to G.S. Miller)
- $35.50 allowed for support of Matilda Gipson, daughter of James Gipson.
- A.F. McKendree $5.45 for pork furnished McClary at the Poor House.
- Jennel Porter $20 for keeping Nancy Clark until 31st of March 1859.
- Dr. V.R. Moss $94 for medical services to paupers up to 31st march 1859.

page 204

- Dr. Hall $19 for medical services for Jacob Winters in 1857. (Issued to H.B. Maupin.)
- Dr. Harrison Walker $6.25 for medical services to Mrs. Selby in 1858.
- (Dr.) H.B. Maupin $46 for medical services to paupers until 31st of March 1859.
- (Dr.) H.B. Maupin $125 for horse furnished to the Poor House for the benefit of the county. (Issued to James T. Herndon.)
- B.F. Swann $15.75 for tools furnished Poor House.
- Archibald Reynolds $3.62 for plowing at the Poor House.
- Alexander McClary allowed $19,75 for labor he performed for the benefit of the Poor House 25th Dec 1859.
- John M. Blake $3.50 for services, order J.T. Herndon.
- James O. Cox $6.30 for goods, Herndon order.

page 205

- Mrssers Howell & Switzer allowed $38.52 for meal & corn to Herndon's.
- James T. Herndon $120.75 for (horse) wagon, chain & shovel furnished Poor Farm for its use.
- Spencer Midkiff $5.75 for corn & (----) furnished Henry Miller, Hy McComas order.
- William G. Fielder $20 for keeping old Mrs. Turley until 31st of March 1859.

- Sarah Heath allowed $122.26 for grain furnished Poor House, 1858,1859.
- John Bell & Co. $25.38 for pork furnished Poor House.
- $16.25 allowed to support Jonathan Fielder's child, Mayabell, an idiot.
- Andrew Johnson $5 for keeping Widow Johnson in 1858.
- John Merritt & Co. $4

page 206

- Isaac Blake Jr. $19.93 for goods furnished paupers.
- Jacob Smith allowed $40 to support Jacob Smith & wife.
- W.B. Wolcott $2.45 for goods furnished paupers last year.
- Jewel Porter $1.62 for taking Mrs. Connor to Poor House.
- R.B. Allen $48.21 for goods furnished paupers.
- S.M. Clark $4.95 for medicine for (Adamsly) Dillon an Overseer of the Poor.
- A. McClary $20 for hogs furnished Poor House - to be paid in hogs 25th Dec 1859.
- William Morrison $9.50. Issued to Wm. Rogers.
- (Dr.) P. C. McCullough $54 for 38 visits and medicine to Jordan Adams during 1858, a distance of 5 miles at $1.50 per visit.

page 207

- William Douthit $10.88 for the benefit of Jordan Adams from April 5th 1858 until 15th June 1858 on order of M. Dillon.
- Henry Miller $28.25 for boarding and clothing for Elizabeth Hissey for 1858 and the same for 1859.
- Sarah Holdryde $30 for keeping James Holdryde for 1859.
- xx Columbus E. Bowen xx
- Mrs. Bowen allowed $30 for keeping Columbus E. Bowen for 1859.
- James T. Herndon $7.90 for meat furnished Widow Smith's family in 1859.
- Jefferson McComas allowed $25 for benefit of Emerson McComas.
- Samuel Teele allowed $4.50 for the benefit of Charles Peyton in 1859.
- Jefferson McComas allowed $2 for the benefit of Preston (Spiesos).

page 208

- F. Sanders allowed $21.73 for wheat sowed on the Poor Farm in 1859.
- William Keaton $12 for keeping Matilda Jordan at the rate of $2 per month from the 25th of Dec 1858.
- A.B. Roberts $2 for the benefit of Elizabeth Holton for 1859.
- A.B. Roberts $15.47 for self for 1859.
- A.B. Roberts $40 for benefit of Susie Wysong for 1859.
- Article between Overseers and A. McClary to be recorded, 31st March 1859.

page 209

- Jefferson McComas $23 for services rendered overseers in 1858 to March 1859.
- Martin Dillon $8 for services rendered Overseers 1858 to March 1859.
- James T. Herndon $8 for services rendered Overseers same.
- A.B. Roberts $15 for services rendered Overseers same.
- William E. Feazel $15 for services rendered Overseers same.

- A. McClary allowed $350 for stewardship of Poor House through 31st March.
- (large ink spot) Of That $150 for purpose of paying hire and physical changes for Poor House through 31st March 1859.
- *Western Bingmian* office allowed $6 for use of W.B. Moore.

page 210

- A. McClary authorized to hire such work as he deems necessary for the Poor Farm to be paid out of the $150.
- Board adjourned. J.T. Herndon President, Wm.E. Feazle clerk.

page 211

At a meeting of the Overseers of the poor for Cabell County held at the Poor House 10th of Sept. 1859. Present: Frederick Miller, Alexander Roberts, Jefferson McComas, James T. Herndon President.

- On motion of J.T. Herndon, Alexander McClary was reappointed superintendent of the Poor House for 1860 beginning 25th Dec 1859 and ending 25 Dec 1860. For which McClary is to be paid $350 and to provide the Board with required bond.

- John Sheff be paid $68 with interest out of the 1860 levy. A.N. Williams clerk protem, J.T. Herndon President.

page 212

- Bond of Alexander McClary with security James Bias and Benjamin Perry to the Overseers of the Poor. $700 lawful Virginia money as steward of the Poor House. McClary agrees to furnish 1 horse, 2 cows, 2 sows and pigs to be used for benefit of the paupers. Value of livestock to be refunded to McClary at end of year if duty preformed. James B. Bias, Benjamin L. Perry, James T. Herndon, Marlin Dillon, A.B. Roberts, Jefferson McComas.

page 213

At a meeting of the Overseers of the Poor at the Courthouse on the 31st of March 1860. Present: James T. Herndon President, G.F. Miller, Marlin Dillon, A.B. Roberts.

- Henry Miller allowed $30 for keeping Elizabeth Hisey until 31st March 1861.
- Mrs. Holdryde $25 for keeping James Holdryde until 31st March 1861.
- Mrs. Bowen $25 for keeping C.B. Bowen, same.
- $30 allowed for benefit of Matilda Gipson, same.
- Mrs. Cook allowed $20 for her support, same.
- $50 allowed (G.F. Shelton) for keeping Jacob Smith & wife, same.

page 214

- $20 allowed for Mrs. Wysong for support of Susan Wysong, same.
- Jacob M. Smith $40 for keeping Jacob Smith & wife, same.
- William C. Miller & Co. $32.40 for goods furnished paupers to March 31, 1860.
- $14.50 Timothy Adkins for keeping Caroline Adkins & child while confined.
- Squire A. Johnson $11.16 for making coffins and finding provision for paupers.
- Miller Solomon & Miller $28.61 goods & provision furnished Old Mrs. Cook and shroud for Charles Paton through 31 March 1860.

page 215

- H.C. Potete $5.24 for 1lb of timothy seed furnished Poor Farm in 1859.
- William (H—ll) (overwritten) $6 for taking John McCardy to Poor House & boarding same for 15 days.
- $10 allowed H.C. Stevens for services rendered Anderson Bowling in his last illness, by himself & wife.
- Howell & Switzer $11.58 for meal and plank furnished Poor House.
- $18.58 allowed John Q. Adams for keeping Jordan Adams prior to 1860.
- $12 allowed A.F. McKendree for washing tobacco and making clothes for (Michael Loller) to 31st March 1860. (Lawter)
- $11.60 to Richard Lunsford for necessaries furnished Charles Peyton when sick.
- Dr. Samuel McGinnis $5 fee for Lucinda Adkins & Caroline Adkins.

page 216

- John T. Hibbens $18.50 for making coffins for paupers through 31st of March 1860.
- $56.33 allowed Dr. Allen B. McGinnis for attention to pauper, same.
- $25 allowed Dr. Rouse for medical attention to William Williams' family when sick in 1859 & 1860, until March 31st.
- $15.45 allowed Dr. H.B. Maupin for medical attention to paupers.
- $30 for benefit of John Forth & family and John Reynolds' children, no charge for rent of house and garten on Poor Farm for 1860. [Poor farm charged paupers rent?]
- James O. Cox allowed $111.83 for necessaries furnished Poor House.
- $7 to J.W. Carter & William Love for moving David Smith's family to Poor House.

page 217

- $13.50 allowed to Washington Angel for keeping Mary Smith.
- Wolcott & Everett $14.60 for chairs & plow for Poor Farm.
- Dr. V.R. Moss medical services to paupers through 31st March 1860.
- G.F. Miller & Co. $25.70 necessaries provided to paupers at Poor Farm, same.
- John Peyton $3 for pork for Charles Peyton.
- A. McClary $55.40 for preliminary expenses at Poor House.
- $4 allowed James Rowsey for conveying Charles Peyton & wife & children.
- $50.25 allowed A.B. Roberts for services rendered and keeping paupers.

page 218

- $350 to Alexander McClary for service as superintendent of Poor House from Jan. 1st 1860 until Jan. 1st 1861.
- County Court to levy $300 to have as surplus for special charges.
- James T. Herndon $161 for keeping paupers and taking them to Poor House.
- Overseers allowed following sums:
- $2 Martin Dillon, $3 G.F. Miller, $15 Wm.E. Feazel.
- Board adjourned until 31st March 1861, this day of March 31st 1860.

James T. Herndon President.

page 219

At a meeting of the Overseers of the Poor of Cabell County, Virginia held at the Poor House on the 21st of July 1860. Present: George F. Miller, Anderson Bias, Larkin Bias, James Miller & James T. Herndon.

- George F. Miller appointed President of the Board.
- Moses S. Thornburg elected clerk of the Board for a term of 4 years from the 1st of July 1860 and he is allowed $15 per each year.
- Motion to let Poor House & Farm out to the lowest bidder lost 2 to 3 vote.
- Board voted to retain Alexander McClary as superintendent of the Poor Farm for 1 year, from 25th of December 1860 and to pay his expenses in exchange McClary is to provide $700 bond.

page 220

- McClary is to have same terms as in previous year.
- Board adjourned. G.F. Miller President.

page 221

- Alexander McClary's bond for $700 with security by James Bias, Alin D. Davis & Anderson Bias. dated 1st of January 1861. (All security signed by (x) mark.

page 222

At the annual meeting of the Overseers of the Poor of Cabell County held at the Court House on 31st of March 1861. Present: George F. Miller President, James T. Herndon, James Willson, Anderson Bias, Larkin Bias.

- Moses S. Thornburg not being present, Wm.E. Feazel appointed clerk protem.
- E. H. Walton $5 for goods furnished Mr. Boyd for benefit of his daughter.
- W. & D.D. Smith allowed $20 for amount paid More's for keeping Wm. Floyd.
- $25 allowed for Mr. Boyd's daughter on order by James Willson.
- H.H. Miller $5.65 for goods furnished for burial of Elizabeth Higsey.
- Dr. H. Rouse $10.50 for medical services rendered Mr. Collins & Fretwell Hensley also $10 for services to J. Quincy Adams.
- Dr. Samuel Williams $15 medical service to Samuel Kinder's wife and others being Ashworth & Betsy Dunbar and Robinson Patton.

page 223

- Dr. V.R. Moss $15.50 for medical service to the Poor House to date.
- Elias Collins allowed $10 for keeping Caroline Adkins' child.
- $30 allowed for support of Matilda Gipson, order to G.F. Miller.
- $20 allowed for support of Old Mrs. Cook.
- Jacob Smith & wife allowed $50 until 31st March 1862, order G.F. Miller.
- $20 allowed for support of Old Sally Ferguson.
  {1860 Census #193-188 Sarah Ferguson aged 84}
- Merritt & Co. $5 for breadstuff furnished John Woods & mother.
- $9.67 allowed G.F. Miller & Co. for goods furnished paupers to this date.
- $4 allowed Old Mrs. Joseph Wentz for keeping Jacob Wentz, a pauper 4 weeks.
- $20 allowed for support of Old Mrs. Turley, order to Wm. (G.-S.) Fielder.
- $14.63 to Wm.C. Miller & Co. for goods furnished paupers.

- Miller Solman & Miller allowed $21 for goods furnished paupers.
- John M. Dial allowed $1.25 for moving Matilda M. Emmons

page 224

- Alexander McClary $17.48, for cash paid out for paupers.
- Dr. A. B. McGinnis $36 for medical services to Jordan Floyd & F. Hensley.
- Eliza McComas allowed $20 for maintaining her 34 year old son Emerson.
- $29.54 allowed James O. Cox, goods furnished for benefit of Poor House.
- H.C. Poteet $6.78 for burial expenses for Jackson Jefferson.
- $19.43 allowed Sampson Handley for (blacksand) work done at Poor House.
- (Dr.) A.M. McCorkle $4 for attending Jackson Jefferson, a pauper.
- Sherod Adkins $5 for things furnished Mrs. Henry Miller in 1859.
- Howell & Switzer $24.57 for meal & flour to the Poor House.
- Sarah Holdryde $25 for keeping James Holdryde until March 1862.
- Mrs. Bowen allowed $25 for keeping James H.C. Bowen.
- James O. Cox allowed $106.43 for goods furnished Poor House.
- $4 allowed to Alba Holton for coffin for Old Man Pearson.
  {1860 census #947-910 Simon, aged 70}

page 225

- J.W. Nelson allowed $10 for keeping Elizabeth Dunbar while confined.
- J.T. Hibben allowed $4 for coffin for (ink spot) Jacob(?) Wentz.
  {1860 Census #184-180 aged 80}
- Hamilton Adkins $10 for keeping and for burial clothes for Simon Pearson.
- $30 allowed for support of John Forth's wife and for John Reynolds' children, order to Anderson Bias.
- (Dr.) H.B. Maupin $3.50 for medical services to paupers.
- Larkin Bias $15 to in support of Jonathan Fielder's child, an idiot.
- Alexander McClary $350 for superintendency of Poor farm and paupers for 1861 until 31st of March 1862.
- Alexander McClary $10 for cash paid to Mrs. Heath for corn for paupers.
- County to levy $400 for specials charges for next year.

page 226

- James T. Herndon $2.50 for Red bedstead for Poor House.
- Robert McClary $4 for stocking 2 cradles for Poor House. (Grain cradles?)
- Following sums to be allowed overseers: each for 2 days
- $2 to George F. Miller, James T. Herndon, Anderson Bias, Larkin Bias and James Willson.
- Adjourned until 31st of March 1862. G.F. Miller President

page 227

At a called meeting of the Overseers of the Poor held at the Court House 5th of October 1861. Present: James Wilson, James T. Herndon, Anderson Bias, Larkin Bias, M.S. Thornburg, clerk.

- James Wilson appointed President Protem.

- Alexander McClary voted to remain superintendent of Poor House for one year commencing on 25th December 1861, provided a bond of $600 is given. McClary to have salary of $300.
- Board Adjourned. James Wilson.

loose page

page 228

- On settlement with the sheriff in 1823 an allowance of $18.61 was found in favor of the Poor. E. McGinnis clerk.
- On settlement with the sheriff in 1824, a balance was found in favor of the Poor in the amount of $99.77 which includes $18.61 from 1823 and $48 for Molly Adkins and $33.16 1/2 in 1824. E. McGinnis, clerk.
- Amount collected in 1825

from 1052 tithes, 25 cents collected from each being	$263.00
balance in hands of sheriff	$ 99.77
Total for 1825 being	$362.77
6% interest on $263 = $ 15.78	
claims paid by overseers $ 316.81 1/4	

- Balance in sheriff's hands 5th Jun 1826 $ 30.18 1/4
  E. McGinnis clerk to the Board of Overseers.
- 4th June 1827 balance in sheriff's hands $ 99.26 3/4

page 229

- Surplus levy to paid to 1861.
- Larkin Bias order $5 to Lucy Deal to support Phebe Deal.

Back leaf of book

1826 claims to pay on Bowen's side of county $18.70
claims to pay (McGinnis) sector $19.69

Peter C. Buffington - Michael O. Donivan for clothes $3.50

issued $1 to Wolcott
$5 to May for necessaries for (M--------) Johnson
3 lines illegible

The end

1860 Cabell County Census - Poor Farm

	Name	Age	Born	Occupation
#815-782	McLeary, Alexander	55m	VA	farmer
	Lucretia	49f	VA	
	Alexander	20m	VA	farmer
	Catherine	9f	VA	
	Charles	8m	VA	
	McCoggle, John	66m	PA	blksmith/pauper
	Smith, Mary	30f	VA	pauper
	Holten, Minerva	28f	VA	pauper
	Hill, Benjamin	22m	VA	pauper
	Smith, Joseph	12m	VA	pauper
	Smith, Nathaniel	3m	VA	pauper

1870 Cabell County Census - Poor Farm

	Name	Age	Born	Occupation
#73-74	McKendree, Aaron F.	65m	VA	farmer
	Catherine	52f	VA	
	William P.	19m	WV	laborer
	Mary S.	16f	WV	school
	Emma M.	15f	WV	school
	Lydia	12f	WV	
	Retherford, Eliot	40m	WV	pauper
	Cannon, Matilda	53f	WV	pauper
	Jourdon, Matilda	26f	WV	pauper
	Shumaker, Nancy	26f	WV	pauper
	Shumaker, Lucy	1f	WV	pauper

DEATHS LISTED BY THE OVERSEERS OF THE POOR

(Either directly or by reference of death)

Note: The fiscal year is not from January 1st, but different with each Board.
Note: Most of these people do not appear on the census.

1813/14 Nancy Coxe
1817/18 Buckel
John Short
1820/21 Jamima Roberts
1822/23 John Brown's mother
Martin Busad's mother
Randolph Marcum s/Josiah
Molly Adkins
1824/25 Richard Vernon
1827/28 Robert Lewis (April 1827)
Mr. Broom
David Withrow
1828/29 Widow Blue
1829/30 Samuel Butcher
Martin Hollenback
1830/31 Rudolph Hoozer (VanHoose)
Mother Osburn
James Halsey
1831/32 H. Harris
Polly Night
H. Hart
1832/33 Joseph Huller
1833/34 Marmaduke Wells
Catherine Hollenback
Thomas Noe
Micager Frazier
1835/36 Old Mrs. Sally Cooper
Joshua Henwood
1836/37 Mary Humphrey (infant)
Sherrod Adkins
William Campbell
Elias Humphrey
Tabitha Russell's child
1837/38 James Toney
1838/39 Betheny Stephenson
1840/41 James Cox
Mary Short
James Kinsloving
Mrs. Elizabeth Riley
Henry Adkins
George Farrow
1841/42 Rebecca West
William Lane
Esther Bullman
1842/43 Tophouse's child
Johh Boughman
Nathan Holten
Nisely (Nicely)
Morris Hudson
Old Nancy (Negro)
1843/44 Mrs. Elkins
1844/45 Taylor's child
1845/46 Andrew Barrett
Joseph Runion
King's child
1847/48 Old Mr. Powell
1848/49 Miriam Cornell/Corwell
Mavel Elkins
1849/50 Burwell Dodd
Levi Rowland
John Adkins
1851/52 Calvin Lucas
Alexander Ruggles
Dodd's child
Hezekiah Hudson
Old Mrs. Plank (1851)
1852/53 Old Phil (Negro)
James Sexton
Mary Curtis
1853/54 Old Mrs. Henry

DEATH LISTED IN OVERSEERS
(con't)

1853/54 Mrs. Beach
A. F. Turley
James H. Sexton
Old Mrs. Teal
Irish girl
Old Elizabeth Adkins
Canton
L. Chapman

1854/55 Martin Higgins
Susan Thompson
Mrs. Kyle
Old Mrs. Mowman
George W. Zirkle
Samuel Kyle (at Cincinnati)
Mother Adkins
Mother Chapman

1855/56 Old Mr. John Lunsford
Wesly Webb
Susan Thompson
Catherine Jewel

1856/57 Alex Cremeans
David Craig
William Webb
Richard Johnson
Thomas Gallaspie

1857/58 J.D. Holdryde
8 coffins for Poor House
Willis Hamblete
Eliza Raynes
David Craigh (twice)
Mrs. Selbee

1858/59 William Jenkins
Nancy Clark

1859/60 9 coffins for Poor House
Charles Patton
Anderson Bowling
John Reynolds

1860/61 Elizabeth Higsey (since 1816)
Jackson Jefferson
Old Man Simon Pearson
Jacob Wentz

BOUND CHILDREN - INDENTURES
(from Overseer's Minutes)

1838/39	Thomas Adkins
	Nathaniel Adkins
	David Dick
	Preston Toppins
	Eleanor Adkins
	Sally Adams
	John Wells
1840-41	Nelson Wiley
1841/42	Elizabeth Adkins
	Hulda Snell
	Steven Bragg
1846/47	Thomas Galaspie
	Linanda Elkins
1847/48	Charles Shoemaker
	2 Roach children
	H. Holten
1848/49	Mary F. Adkins
	Clarinda Adkins
	Jonas Adkins
	Sarah G. Adkins
	Elizabeth Carpenter
1849-50	Sinate Hudlin
1851-52	Manual Adkiins
1856/57	Elizabeth Crump
	Elizabeth McComas

ORPHANED CHILDREN
(from Overseer's Minutes)

1822/24	Sarah Blankenship
1824/25	Daniel Bogus
	ch/Betsey Snell
	Joseph Gates
1831/32	ch/Elizabeth Tally
1833/34	John Porter
	William Porter
	Martha Porter
	Peggy Eplin
	Anderson Wells
1835/36	ch/Josiah Henwood
	ch/William Campbell
	ch/Sherrod Adkins
	John Humphrey
	Mary Humphrey
	Francis Humphrey
1836/37	Ida Adkins
	Malvina Adkins
	John Toney s/James
	ch/Rebecca Toppins
1840/41	3 Roach children
1841/42	Lucinda Adkins
	4 Rose children
	George Jordan
	2 ch/Nathan Holten
	2ch/Widow Roach
1842/43	Steven Bragg
	Dodd children

CABELL COUNTY DOCTORS

1813/14	Dr. Benjamin Brown	
1818/19	Dr. Thomas Collens	
1822/23	Dr. Shangulson	
1825/26	Dr. Louis Spangler	
1826-27	Dr. James S. Hepburn	
1827/28	Dr. Edward Jones	
1829/30	Dr. John Talbott	
1830/31	Dr. Archibald McLewskey	
	Dr. James H. Hereford	
1835/36	Dr. Joseph Shallcross	
	John McGinnis (coroner)	
1836-1849	Dr. John Seashols	ads
1842/43	Dr. R.C. Dorviner	
	Dr. William Payne	
	Dr. S.J. Yates	
1842-1856	Dr. Henry B. Maupin	
1850-1856	Dr. Maupin & Brother	
1845-1850	Dr. P. H. McCullough	
1847-1857	Dr. G.C. Ricketts	
1847-1858	Dr. A.M. McCorkle	
1848-1854	Dr. Joseph Sidebottom	
1849-1854	Dr. W.W. McComas	
1849/50	Dr. Milton McCoy	
1853/54	Dr. J.G. Harriman	
1856/57	Dr. William Curry	
1856-1860	Dr. V.R. Moss	
1858/59	Dr. Hall	
1859/60	Dr. Samuel McGinnis	
	Dr. H. Rouse	
1860/61	Dr. Sam Williams	

COFFIN MAKERS OF CABELL

men who charged the Overseers

E. Wellington 1827,1856
John Merritt 1831
Windon Emmons 1832
James Plymale 1835
Thomas Joy 1836
Epps Johnson 1837
Dingess Henderson 1841
John Hannon 1841
William Merritt 1842
Sam A. Childers 1845
John Hibbens 1845, 51, 58, 59, 60
Edmund Rece 1845, 1851
Jeremiah Flint 1847
Rufus Batzel 1849
Sam Childers 1849
Jacob Miller 1850
Laven Swann 1850
John T. Hibbens 1851
Edmund C. Rece 1851
Benjamin L. Perry 1851
Andrew Johnson 1852
Smoot Johnson 1852
Broaddus Perry 1855
John W. Dick 1855
Perdue 1855
John Dick 1856
W.B. Perry 1857
T.J. Hayslip 1857
Squire A. Johnson 1860
Alba Holten 1860
J.T. Hibbens 1860

COUNTY STORE KEEPERS

1813/14 Benjamin Brown
1817/18 Tiernan & Gardner
1818/19 Garrett & Everett
1830/31 John Russell
1837/38 John Everett Jr.
1840/41 Holderby & Miller
Frederick Moore
1841-42 William Merritt
Charles T. Love
William Jordan
1842/43 Charles L. Roffe
Samuel M. Johnson
1848/49 William C. Miller & Co.
James Garrett
Thomas Merritt
1849/50 Edward Nixon
Eli H. Walton
William M. Williams
1852-53 James Adkins
1853/54 V.D. Letulle
1854/55 John S. Nicholas
1857/58 John M. Rece
1858/59 Wolcott & Everett
Miller Solomon & Miller
John Merritt & Co.
1860/61 James O. Cox

OLD POOR FARM CEMETERY

(article in Huntington newspaper)

burials

Bryant Dangerfield - a teacher from NC

Charles Jones - a fiddler from Somerset, KY

lived on Madison Creek

Michael Loller - a carpenter from

Rockbridge Co. VA

(Loller=Lawler)

1900 Cabell Census
"Inmates of Infirmary"
McComas District
#14-14 Wm. McKendree

Adkins, Elba	8m
Albright, Pantha	50f
Albright, Margie	17f
Albright, Cleveland	15m
Albright, Lewis	11m
Carroll, Albert	47m
Elkins, Lewis	29m
Elkins, Jane	30f
Elkins, Otta	9m
Elkins, Mary	1f
Estep, Lottie	57f
Estep, Martha	28f
Estep, Silva	15f
Estep, Wallie	9m
Estep, Reece	7m
Estep, Stella	5f
Foster, Rachel	58f
Gibson, Mary	44f
Hisley, Henson	11m
McComas, Charles	unk
Plybourn, Giles	73m
Rabourn, James Sr.	50m
Reybourn, James R.	6m
Rabourn, Willie	4m
Raybourn, Bellgora	27f
Raybourn, Viola	7f
Shumaker, Nancy	57f
Walls, Minnie	10f
Ward, John	53m
Wisley, Floyd	21m

1910 County Infirmary
(p4277)

(m)married (w)widow

Adkins, Mathew(m)	45m
Adkins, Amanda(m)	38f
Adkins, Ana	2f
Albright, Lewis	19m
Earls, Malinda	31f
Earls, Ethel	7f
Earls, Inez	4f
Estep, Lottie	69f
Estep, Sylva	28f
Estep, Martha(m)	36f
Estep, Della	6f
Estep, Osa	3m
France, Emily(w)	45f
Hall, Catherine	62f
Hill, Lorenza	12m
McComas, Chas.(w)	48m
Morris, William	50m
Rayburn, James (w)	50m
Rayburn, Lewis	15m
Shumaker, Nancy	65f
Thomas, Isabella	3f
Waldron, Evelyn(m)	40f
Wroten, Linnie (m)	33f
Yates, Allen	8m

1920 Cabell Census(9424)
5B-6A McComas District
Trace Creek
72-76 McKendree, Wm.

Adkins, Amanda(w)	46f
Adkins, Annie	12f
Albright, Lewis	25m
Brumfield, Geo.(w)	65m
Cook, Pauline	5f
Earls, Malinda	43f
Estep, Lottie	77f
Estep, Sylva	37f
Estep, Martin	23m
Estep, Mary (w)	53f
Estep, Lizzie	16f
Germand, William	8m
Holdbrook, Jane	50f
Holdbrook, Vilie	6f
Holdbrook, Mertie	8f
Hughes, Rosa	18f
Hughes, Lillie	10f
Hughes, Evelyn	4f
Hughes, Donald	6m
Hughes, Clodine	1f
Leonard, Florence	25f
Leonard, Gladys	1f
McComas, Laura	36f
McComas, Paul	4m
McComas, Noma	1f
Neil, Levi	68m
Rayburn, James(m)	64m
Ross, Malinda (w)	51f
Ross, Robert	14m
Ross, Delbert	13m
Ross, Spicy	11f
Ross, Annie	10f
Ross, Arting	7f
Shumaker, Nancy	78f
Thomas, Isabelle	12f
Wroten, Armilda	8f

FEE BOOK

1826- 1839

CABELL COUNTY, VA/WV

WESTERN VIRGINIA
COUNTY BOUNDARY LINES

All researchers should be aware of the differences in county formation in eastern and western Virginia. The first county units (known by severals names) were created along the eastern coast of Virginia by Englishmen who expected to have constant contact with Great Britain. These men built their homes near the ocean or major streams and did almost all busy and travel by water. It was only natural that all counties have "a water boundary" or access to the rivers leading to the ocean and Great Britain. The eastern Virginia counties (to the Blue Ridge) are all separated by a river.

As the pioneer moved west, two things happened. The topography changed making it dificult for the people to reach the ocean; and the people began to rely on internal trade instead of depending on English manufactures. Virginia had vast lands to the West, but no one knew anything about the land by which to make the required county boundaries. A new method of county creation came into being. A county west of the mountains was all the land drained by a certain river to the diving ridge between one river and the next.

Originally Augusta County (the first county west of the Blue Ridge) was all the land drained by the Ohio River plus the original Virginia Charter "to the western sea". Although this hugh territory could not be governed as a single unit, the "watershed boundary" became the dividing line for almost all the western counties of Virginia (both Kentucky and West Virginia).

The original boundary of Cabell County was the Big Sandy River,(that river being the line between Virginia and Kentucky), the Ohio River on the west (the line Virginia accepted for the creation of the Northwest Territory), the Little Guyan on the northeast (at a certain point the line moves to the watershed ridge), while the southeast line is the ridge between Mud River and the Kanahwa River. The southern boundary line was another "western" invention, the imaginary line. As counties were created from the original Cabell County, their boundary lines were the watershed ridges in the region.

NOTES: There is no explination for the date regression.
Perhaps original book was dated front - back.

The Hite family was prominent in Cabell County.(descendants of Josh Hite).
John W.Hite is often misread John White.

Several persons make entries on each page, allowing for many mistakes in interpertation of names - (due to varied handwritting).
Frame -France W.Hite-White Newman-Runion etc.
(Appears each lawyer wrote his own entries.)

I make no attempt to explain legal notes. chy=chancery, caps-? as many abbreviations are used in entries. assee-assignee(with double s sign),

County has all of the following double family names:

Burkett and Beckett
Brown and Drown
Love,Lowe,Lour,Loar and Lower
Dean and Bean
Hite and White
Hannon and Haner and Haney and Harman
Wilson and Wilcox
Seamonds and Simmons and Sammons

which naturally adds to the handwriting confusion.

I have tried to match difficult names with additional information such as repeated cases or acquaintances.

CABELL COUNTY FEE BOOK 1826- 1839

The county charged a fee to enter each court case in the books..

chancery-chy assee-assignee paid-pd AB-assult & Battery
vs-verses decd.-deceased plf-plaintiff def-defendant
do-ditto att-attorney comth - commonwealth
(The clerk used many abbreviations in the original.)

1836

pg 1 (crossed out) XX George Cheek who sues for the use of Newton Gardner vs Elizabeth Derting, John Merritt, George Merritt, Jacob Merritt, Thomas Merritt, Melchor Merritt, William Stroop and wife Margaret, John Dundass and wife Ann, Joseph Wintz and wife Polly, heirs at law of William Merritt, decd. - debt $292.24 damage $50 This is an action of debt for money due on a Bond of Wm.Merritt, decd. with collaterial - no bail refund XX
Laidley for tax Wilson & Laidley PV
_____ (crossed out) XX Joseph (Dennison ?) vs Thomas C. Collins and Edmund McGinnis XX in chancery
_____ P & L Minages vs G. M. Rutherford debt tax pd
_____ McGononigle & Co. vs Isom Adkins debt tax pd

pg 2 Jacob Piles vs G. M. Rutherford lease tax pd
_____ Jas. Snodgrass vs Andrew Barrett debt tax pd
_____ Thos. McCallister vs Jas.Wheeler debt tax pd
_____ Pannel Blake vs Philip Baumgardner debt tax pd
_____ F.G.L. Beuhring vs John Hatfield debt tax pd
_____ same vs ---Everett debt tax pd
_____ same vs L. C. Swan debt tax pd
_____ William McCoy vs Joseph Davis debt tax pd

pg 3 W.L.Thompson vs Chas. B. Riggs debt tax pd
_____ ape. John Samuels D. Lety Scal on Hatton's debt

_____ Merritts heirs vs Morrow adm cov - John Merritt for tax
_____ John Luther McConnell to pay D copy bill vs Chapman $1.35
_____ Jo Davis assee vs N. Webb debt plf for tax
_____ Moses McCormick vs Saml. Wilson debt plf tax
_____ Saml. Short vs John Vanhorn assee
_____ Wm. Garrett vs Jessee Perdue case tax pd
_____ A.Holderby vs Wm. Hite plf for tax

pg 4 A.Holderby vs P.Keenan debt tax pd
_____ 1826 May John Samuels D
County seal on Edmd. McGinnis ans $2.00
ditto on Allen McGinnis 2.00
ditto on Coffland 1826-plot & survey 2.00
ditto on Wolfington P atto 2.00
Bloomer & Mc() (Gorby ?) $8.00
do on Ward vs Campbell(?) 2.00 total $10.00
1826 May Allen McGinnis D
3 county seals and certificates 7.50 pd 1.50
1826 May F.G.L. Beuhring D certificate on Boomers record .50
_____ Andrew Walker vs Isaac Hanley debt Laidley for tax pd
_____ Jesse Perdue vs Leroy Garrett case
_____ B. Davis vs Bailey Hagerman debt
_____ Chas. Rigg vs F.G.L. Beuhring

pg 5 Wm. Clark vs Saml. Wilson chy tax pd
_____ John Laidley vs Saml. Wilson debt Laidley for tax pd
_____ John Chadwick vs John Bellamy debt tax pd
_____ Danl. Bloomer for use Beuhring vs Benja. Martin - Beuhring for tax
_____ R.Worthington vs Sarah (Mary) Worthington & heirs chy - Everitt, tax & costs
_____ 1826 Jul 8th Andw. Fraley D .69
copy Jas. Fraley's answ. .62
do for Wm. Snidow .43
comth to take ------- 1.74

pg 6 Elisha McComas (adm of estate of William McComas,decd)
sues for the use of Saml. Barrett
_____ Jesse McComas & Moses McComas debt $88.50 damage $50 - tax pd Laidley
_____ Isaac & William Chapman vs James Fry debt $21.68 damage $50 - tax pd att
Laidley PV
_____ Phil Chapman vs John Laidley adm chy
_____ Rufus Webb & wife Malinda vs Wm. Hanley Case damage $200

pg 7 Sep 1826
_____ Charles Payton & wife Jincy vs Samuel Hensley & wife Betheny debt $35.00 damage $50 Laidley PV
_____ Frederick Moore assee of Benjamin Martin (assee of Anthony Hampton) vs Samuel Short damage $100 tax pd Laidley PV
_____ Frederick Moore vs Daniel Ratcliff & Wm. Snidow debt $50
_____ Jas.McDonals vs John Wellman damage $100
_____ A. Holderby vs Wm. Hite debt plf for tax
_____ James Holderby vs ( ) Morris heirs tax pd

pg 8 Joseph Turner vs C.W. Drechsler (adm of Levi Spengler) chy
_____ James Shelton vs William Jenkins damage $200
_____ George Alderson (?) & Thomas Crea (merchants operating as the firm of George Alderson & Co. vs George Crawford debt $58.21
_____ Thomas Smith vs Robert Forth damage $100
_____ William Stevens(?) guardian for Phebe Blankenship
_____ Calloway & Letty Blankenship vs Jesse Blankenship (adm for Nancy Brown (very unclear)

pg 9 Joseph Davison vs Nathaniel Webb chy account for year 1826
_____ John Deatley vs Thos. J. Hinch damage $300
_____ Chas. W. Drechsler vs (adm of L. Spengler) vs Joseph Turner
_____ 1827 Feb F. Tiernan & Co. copy recd. Geo. Morrison county seal & certificate $2.50 total $3.48
_____ P. Merritt vs T. Witcher debt caps awarded

pg 10 James K. Craig vs Charles Walker debt $57.60
_____ George W. Kouns (assee of H. Catlett) vs Levi Shortridge
_____ John Leathers vs P. Chapman & Co. - copy of answer of def Chapman
_____ 1827 Mar 24 John Leathers McConnell to pay copy answer
_____ A. Holderby vs John & Wm. P. Hereford debt $50.38
_____ Thomas Wyatt vs William Jenkins an action for work & labor

pg 11 E.J. Duncan(?) vs M. Moor debt
_____ William Heath vs James Barrett slander
_____ John Samuels to comth D to county for Hinch's adm letter
_____ Isabella Night vs Joseph Wintz and Windle Wintz debt
_____ Michael C. Collins vs Nathaniel Webb & Thos. C. Collins
_____ Lindsey Cremeans vs James H. Hereford & Frederick G.L.Beuhring

pg 12 Pennill Blake vs Jacob Baumgardner, James T. Carrell & David Hashbarger
_____ Frederick G.L. Beuhring vs Andrew Hatfield damage

_____ Frederick G.L. Beuhring vs Wm.G. Noble debt
_____ Joseph Davison vs Nathaniel Webb account for year
_____ John Samuels D copy of seal on Bostick deed $2.00
_____ Edwd. Barrett vs Byrd Brumfield debt
_____ John Talbot vs William L. Thompson damage

p 13 Daniel Bloomer for use of F.G.L.Beuhring vs Bery & Martin (?)
Beuhring for taxes
_____ Absolum Holderby assee of Elisha McComas vs Benjamin Davis debt
_____ Absolom Holderby vs Thos. Morris heirs
_____ Jesse Blankenship assee of Thomas J. Lusher(?) vs William Stowers
_____ Salley Callaway (by Elijah her father) vs Hiram Bloss damage $500

p14 Jesse Blankenship vs Wm. Stowers damage $50
_____ Jesse Martin vs Samuel Short damage $200
_____ Joseph L. Fry vs William Hite
1827 Oct 11 continued to November term
_____ Hannah Huddleston vs David Jarrett debt $30
_____ Absolum Holderby vs Isaac Blake damage $100

pg 15 Benja. Martin vs Saml. Short case
_____ John Vanhorn who sues for the use of Ben Martin & Martin Mims
in covenant vs Samuel Short
_____ James Blake vs William Jorden damage $100
_____ J. Samuels account for Oct. 23,1827 Talbots deed $2.00
_____ Jas. H. Hereford vs Fred. G.L. Beuhring damage $1000
_____ John Samuels D county seal on Garrett's(?) papers $2.00
_____ 1827 Nov. Laidley & Tiernan D copy Garners bill , seal & certificate $24.58

pg 16 Charles W. Drechsler who sues for the use of Thos. Paultney(?)
vs for James McGinnis debt $24.22
_____ same vs Henry T. Dundass & John Dundass
_____ Wm. Love (adm of Dd. Jarrett vs Jas. H. Hereford & Jas. Cox
_____ John Hansford D 18 Nov 1827
copy of deed from McComas to Morris .70
same to Thomas Morris .70
_____ (crossed out) XX Wm. Stowers vs Wm. Hite & Wm. Hatten XX

pg 17 - 1828 Jan 10 Wm. L. Thompson D copy of record Talbot $1.76
less $1 pd by D. Witcher - 1.00
_____ John McComas vs Wm. McComas in chy
_____ Thomas Bellamy (who sues for the use of Matthew Bellamy)

vs Philip Bombgardner-jailor of Cabell County
This is an action of debt brought 17 feb 1823 of several acts to recover reward for taking runaway slave in the state of Ohio and committing slave to jail and $1.20 for mileage.
_____ James Templeton who sues for the use of Joseph Gardner(decd ?)
Thomas C. Billips and William Billips debt $115

pg 18 Pennell Blake assee of William Deal vs James Webb debt $33.60
_____ Frederick Moore vs Ephraim Lockwood covt. broken damage $300
_____ John L. Wacker vs Frederick Moore(adm of John Emrath) damage
Wm. McComas for tax Wm. McComas PV
_____ Leroy Newman assee of James McFerren (assee of John McFearan)
vs William Fullerton
_____ John Emrath adm vs C.G.--------
_____ H.W. Thompson vs Moses Marcum - Ward PV

pg 19 William Averrell who sues for the use of William Hatton vs William Hill and Ephraim E. Hill debt $40 damage $20 Clark PV
_____ John Samuels D 27 May 1828
County seal on Theolicres decree $2.00
_____ 2 Jun 1828 Peter Dingess & Henry Farley D copy Elkins record .67
_____ George W. Kouns D copy Hatton record 1.00
_____ 3 Jun Fredk. Moore copy of Short record 2.70
_____ Mary Teays (executrix) of Stephen Teays decd. vs John Thomason
_____ Andrew Bierne & William Patton merchants trading under the stile(style) of Bierne & Patton vs Patrick Keenan debt $132

pg 20 D. Garrett vs F. Moore case
_____ Peter Dingess D copy Wade vs Stewart .70
_____ O. Merritt vs Hy Payton assult & battery tax pd
_____ Solomon Adkins vs Frederick G.L.Beuhring debt $156 McComas PV
_____ John Plymale assee of James K. Bean (who was assee of Grief Talley)
vs Richard Brown debt
_____ Fredk. Moore (adm estate John Emrath) vs George W. Kouns case

pg 21 James Cox vs E. Morris heirs tax & costs
_____ William Frasure assee of Fredk. Moore vs John Wellman debt $98
_____ Robt. Wilson vs Stephen Wilson chy
_____ James Coalter assee of John Billips vs William Billips & Richard Billips
Laidley for tax & cost
_____ Rufus Leonard assee vs Samuel Short debt $36.56 1/2

pg 22 Robert Pogue vs J.W. Powell debt $22.20 Clark for tax
_____ C.W. Drechsler ve Frederick Moore (adm of estate of John Emrath) debt $111.84 Clark for tax
_____ James Toney vs Thomas Spurlock AB $1000
_____ Governor of VA (who sues for the use of Thos. Wilson) vs Jacob Dean
_____ Charles C. Johnston (assee of Edmd.McGinnis) vs Henry L.Dundass, John Dundass, Thomas Dundass debt $75 damage $50

pg 23 David Jarrett vs Fredk.Moore case
_____ John Laidley assee of Absolom Holderby vs John Bryant debt $111
_____ E.M.H.Winfield vs Jn. Plymale case
_____ 1828 Oct 27 P. Keenan to clerk of Cabell County D
copy of record Theoliere vs Swan $8.22
_____ 1828 Oct John Samuels D
for county seal Thomason record vs Ward on Dr. Green $4.00
_____ 1828 Oct 27 J. Laidley & F. Tiernan
copy of P. att. Jerome to Hereford .43
do deed of trust Jerome to Tiernan 2.40
_____ 1828 Oct 28 F. Moore & B. Martin D copy of answers Short .58
_____ 1828 Oct 31 John Dingess copy of Jacob Stallings will .52

pg 24 1828 Nov 3 Wm. Hatten D copy of Hatten bill vs Kouns & Catlett .35
copy of G.W. Kouns answer .36
_____ James McCallister vs Jon Briant debt
_____ 1828 Nov 4 Leroy Newman D copy of Fullerton's bill .86
_____ Absolom Holderby(assee Francis M. Burns) vs Walker J.L. Sanford
_____ 1829 Jan P. Keenan D copy of record McComas vs Lucas 1.20
copy Lucas bill & Keenan vs Lucas 1.33

pg 25 1829 Jan 27 Jesse Blankenship D copy of Stowers(?) bill .58
ditto Peter Blankenships bill .52
_____ 1829 Feb Wm. Fullerton D
copy of bill Newman & al .86
_____ Joseph Robertson vs Rachael Donathen
_____ 1829 Feb 25 H. Catlett & Wm. McComas to pay D
copy Kouns assee vs Hatten .58
county seal & certificate 2.50
John Samuels county seal 2.00
_____ Blake assee ve Hite debt Clark for tax
_____ A. Plymale assee vs Jesse Blankenship
_____ C.C .Johnson (adm of Preston) vs Solomon Cook
_____ same vs Jacob Hite

pg 26 John Kirk vs Robert Wellman McComas for tax
_____ A.F.------ vs John Deatley AB
_____ Nancy Hinch (widow of Samuel Hinch) vs Ransom Dial chy
_____ John Plymale vs Richard Brown
_____ William Jarrett an infant under 21 years and Valentine Alexander(?) his next friend vs James T.Carrell - Jacob Baumgardner issued in chy
_____ John Barrett (guardian of the infant children of James Alford) vs Sarah Alford, William & Richard Heath, John Ray & Abraham Sires issue in chy tax pd
_____ George Keeton vs William Conner $3000 for slander

pg 27 James Haskins vs John W.Russell case
_____ Fredk. Moore vs Brice Stokes debt
_____ P.S. Smith(sues for the use of Henry Thomason) vs Henry Thomas
_____ William Hatten vs Stephen Wilson debt $37.50
_____ William Hatton vs S. Dean debt
_____ Fredk. Moore vs Brice Stokes debt

pg 28 Rachel Donanthan vs Fredk.Moore (adm estate of Jno.Emrath)
_____ John L. Walker vs Fredk.Moore (adm of John Emrath decd) chy
_____ John Gilkerson vs John Smith chy
_____ 1829 Jun 10 Wm. McComas D copy of record for Catlett -of- Kouns assee vs Shortridge county seal & certificate $3.10
_____ 1829 Jun 10 John Samuel same $1.00
_____ 1829 Jun 22 John McComas D copy record Wm. Fry vs Jas. H. Johnson -seal/certi $3.52

pg 29 1829 Jun 23 Fredk. Moore D to take deposition in case of Garred .43
_____ 1829 F.G.L.Beuhring D case vs Hatfield
_____ Edward Franklin vs John Spears debt
_____ George H----- vs Charles W. Drechsler & F.G.L.Beuhring debt $327
_____ George Bierne vs Isaac Hanley
_____ (Dawson-Damron) Blackamon assee vs Jacob --- & James McGinnis debt $82

pg 30 1829 Aug John Samuels D county seal Buffington deed 1.50
_____ Aug 15 John Toney D copy deed of Squire Toney to J & W Toney .70
_____ Jas. Perry & Henry Perry Jr. D copy of White's bill chy .88
_____ Aug 22 Ransom Deal D copy of Nancy Hinch's bill .25
_____ John Spears vs Edward Franklin damage $200
_____ Samuel F. Clark vs Thomas F. Lusher(Luster)
_____ 1829 Aug 26 Rachel Donathan D copy of Robertson's bill .46

pg 31 Sep 1st 1829 Joseph Malcomb D copy deed Jordan from Bennett
_____ 1829 Oct William Fullerton copy of record $6.66
_____ Francis Tiernan vs Elizabeth Durton debt $28.91
_____ Francis Tiernan vs Levi McCormick debt $86.13
_____ (crossed out) Francis Tiernan vs Wm. Hite debt
_____ (crossed out) same vs John B. McGinnis
_____ same vs Wm.Hite $54.67
_____ same vs John B. McGinnis debt $53.39

pg 32 same vs Leroy Garret debt $120
_____ Tiernan & Garnder vs John B. McGinnis debt $29.71
_____ same vs Wm. Hite debt $26.47
_____ same (assee of John W. Hite)vs Greenville Newman & Wm.Spurlock
_____ James White & Co. vs T.W. Powell debt $60
_____ F.G.L. Beuhring vs Obadiah Merritt caps trespass

pg 33 F.G.L.Beuhring vs Obadiah Merritt & Pellington Merritt damge
_____ Benjamin Davis & wife Sarah vs Paul Davis & Mary his wife
damage $1000 slanderous words spoken by Mary Davis against Sarah
_____ John Bowyer vs Saml. Short caps Clark for tax
_____ Martin Moore asse vs Caleb Witcher, Jerh. Witcher & William
Morrison debt $120 Shelton for tax
_____ Jacob Hite vs Wm. Mather(?) damage $100

p34 Philemon Chapman vs James Buffington damage $300
_____ Jesse Toney (adm for estate of Ratt Rainy decd) vs Jesse Blankenship
damage $100 Toney for tax Laidley PV
_____ Fredk.G.L.Beuhring assee of David Harshbarger vs Henry T. Dundas
_____ F.G.L. Beuhring vs Jacob Hite caps
_____ John Samuels D county seal for Collins record $1.00
ditto on Lysles Deed manumintion (?) 1.00
_____ Wm. McComas Jr. D county seal Lysles deed 2.02

pg 35 John Samuels D county seal for two powers of atty for Letulle $2.00
_____ Letulle D certificates for two powers of atty 1.00
_____ Thomas Arthur vs David Harshbarger case $1000 slander
_____ Benjamin White vs Robert Hensley & Cat. T. Clark debt
_____ Tiernan & Gardner vs John McComas debt
_____ Lewis Summers & Manoah Bostick vs Greenville Newman, Joseph Newman
& Alexander Hazlett

pg 36 Lewis Summers & Manoah Bostick vs Anthony Plymale & John Plymale debt

_____ same vs John Stith debt
_____ same vs Edward W.H. Masfied(?)(Worsfied) debt
_____ same vs John Meadows debt

pg 37 same vs Brice Stokes debt $500
_____ same vs Augustus Damrell debt $200
_____ same vs Benjamin Davis debt $300
_____ Johnson & Chapman vs David Fry
_____ Wm.Chapman vs David Fry

pg 38 (crossed out) Rachael Donathan vs James Wellman debt
_____ Robt. Wilson for the use of Stephen Wilson vs John Toney debt
_____ Jesse Blankenship who sues for the use of John W. Hite vs Wm. Stowers, James Miller, Christopher Keezer debt with collaterial
_____ copy of bill in chy Jesse Blankenship vs A. Plimal to John Chapman atty at case A. Montgomery to Milton Ferguson to pay
_____ Ben Maxey vs Danl. Morgan

pg 39 Isaac Chapman & William Chapman vs John Canterberry debt $23
_____ 1830 Jul 20 A. Holderby D copy of Lucas bill & Keenan's answer $1
_____ George W. Kouns vs John Toney caps
_____ 1830 Jul 20 Milton Ferguson D copy Blankenships bill .48
_____ 1830 Jul 20 William Morrison D copy Judge Moore's--- to Witcher
_____ Jas. Holderby & Co. assee vs John Gilkerson & al debt
_____ Jas. Gallaher vs G.W. Kouns debt $50 damage $50

pg 40 September 1st 1830
1830 Sep 17 Gabriel Plymale D copy Perdue's bill .52
_____ And. Berrie, Martin Mims, Jno. H. Allison & Chs. Tiernan(?) under the firm of A. Berrie & Co.(?) vs John Wellman
_____ same vs Saml. Short
_____ same vs Benj. Martin
_____ 1830 Oct Henry Clark D (marked out) $1.15
_____ Oct 24th 1830 John Samuels D county seal Berry's deed $1.00
_____ Jas. Brice assee vs John Morris debt

pg 41 Imri & Loyal Wilcox vs James Cox debt
_____ A.Holderby vs Jacob Hite debt
_____ same vs Wm. Hite
_____ same vs Elisha McComas
_____ same vs David Fry
_____ Wm.Prate for use of Jo Gardner vs Thomas Arthur

_____ Gabriel Plymale & wife Mary vs James Ferguson & wife Lucy slander

pg 42 Stephen Wilson vs George E. Kouns, John C. Kouns & Jacob Kouns
_____ Christopher Keezer vs John Blankenship, William Stowers, James Miller & George Calloway
_____ Edward Damrell assee of Griffing W. Rutherford for the use of Peter Newman vs Stephen Wilson, George W. Kouns, late parterners under the name of George W. Kouns & Co. debt $97.10
_____ Benjamin F. Gardner vs Jacob Baumgardner
_____ James Leonard vs Isaac Hanley J. Laidley PV

pg 43 Jesse Toney (adm) vs Jesse Blankenship called as witnesses Jno.Madison, Christopher Keezer, Wm. Miller, John Toney.
_____ (crossed out) A. Holderby vs Andrew McCallister
_____ G.W. Gardner assee vs A. Shelton debt $77.33
_____ John Samuels D March 5th 1831 copy of Hite's certificate etc. $1.50
same seal on Barrett term of adm 1.00
_____ Andrew Barrett D Mar 1831 seal on letters & certificate 1.50
_____ Francis Tiernan vs James McGinnis debt

pg 44 Geo.W. Kouns & Co. vs John Toney
_____ John A. Talbot vs Jas. Baumgardner debt
_____ Robt. Wilson vs John Toney
_____ George W. Kouns for the use of John & Jacob Kouns vs Wm. Brumfield
_____ Peter Leech vs Wm. Ratcliff chy
_____ Henry Hampton vs Richard Brown damage $200
_____ R. Adkins assee vs Wm. D. Bellamy debt

pg 45 1831 Apr 25th John Thompson D
answer to Shelton & copy of order R. Hereve(?) .84
_____ 1831 May John Shelton D copy of Thompson bill .43
_____ Fredk. Moore assee Renyerd Anderson vs John H. Allison and Martin Minns
_____ (?) vs A. Bowen --Thos. Gilkerson, Ben & Moses Davis (??)
_____ Stephen Spurlock D seal & certificate $2.55
_____ John Samuels D for Burwell Spurlock 2.55
_____ 1831 Jun 2nd Ransom Dial D copy of Hinch record $2.85
_____ 1831 Jun 6th John Samuels D seal $1.00

pg 46 A.Rece D certificate & cty seal 2- .50
_____ Tiernan & Gardner vs Martin Moore debt $59.00
_____ Thomas Wyatt vs William Billips Jr. chy
_____ Jesse Toney vs St. Mark Russell damage $100

_____ T. & L. Wilcox assee of Merrit Clark vs James McCondon debt $30
_____ Jos. Dick vs John Peyton AB

pg 47 Esom Hannan vs Jesse Toney covenant
_____ James Holderby D 1831 Sept 9th copy of Laidley's deed .36
20th copy of course of Hugh Paul's lot .14
_____ 24 Sept Benjamin H. White copy record J.G. Perry $2.62
_____ Peter Scales vs Saml. Hensley & Jas. Butcher debt $60
_____ 1831 Oct 15th Peter Leach D copy of Ratcliff's answer .18
_____ 1831 Oct 15th Robt. Wilson D copy deed for Toney .39
_____ Jno. Spears vs E. Franklin issued suppoena Tabitha Russell, Thomas McComas, Roland Bias, Richard Adkins, Ransom Dial
_____ Peter Blake vs Simon Reynolds & Jas. Brown debt $30

pg 48 A.Beirne & Co. assee vs James Copley debt $75
_____ 1831 Nov 29 John Samuels D county seal on Hull's petition $1.00
_____ 1831 Dec 8th Wm. & Jas. Buffington vs Robt. Adams heirs
_____ Thomas Kilgore vs Wm. Brumfield damage $100
_____ J & L Wilcox vs G.H. Haynie debt
_____ same vs John Hatfield debt
_____ same vs P. Newman debt $32

pg 49 same vs Joseph Newman debt $35
_____ same vs Hansford Haynie debt $31.50
_____ same vs James P. McGinnis & Paul Davis debt $35
_____ same vs Joseph Riggs debt debt $30
_____ same vs Stephen Wilson debt $30
_____ same vs Samuel Dean debt $30
_____ same vs George H. Haynie debt $33.38
_____ same vs Overton White debt $25
_____ same vs William Perry debt $30
_____ same vs John Toney debt $30

pg 50 Joel Estes vs Obadiah Merret debt $30
_____ J & L Wilcox vs Jesse Adkins debt $28.67
_____ John Hollenback vs John Shelton, Jesse Toney & Paul Davis debt
_____ Richard Packwood who sues for the use of Edward Ferguson vs Samuel Davis debt $32.69

pg 51 Fredk. Moore vs E. McComas case
_____ 1832 April 4th William Hite D copy of inquistion of Jo Gatewood .24
copy deed for Cary Marshall .82

_____ Prenty Chub D copy of deed of trust from McComas 1.44
_____ Martin Hollenback & wife Elenor vs Henry Hampton debt $600, damage
$1000
_____ Thompson Bell vs Daniel Ratliff - Wm.P. Bell desires a copy of record be sent to Fredk. Moore at the Forks of Sandy- Wm.P. Bell to pay fee upon delivery W. McComas

pg 52 Robert Wilson vs John Toney debt
_____ Lewis Summers & Manoah Bostick vs Absolom Queen & Johnson C. Hatton
_____ James Ferguson vs Joseph Robertson & Jesse Robertson
_____ John Ward D 1832 May 18th seal, copy, certificate $2.00
_____ Fredk.G.L. Beuhring assee of Stephen Marcum vs Thomas Chandler

pg 53 Bartron Clark, William Johnston, & Benjamin Whristan(?) trading under the name of Barton Clark & Co. vs Samuel Wilson
_____ 1832 July 23 Haytten Frazur D copy Sally Loves(?) record .30
_____ W & B Johnson vs J. Campbell & al debt
_____ G. Grason assee vs G. Newman (?) debt Wade Hampton tax pd
_____ Wm. Blackamon vs Wm. Mather covenant
_____ M. Cowles for the use of J & L Wilcox vs Nicholas Couplevarger(?)
_____ J & L Wilcox vs Danl. Ratcliff debt

pg 54 Justices for case of Drechsler vs F. Moore & al debt $1000
_____ 1832 Aug 8th John Toney D copy Lewis Russell's deed .20
_____ 1832 Aug Wm. Mails D copy Lee Spa vs Vincient Nowel .36
_____ 1832 Sept 15th Sampson Sanders D copy order -----------
_____ V.W. Southall vs Willis McKeand debt
_____ Greenville Newman vs Charles Tiernan damage
_____ Chas.W. Drechsler D 1832 Sept 9th copy order Emrath adm .08
_____ 1832 Oct 12th John Samuels D county seal $1.00
_____ 1832 Oct 19th John Waitt D copy bill of sale .52

pg 55 Robt. Wilson vs John Toney 2 suits costs $3.47
_____ Isaac & Wm. Chapman vs John Canterberry
_____ James Leonard vs J. Hanley costs
_____ A. Bierne & Co.(assee of Jno. Burchett) vs James Copley debt $75
_____ 1832 Dec 1st John Gilkerson D abstract Holderby's adm .18
_____ P.B. Doudall vs W. McKeand debt
_____ make out record for S. Wilson vs Kouns

pg 56 Absolum Holderby vs Charles B. Riggs debt
_____ Joseph Gardner vs Thomas Arthur, Patrick Morrison and William Morrison

_____ John Deatly (adm of John Deatly) vs Elizabeth Biass (late E. Deatly)
and Andrew Bias debt $35.50 Talbot for tax
_____ 1833 Feb John Dingess D copy of Keand deed to Hensley heirs .25
copy deed of trust Hensley to A. Bierne .18
_____ John Deatley adm vs A. Bias & al damage $200

pg 57 1833 Feb 12th Edwd. Franklin pd $3.00 on fee bills
_____ (crossed out) Wm. Conner vs Ruel Porter
_____ (crossed out) Wm. Conner vs Alexander Porter case $1000
_____ Martin & Isaac Frampton (merchants trading under name of M & I
Frampton vs Jesse Toney debt $76.18
_____ Mathias Walker & Isaac Miller vs James Miller debt
_____ John Talbot vs Isaac Miller and Nancy Miller (late Nancy Miller)

pg 58 Floyd Turley vs George Hatfield damage
_____ Gabriel Plymale vs Elliott Rutherford & Robert Rutherford debt
_____ John Deatly vs Rolin Bias & James Wilson trespass, AB
_____ Peter Scales vs John D. Canicson(?) AB
_____ N. Canterberry vs Thomas Duckham & Saml. Beatty debt
_____ John Samuels D county seal on Philip C. Buffington certificate $1

pg 59 John W. Hite vs Frederick M. Moore debt
_____ Wm. Ferguson assee vs Jn. Perdue debt
_____ Absolum Holderby vs Thomas Mosely debt
_____ Harvey Lusher vs Nicholas Messinger trespass
_____ Peyton Newman (by John Newman his father & next friend)vs Philip Derton
_____ Weiley Farguson vs William S. Thompson

pg 60 Jesse Blankenship vs Jesse Toney (adm Keith Reins) case
Mrs. Blankenship for tax
_____ Joseph Coffman, Austin E. Recca and Henry Chapell (parteners in trade
under the name of Joseph Coffman & Co. vs Thomas Kilgore - trespass
James M. Laidley - Benj. H. Smith PV
_____ 1833 Jun Fredk. Moore & John Wellman D
copy of def plea in McConnell case $1.22
_____ 1833 Jun S. Thornburg (ex Mal Strup) copy of M. Strupe's will .26
_____ 1833 Jun John T. Cookus D copy inquisition Hogan's lot .25
_____ 1833 July 5 Sheriff of Cabell County D to treasury
license money for exhibit show from Joseph T. Bailey & Co. $30.00

pg 61 (crossed out) John Morris vs Stephen Spurlock
(adm of estate of William Spurlock) debt $150

_____ (crossed out)Thomas S. Buskirk against Stephen Spurlock (adm of estate of William Spurlock) debt & damage
_____ Luke W. Billips vs Stephen Spurlock (adm of Wm. Spurlock) debt
_____ John Scales vs William Mails case

pg 62 John Scales vs William Mails case damage slander $500
_____ Arthur F. Turly vs William Mails slander
_____ William Dirten vs Absolum Holderby action due for work & labor

pg 63 1833 Jul 23rd Peter B. Dowdall D copy McKeand bill .52
_____ John Smith vs Spurlock's adm debt
_____ L. Summers vs Spurlock's adm covenant
_____ Saml. Booth assee vs Wm. Spurlock's adm debt
_____ Thomas Hereford (adm of James Wilson dec) vs Elisha McComas debt
_____ Thos. Hereford (adm James Wilson) vs Patrick Keenan & Elisha McComas

pg 64 F.G.L. Beuhring vs Andw. Morris debt
_____ F.G.L. Beuhring vs Peter Barnheart debt
_____ Nicholas Messinger vs Samuel Wilson caps
_____ James Wilson vs John Deatley caps
_____ Catherine Bragg vs Mark Adkins
_____ Robert Holderby vs Burwell Spurlock (adm of Leroy Garrett) debt

pg 65 John Everett Jr. & James Russell merchants trading under the name of Everett & Russell vs Burwell Spurlock (adm of estate Leroy Garrett) $61.52
_____ John Plymale vs Burwell Spurlock (adm of Leroy Garrett) debt
_____ John C. Kouns & Jacob Kounts (trading under the name of J.C.& J. Kouns vs Burwell Spurlock (adm of estate of Leroy Garrett) debt
_____ Tiernan & Gardner D 5 abstracts against Wm. Hite, John B. McGinnis, Greenville Newman & Wm. Spurlock, John McCune & Thomas Arthur & al
_____ John Samuels D seal on Kouns certificate $1
_____ J. Kouns D seal & certificate $1.37

pg 66 Burwell Spurlock (gauardian of Benjamin Russell & Sally Russell) vs Stephen Spurlock (adm of Estate of Wm. Spurlock) damage $500
_____ Burwell Spurlock (adm of estate of Reuben Adkins decd) vs John Wood debt

September 1st Term 1833

_____ Joseph Newman vs David Heshbagger case

pg 67 John Poteet vs Burwell Spurlock (adm of estate of Leroy Garrett)

_____ Thomas A. Hereford (adm of estate of James Wilson decd) vs Richard Billips
_____ James Russell vs Martin Moore debt
_____ Martin Moore vs Jeremiah Witcher slander

pg 68 Absolum Holderby vs John Spears debt
_____ John Plymale vs Harvey Garrett debt
_____ Catherine Bragg vs Mark Adkins - suppeonas for Matthias & Polly Plumbly, Alexander Adkins & Jacob Bragg for plf
_____ Joseph Newman vs David Harshbagger - suppeonas for Wm.Simmons, Thos. Becket, Claybourn Howard for plf
_____ Payton Newman (by guardian) vs Philip Derton - suppeonas for Anthony Shelton & xxx Flinn for plf
_____ 1822 Nov 4th Patrick Morrison D copy 4 notes on Wishon to P. Keenan .21
_____ John Ward (adm of Nancy Gilkerson, decd) vs Paul Davis case
_____ Jas. Conner vs Spurlock's adm.

pg 69 Benja.B. Nicholas assee of John Tiernan vs Ignatius Tiernan debt
F. Moore for taxes Rece PV
_____ Lewis Summers & Manoah Bostick vs James Perdue debt
_____ same vs Benjamin Stevenson debt
_____ same vs William Rutherford debt
_____ same vs Elliott Rutherford debt

pg 70 Morris Blake(an infant under the age of 21 (by Peter Blake his next friend) vs David Harshbarger AB
_____ 1833 Dec 18th John Samuels D seal on H. Fourniers (?)deed
_____ 1833 dec 31st Richd. Lovejoy D marriage license $1.00
_____ William Thompson vs John McHenry debt
_____ James Bartram vs John McHenry & Johnson Thompson debt
_____ Anderson Roberts vs Thomas Harman case

pg 71 George Hudson vs Francis M. Burns debt
_____ 1834 Feb Wm. Morris (adm of estate of Ester Russell decd) D copies of Mark Russell & Ester Russell wills .52
_____ Henry Cushing vs Joseph Rutherford debt
_____ George Hudson vs Benjamin Brown (adm of William Brumfield) debt
_____ Jno. Plymale vs same debt

pg 72 Joseph Ewing vs Thomas Cartmill damage
_____ Joseph Ewing, Francis Tiernan & Andrew Biern merchants trading under the name of J. Ewing & Co. vs Thomas Cartmill debt
_____ Joseph Ewing assee of John Dean vs Greenville Newman and Peter

Newman debt & damage
_____ Isaiah Adkins vs Jonas Heath debt
_____ Edmund McGinnis vs Benja. Davis debt
_____ 1834 Mar 15th Benja. Brown (adm of Wm. Brumfield) D
copy of Brumfield's will .32
_____ commonwealth vs Geo.R. Miller suppeonas for Richard Roberts &
Finley Thompson

pg 73 make letters of adminstration on estate of Henry Loar decd and
send to Louisa charge to adm. M. Rece
_____ I order you to issued all suppeonas as necessary for all courts
John Laidley April 1834
_____ 1834 Apr 8th Stephen Wilson D copy of G.W. Rutherford deed to
Kouns & Co. .52
_____ 1834 Apr 21th Geo. Dial, Thos. Dial & John Dial Jr. vs William Mather
trespass John Dial for tax
_____ Philemon Chapman vs Willis Moore, Allen McGinnis, Wayne McMahan debt

pg 74 James Douglas vs John Toney debt
_____ 1834 May 15th F.G.L. Beuhring abstract of Harshbarger vs H.T. Dundas .18
_____ J. Holderby & Co assee of G.W. Gardner vs Anthony Shelton &
Martin Moore debt
_____ Daniel Peterson vs Thos.V. Buskirk debt
_____ 1834 Jan 29 Thomas Kilgore SCC(sheriff Cabell County) D
pedlars license for G. Hudson & Co. $100.00
_____ 1834 May 16th license to Miller, Mead & Delavan & Co. to exhibit show $30
Levi McCormick

pg 75 Enoch Adkins vs Jacob Adkins debt
_____ William Ferguson vs John Laidley (adm of Charles Smith decd) debt
_____ Absolum Holderby vs William Morrison debt
_____ same vs Thomas Arthur debt
_____ George Hudson vs John Wellman debt
_____ Haine(?) vs Michael Burks debt

pg 76 George Hudson vs William Buckhanan debt
_____ Isom Adkins D abstract case of Saml. Davis vs Edmd. Ferguson .18
_____ Martin Moore vs Jerry Witcher - suppeonas issued for Pellington Merritt,
Sarah Butcher, Dodridge for plf
_____ John Laidley vs Roland Bias
_____ Jun 24th 1834 commonthweath vs George R. Miller for Richard
Robertson, Finley Thompson, for deed Jerh.Wellman

_____ A. Holderby & Co. vs A. Shelton & F.G.L. Beuhring debt

pg 77 Joseph Wheeler, William Miller, Rhodes Westcot merchants
trading under the name of Wheeler, Miller & Co. vs Stephen Wilson
_____ same vs David McCormack debt & damage
_____ same vs John B. McGinnis debt Cormack
_____ same (assee of James Crawford) vs David McCormack & John McCormack

pg 78 make out a copy of deed from Wm. Dingess to Wm. Jeffery and
change to Wm. Jeffery of Logan County (clerk "cannot find this deed")
_____ Joseph Wheeler, William Miller & Rhodes Westcot merchants
trading under the name of Wheeler Miller & Co. vs John Toney case
1834 Jul Thomas Hannan D copy of Roberts record $1.45
_____ James Reynolds D copy of bill Wm. (Suit)? vs Lunsford Tony's(?) heirs .53
_____ Thomas Becket who sues for the use of James Wheeler vs Thomas McComas
_____ Absolum Holderby vs Roland Bias debt $173.41

pg 79 John H. Fulton & Beverly R. Johnston (adm of estate of Charles
A. Johnston decd) vs William Morris debt $125
_____ same vs Joseph Swann & Levin C. Swann debt
_____ same vs John McGinnis covenant
_____ Jno. Ward judgment case (?) C.C.Johnston
_____ Herraw Fournier vs James Brown and Thomas S. Brown debt
_____ John Everett Jr. & James Russell merchants trading under the name
of Everett & Russell vs Benja. Brown (adm of estate fo Wm. Brown)

pg 80 Appearances November Term 1834
_____ Jacob Kouns assee of Anthony Hampton vs Stephen Wilson debt
_____ John C. Kouns & Jacob Kouns trading under the name of J.C.& J. Kouns
vs Stephen Wilson debt
_____ Henry Hampton vs William Thomason trespass
Sep 1st 1834
_____ F.G.L. Beuhring & Co. vs Saml. Ferguson
_____ Spurlock's adm vs Gilkerson's debt

pg 81 (crossed out) Jeremiah Roberts who sues for the use of George Carr
vs David R. Lacy debt
_____ Horace Fournier vs John Wheeler, Pleasant Roberts, William Beckett debt $55
_____ John A. Hite vs Henry Job debt
_____ Henry Goodwin vs Nathan Holt trespass
_____ Andrew F. Hatfield vs James M. Condon debt

pg 82 Jacob Kouns vs George W. Kouns & Stephen Wilson covenant
_____ D. Peters vs Buskirk plf clerk
_____ Martin Frampton & Isaac Frampton merchants trading under the name of M & I Frampton vs Richard Brown
_____ Robert Holderby assee of John W. Hite vs Joseph Rutherford, Luther Ritchie & F.G.L. Beuhring debt & damage
_____ Francis Tiernan & Joseph Gardner merchants trading under the name of Tiernan & Gardner vs Henry Peyton debt

pg 83 same vs Anthony Shelton debt
_____ 1834 Nov 28th copies of 3 orders Jas. Poage .54
_____ John Hatfield & wife Susan vs John W. Ferguson slander
_____ Philemon Chapman vs Elisha Johnson debt
_____ Samuel Hatten & wife Elizh. vs Sugar Johnson

pg 84 Wm. Johnson vs Samuel Hatten & wife Elizabeth
_____ 1835 Jan 26 Geo. Hudson D abstract of Brumfield answer .18
_____ Absolum Holderby & Solomon Thornburg (merchants trading under the name A. Holderby & Co). vs Henry Clark debt
_____ Newton Gardner vs Peter Grass
_____ Absolum Holderby & Solomon Thornburg (merchants trading under the name A. Holderby & Co.) vs Jacob Merritt debt

pg 85 (crossed out) Jacob Bragg & wife Ester vs Bartlett Adkins & wife Mary, Sarah Hatton, Charles Wm. Hatton, Joseph Hatton, George Hatton, James Holton, Parker Adkins & wife Jane, Elizabeth Hatton, Wm. Adkins & wife Rachel, Phebe Hatton
_____ Peter Fulkerson vs F. Moore appeal
_____ fee $3.27 Jos. Ewing vs Newman

March 1835
_____ (crossed out) commonwealth vs Samuel Short
_____ (crossed out) E. Damrell vs S. Wilson
_____ Peter Sullivan vs Hiram Pauly attachment

pg 86 Richard Brown vs Martin Frampton & Isaac Frampton (survivors of he late firm of Martin Frampton, Isaac Frampton & William Frampton)
_____ Wm. Ballard vs J.C. & J.Kouns debt Robt. Holderby for taxes
_____ Jas. Buffington vs Kouns Poge & Co.
_____ John Russell vs Kouns Pouge & Co.
_____ Jas. Douglas for use of R. Holderby vs J.C. & J. Kouns
_____ 1835 Apr 6th Jacob Dean D

pg 87 Benjamin Brown (adm Wm. Brumfield, decd) vs Jacob Kouns & James Butcher - J.M. Laidley PV
_____ same vs Allen T. Brumfield & John H. Brumfield
_____ John T. Cookus vs Ellenor Worthing
_____ John T. Cookus vs Catherine E. Cookus, John M. Cookus, Sarah W. Cookus, Nancy M. Cookus

pg 88 Richd.W. Thompson vs John M. Henry
_____ Harry Cushing vs J. Rutherford & Wm. Kouns
_____ 1835 April 22nd John T. Cookus D copy deposition Morrison heirs
_____ 1835 April 23rd Robt. Holderby copy deed Wm. Hite & wife to Charles W. Smith .38
_____ Benjamin Johnson vs Isaac Mynes appeal witness for def Edwd. Grass, Wm. Grass, James Heath, Andrew Barrett
_____ John M. Hampton (who sues for use of Hasting Knight)vs John Forth covenant

pg 89 1835 May 6th Stephen Wilson copy deed G.W. Kouns .60 record Jacob Kouns .18
_____ 1835 May 6th Solomon Thornburg (adm of Wm. Fullerton decd) 5 copies of Wm. Fullerton's will for Agga, Lewis, Anna, Jack and Richard at .50 each $2.50 seal & certificate $6.87
_____ Alexander W. Handley & John W. Griffin (merchants trading under the name Handley & Griffin) vs James Reynolds
_____ F.G.L. Beuhring & Co. vs William Mails
_____ 1835 Mar 16th John Plymale D
_____ 1835 May 19th John Samuels D $1
_____ Elias Adkins assee of Henry Miller (who was assee of George Spears) vs Bardell(?) Johns

pg 90 John Plymale (assee of Peter Newman) vs William Freeman & Wade Hampton
_____ John Hatfield (assee of Peter Newman who was assee of William L. Gholston) vs Frederick Berger
_____ 1835 Jun 16th John Samuels D seal on John D. Carmeans deed $1
_____ 1835 Jun 22nd Wm. Thompson D
_____ H. Catlett & Co. assee vs John Woods
_____ Nathan Holt vs Hy Goodwin -- Saml. Short Jr. & John McHenry for Holt
_____ 1835 Jun 26 F. Moore vs Jo Fulkerson-- Jos.R. Ward & Saml. Short Jr.

pg 91 June 26 1835 Wm. Thompson vs Hy Hampton suppeonas for Jas. Ferguson, Thomas Marcum & Stephen Marcum
_____ Peter Sullivan vs Hiram Pauley & William Thompson debt
_____ comth vs O. Ross suppeonas: John Stevenson, Madison Ross

_____ Absolom Holderby vs John Poteet
_____ (crossed out) Isaac Myries vs Benjamin Johnson trespass
_____ 1835 Jun 25th Andrew Crockett copy record of Chapman .58

pg 92 1835 Jun 10th Thomas Cartmill D copy record Ewing $1.68
_____ Absolom Holderby vs Philip Wintz
_____ Absolom Holderby & Solomon Thornburg (merchants trading under the name A.Holderby & Co.) vs James M. Condon debt
_____ same vs Isreal Heath
_____ John Campbell (who sues for the use of George Ward) vs Isaiah Perdue

pg 93 Littleton W. Tazewell (governor VA) ( ) of John Floyd (who sues for the benefit of J. Bellamy) vs Asher Crockett debt $2500
_____ N. Vallentine vs Jas. Wilks debt
_____ Fredk. G.L. Beuhring vs Wayne McMahan
_____ 1835 Jun 15th John Samuels D county seal $1.00

pg 94 Josiah Stallings vs Commonwealth- suppeonas Jacob Douglas,
_____ Mansfield---
_____ Wm. Burkett vs L. Fields case
Returns to the November Term 1835
_____ James Douglas who sues for the benefit of Robert Holderby vs John G. Kouns, Jacob Kouns and George Poague debt
_____ 1835 Aug 24 J. Laidley $5 on account - case of John Hatfield
_____ William McComas vs William Mails, Henry Peyton and Henry Partelow debt
_____ William Hutchinson (who sues for the use of Paul H. Davis) vs John Caughlan & James Poague

pg 95 J.W. Ferguson vs J.B. Green & Co.
_____ 1835 Sept 11th sheriff recieved $30 tax from J.B. Green & Co. to exhibit public show
_____ Alfred Ellis vs Jas.M. Walden caps
_____ 1835 Sept 28th Stephen Wilson D copy of E. Damrell record $2.12
_____ Rachel Butcher vs Pellington Merritt debt
_____ Cats Cale vs Thompson (?)

pg 96 James Lower vs Michael Burk & wife Lydia damge $500
_____ James Loar vs Judah (alias Mary Ann Loar) debt $500
_____ 1835 Oct 1st Anthony Lawson D
_____ 1835 Oct 7th Frederick Moore D copy record P. Fulkerson seal $1.62
_____ Elizh. Arthur vs Wm.A. Davis $5000
_____ 1835 Oct 2nd (xxJohn D 1826-ingess Dxx) Anthony Lawson D

copy of deed Nancy Dingess to P. Dempsy .62
_____ 1835 Oct 13th Stephen Wilson D-2 deeds Wm.A. Allison to G.M. Rutherford

pg 97 F.G.L. Beuhring & Co. vs Sanders Archer
_____ 1835 Oct 15th Stephen Wilson D copy deed Geo.W. Kouns to J.C. Kouns
.58 copy will John P. Duvall .60
_____ 1835 Oct 19th Fredk.G.L. Beuhring D
copy deed of trust from Israel Heath to Manuel & Grant .44
_____ Mary A. Alford vs Bias Humphrey(ink spot)
_____ 1835 Oct 27th Redman S. Conden D copy record of Jas.M. Condon
_____ 1835 Oct 27th John T. Cookus copy record E. Worthington & al .18
_____ comth vs John Hatfield debt

pg 98 R. Martin vs W.B. Mahony caps
_____ M & I Frampton vs St. M. Russell debt
_____ same vs Wm. Mays debt
_____ Hy Luther (adm) vs G. Newman
Appearances - March Term 1836
_____ Sarah Defoe vs Littleberry Adkins Jr. & wife Delpha AB

pg 99 John Samuels seal on manumintion of Abraham & Lucy $2.00
_____ 1835 Dec 26th F.G.L. Beuhring copy of W. McMahan bill .25
_____ John Toney vs Lewis Russell
_____ F. Burkett vs D. McCormack case
_____ 1836 Jan 8th J. Laidley pd tax on all writs for which he was liable
_____ 1836 Jan 9th John Samuels seal on Carmeans deed

p100 Robert M. Hall vs Wilson Cox debt
_____ John Spears vs Frederick G.L. Beuhring caps
_____ John W. Griffin (adm of G. Spears, decd) vs Burwell Johnson & Merritt Johnson
_____ George Hudson vs Charles B. Rigg debt
_____ Adam Heller vs Philemon Chapman slander

pg 101 John Samuels make out copy of deed of trust from John Deatly to Charles L. Roffe for F.G.L. Beuhring and file with Deatly & Deatly
_____ Ephraim Lockwood vs Samuel Craig damage
_____ Joseph Gardner & John Everett Jr. (merchants trading under the name of Gardner & Everett) vs Paul Davis debt
_____ Francis Tiernan & Joseph Gardner(merchants trading under the name of Tiernan & Gardner) vs Paul Davis
_____ Wm. Biggs (adm of John M. McConnell decd) vs Elisha McComas

_____ F.G.L. Beuhring & Co vs George Stephenson debt

pg 102 Jonathan W. Riley vs William Irby trespass
_____ Smith vs Thompson - suppeonas: Patrick Napier, Edmund Napier, William Walls, Samuel Leaves, John McHenry, Nathaniel Holt to July court - Mansfield
_____ Asher Crocket for the use of F.G.L. Beuhring & Co. vs Daniel Davis
_____ F.G.L. Beuhring & Co. vs Rowland Bias caps
_____ same vs Benja.H. Defore debt
_____ Horatio Catlett & William Williams(merchants trading under the name of Catlett & Williams) vs Wade Hampton debt

pg 103 Thomas Dennison (who sues for the use of John P.B. Maxwell) vs James Brown & Simm Reynolds debt
_____ Edward Ferguson vs George Adkins slander
_____ Philemon Chapman vs Adam Keller case
_____ Spears vs Beuhring auppeonas: John W. Hite, John Peyton, Josiah Swan, William Spears, Jonathan Peyton
_____ Percival L. Smith vs Wade Hampton debt

pg 104 Jacob Adkins vs Patrick Napier damage
_____ John Morrison vs Frederick G.L. Beuhring debt
_____ Joseph J. Mansfield vs Samuel Helton & wife Elizabeth
_____ Robert Ross vs Lewis Adkins covenant - John Ross witness

pg 105 William Turner vs Edmund McGinnis case
_____ 1836 Jul 26th John Samuels D seal Jas.W. McGinnis deed $1.00
_____ James Ferguson vs John Vaughan damage
_____ The clerk will dismiss the suit I brought against Helton & wife - J.J. Mansfield
_____ James Brown vs Nancy Walten chy
_____ Martin Moore vs Wm. Morrison debt
_____ Haney & Griffin vs Wm. Morrison
_____ P. Ellington vs F. Burkett

pg 106 John Morris vs Joshua M. Chapman debt
_____ William Mather vs Jos.B. Malcom debt
_____ 1836 Sept 21th Stephen Wilson D copy od deed from Wm. Allison & al to J.H. Allison & al to Garrett & wife $1.04
_____ 1836 Oct 1st Wm. & Jas. Buffington D copy Wm. (Freutel)(?) will
_____ Philemon Chapman vs Adam Keller suppeonas : John McKean, James McKean, John Connwell, Philip Bumgarner
_____ James Brown vs Hugh Bowen suppeonas: John McCaskey, Thomas S. Brown

_____ A. Holderby vs James Pennell (adm of Elias Humphrey) debt

pg 107 James Ferguson assee vs G. Newman debt
_____ John Spears vs Beuhring suppeonas: John W. Hite, Josiah Swan, John Peyton (son of young Henry Peyton) Benjamin Spears & William Spears
_____ William Thompson vs comth suppeonas: A.C. Thompson, Samuel Lavin, William Marcum, William Watts
_____ 1836 Aug 24th John Samuels D seal on Katy's manumintion $1
September 1st 1836
_____ James Ward Jr. (who sues for the use of Catlett & Williams) vs David McCormack & Joseph Kelly

pg 108 John Capeheart vs Alexd. Roberts debt
_____ John Laidley vs Allen McGinnis debt $450
_____ (crossed out)Warren B. Mahone vs James Shelton caps
_____ Beverly R. Johnston & John H. Fulton vs Leven C. Swan debt

pg 109 Daniel Witcher vs Green Rigg & Charles B. Rigg debt
_____ Absolum Holderby & Alexander H. Gardner (merchants trading under name of A. Holderby & Co.) vs Pellington Merritt debt & damage

pg 110 Kelly Ferguson (constable of Cabell County) who sues for the use of Edmund Napper vs Hiram Pauly debt
_____ Thos.J. Turner vs F. Burkett debt
_____ Martin & Isaac Frampton merchants trading under the name of M & I Frampton vs George Martin
_____ Absolum Holderby vs Willis McKeand, Alexander McKeand, John McKeand Jr., John Samuels, William McComas chy

pg 111 Adam S. Hatfield (assee of Joseph W. Roffe) vs Elijah Seamonds, Jr. & Elijah J. Seamonds Sr. debt
_____ Peters vs John Toney suppeonas: John Plymale, John Wilson, Ambrose Johnston. Mansfield for tax
_____ Dec 26th 1836 Daniel J. Smoot D copy deed Dingess & French to Jas. Workman .30
_____ 1836 John Samuels D seal for Daniel Davis $1
_____ 1837 Jan 7th Stephen Wilson D Kouns record $2.76
_____ 1837 Jan 7th F.G.L. Beuhring (?) .87
_____ 1837 Jan 7th Edmund McGinnis record Turner .80

pg 112 Waugh vs John C. Kouns & Jacob Kouns (partners in JC & J Kouns) debt
_____ Levi Shortridge vs John C. Kouns, George Pogue and Jacob Kouns

(partners in JC & J Kouns) debt
_____ Stephen R. Johnson (who sues for the use of Levi Shortridge) vs
John C. Kouns & Jacob Kouns (partners in JC & J Kouns)

pg 113 (crossed out) John Condon vs Seabird Webb AB
_____ 1837 Feb 2nd John Samuels D copy of Letulle naturalization $1
_____ Charles L. Roffe (assee of William Mather) vs Willis McKeand
_____ Frederick G.L. Beuhring & Chas. L. Roffe (merchants trading under the name of F.G.L.Beurhing & Co.) vs Enoch Adkins debt
_____ James C. Waugh vs John C. Kouns & Jacob (partners JC & J Kouns)

pg 114 Absolum Holderby and Alexander H.Gardner (merchants trading under the name of Absolum Holderby & Co.) vs Willis McKeand
_____ Winston Noel (who sues for the use of Absolum Holderby) vs Willis McKeand & John Williams
_____ John Deatly (adm of James Deatly, decd) vs Anderson Bias & wife Elizabeth (late Elizabeth Deatly) debt

pg 115 Eldridge Smith vs Samuel Wilson debt
_____ John W. Hite vs Roland Bias debt
_____ 1837 Mar 8th John Samuel D seal on Lockwood to Thomas $2
_____ James Rouse, Joseph Ewing and Levi Shortridge (merchants trading under the name of James Rouse & Co.) vs John C. Kouns & Jacob Kouns (partners in JC & J Kouns)
_____ Hy Knight vs J. Hansly

pg 116 make out copies of deed from Asher Crocket to John Meadows 1822
also John Meadows to Saml. F. Clark 1836 to be filed in suit
Davis vs Crocket James M.Laidley 28th Mar 1837
_____ Margaret Loar vs Judith Loar-witnesses summoned to June court
Michael Loar, Shelton Parks
_____ 1837 Apr 7th Burwell Johnson D copy of Rogers deed to Lucas
_____ 1837 Apr 13th Gabriel J. Cadecott(?) pd for record
_____ Jacob Grass vs Wm.R. Heath & Richard B. Heath debt
_____ comth vs J. Stephenson (ink spot)

pg 117 Sheriff of Cabell Co. received from James Brice & Co. $100 tax on clock pedlars Apr 19th 1837
_____ Absolum Holderby & Alexander H. Gardner (merchants-A. Holderby & Co.) vs William R. Heath debt
_____ David Campbell (governor of VA) for comth vs David Baily debt
_____ Sugar Johnston and Christopher Cites vs Burwell Johnston, Jacob Adkins

and John Johnston
_____ Beverly R. Johnston (guardian for infant heirs of Charles C. Johnston, decd) vs Thompson Morrison debt

pg 118 Elijah H. Morgan vs Edmund McGinnis debt
_____ Richard McCallister vs James Beckett debt
_____ Alexander B. McKeand vs William R. Heath and Richard B. Heath
_____ 1837 May 22nd Jas. Buffington D copy Buffington will $1
_____ Joseph Wheeler, Wm. Miller, Rhodes Wescot D 1837 May 22 copy Lowry bill $1.29

pg 119 Ward (for the use of Catlett & William) vs McCormack
_____ 1836 Jun 3rd St. Clair Emmons D copy Davis plea $2.10
_____ A. & E. McGinnis vs Daniel Ray caps
_____ E.McGinnis vs Daniel Ray
_____ James Plymale vs William B. Reneck debt
_____ Phileman Chapman vs John Cundiff, John Chapman & William Chapman

pg 120 Lantz Richmond (who sues for the use of William Ferguson) vs William Thompson & Absolum Queen debt
_____ Fredk.G.L. Beuhring vs Edmund Ferguson debt
_____ John Peyton vs Comth- suppeonas: Roland Bias, Emberson Turley, Leonard McCormick
_____ Absolum Holderby & Alexander H. Gardner (merchants by name Absolum Holderby & Co.) vs Madison McComas

pg 121 Roberts vs comth suppeonas: Jones Roberts, James Paul
September 1st Term 1837
_____ Hudson & Waters vs Mather Rutherford debt
_____ Strather & McCormack assee vs James F. Clark debt
_____ same vs Stephen Kelly
_____ same vs Isaac Newman
_____ same vs Thomas Christian
_____ same vs Wm. Allison

pg 122 Fredkerick G.L. Beuhring vs Roland Bias debt
_____ John W. Hite vs William Morrison & John Morrison
_____ Elijah H. Morgan vs William Turner trespass
_____ Percival L. Smith vs Phileman Chapman

pg 123 same vs Jonathan W. Rig
_____ same vs Wm. Cyrus

_____ same vs Robt. W. Hanly
_____ 1837 Sep 25th Stephen Spurlock D copy Russell Mays record $1.63
_____ 1837 Feb 25th F.G.L. Beuhring D copy deed Calloway to Crockett
_____ Robert Holderby vs William Peters debt
_____ same vs Beckett (Ben Kitt ?)

pg 124 James Ferguson assee of Sherod Adkins (asse of Henderson Drake-assee of Edward Franklin) vs Emanuel Sison debt
_____ John Samuels vs William Williams, John Scales and Patrick Morrison debt
_____ James Poteet (assee of Joseph Gardner) vs Edmd. McGinnis
_____ Absolum Holderby & Alexander H. Gardner (merchants of Absolum Holderby & Co) (who sue for the use of Epps Johnston) vs Samuel Dean

pg 125 same vs Leven Swan caps
_____ same vs Elijah G. Seamonds debt
_____ same vs Joseph Riggs debt
_____ same vs William Messinger debt
_____ same George McComas debt
_____ same vs David Lucas debt
_____ same vs Elias Carpenter debt

pg 126 N. Holt vs Frazier & wife case
_____ Andrew M. Henderson & William C. Miller (merchants trading under the name of Henderson & Miller) vs William Hite
_____ Henderson & Miller vs John Morris debt
_____ Wm.C. Miller vs John McClasky debt
_____ Absolum Holderby & Alexander H. Gardner (merchants trading under the name of A. Holderby & Co.) vs Jacob Vaughan debt & damage

pg 127 same vs Jacob Adkins debt
_____ same vs Sanders Arthur debt
_____ same vs Burrel Wilks debt
_____ The above 13 suits are bought for the benefit of Wayne McMahan and Stephen Moore who are liable for costs
_____ same vs William Mather debt (same endorsement)
_____ Strother & McCormack assee vs Hy Clark
_____ Robert Holderby vs David McCormack

pg 128 Robert Holderby vs A. Carter debt
_____ Fredk.G.L. Beuhring & Charles S. Roffe (merchants trading under the name of F.G.L. Beuhring & Co.) vs Thomas Beckett and Moses Becket debt
_____ 1837 William Ferguson (adm of Saml. Ferguson) copy of will $1.52

_____ Wilson & Frampton vs Detz & Hull(?)
_____ same vs S. Hensley (?) ---J. Laidley

pg 129 Blackburn & Barrett vs Samuel Smith debt
_____ Willis McKeand (assee of A. Holderby & Co. who sues for the use of James Kinsolving) vs Warner B. Mahone caps Mansfield PV
_____ A. Holderby vs F. Burkett & al W. Mahan & S. Moore for tax
_____ same vs J. Grass & al (same for tax)
_____ Jas. Buffington D Jan 22nd 1838 copy ---- Will
_____ same D seal for T. Buffington $1.37
_____ 1838 Jan 22nd John Samuels D seal & certificate T. Buffington $2

pg 130 1838 Jan 26th John Samuels D seal Davis record Emmons suit
_____ 1838 Jan 26th Elias P. Davis D Emmons record $3.88
_____ James Garrett vs E.S. Hanly, Thomas E. Hanly & John M. Hanly
_____ George P. Brumfield (who sues for the of Jos. Gardner) vs Wade Hampton
_____ Jos. Gardner vs Wade Hampton

pg 131 Henry Miller vs David McCormick debt
_____ Catlett, Bates & Co. vs William Mather & Overton White
_____ A. & E. McGinnis vs Jacob Hite debt
_____ Joseph Mansfield vs Bostick Brumfield & Allen Brumfield debt
_____ Thomas T. (Train)(?) assee of James Bell vs John G. Wright debt

pg 132 J. Laidley credit of $4 to be applied toward fee bill
_____ Jesse Tony vs Joseph Nagle case
_____ James Douglas vs Henry Miller debt
_____ Edmund McGinnis vs James Bates debt
_____ Samuel Ross vs Mary Blankenship (adm of Ralph Blankenship)
_____ P.S. Smith vs Henry Clark

pg 133 (crossed out) Henderson & Miller vs Wm.B.Renwinds(?)
_____ Henderson & Miller vs Jacob Hite debt
_____ (crossed out) Henderson & Miller vs Luke Adkins debt
_____ William Watts vs comth- suppeonas: Polly Bartron, Thomas Bartron, Solomon Barton, John Queen
_____ 1838 May 11th N. Bail Strothers D copy record McKeand
_____ John Cameron vs Valentine Herndon debt
_____ Austin Smith vs Burwell Wilks debt

pg 134 Thomas Price vs Henry Bussey debt
_____ William Turner vs Henry Clark debt

_____ Archibald Hanly (who sues for the use of Shankring & Hamilton) vs Isaac Hanly debt

_____ James Holderby & Robert Holderby (merchants trading under the name of James Holderby & Co. sue for the use of James Holderby) vs Phillip Wintz

pg 135 (crossed out) Absolum Holderby & William C. Hite vs Arthur F. Farley debt

_____ J. Laidley (adm) vs Miller & Holderby debt

_____ Thompson vs ------ unlawful retainer witness: Lewis Frasier, Goodwin Lycan

_____ Henry K. ----------- vs John Russell debt - John Cameron for tax

_____ Hugha Bowen vs John H. Brumfield, Henderson P. Brumfield, Allen F. Brumfield, Jorden Brumfield, John Hatfield & wife Susan, Bostick Brumfield.

pg 136 John & S. Miller vs John Bail & al debt

_____ Milton Ferguson & John Everett Jr. (merchants trading under the name of Milton Ferguson & Co.) vs George Stephenson debt

_____ James Webb vs Walker J.L. Sansford debt

pg 137 John Porter vs Walker J.L. Sanford debt

_____ Beverly R. Johnston (guardian for John P. Johnston and Eliza M. Johnston) vs John Payton debt

_____ same vs Samuel Hensley debt

_____ Isaac Patrick (adm of Henry Rodgers) vs David R. Lacy debt

pg138 Smith Syres vs comth- suppeonas: Anthony Plymale & John N. Smith

_____ Percival S. Smith vs William Mather, Joseph Rutherford, Henry Maupin (merchants trading under the name of Mather, Rutherford & Co.) debt

_____ James (ink spot) grass (Snodgrass ?) vs Walker J. L. Sanford debt

_____ William Dingess vs Thomas C. Bails, Richard Bails, Perceder Bails, and John Bails (partners trading under the name of T.C. Bails & Brothers) debt $260

pg 139 John Cameron vs Valentine Herndon suppeonas: John Dundass, Thomas Dundass

_____ Robert Holderby vs Richard Brown debt

_____ John Plymale vs Henry Clark & B. Brown debt

_____ 1838 Jul 25th John Samuels D. seal Barrett's record

_____ 1838 Jul 28th Andw. & Jas. Barrett D copy record S. Reynolds

_____ J & S. Miller vs Thos. Davis debt

pg 140 David Turner & Octavius Church vs Willis McKeand debt

_____ Solomon Hensley vs Daniel Witcher debt

_____ B. Maupin vs G.W. Michell

_____ Beuhring vs Jas. Webb Jr. debt

_____ same vs P. Burnes Jr. debt

pg 141 Samuel Childers vs ------,--- -- , Lewis Roffe , Absolum Bias, Wm. Johnston
_____ 1838 Sep 15th James Ford D 2 deeds Spurlock to R. Adkins
and Andrew from R. Adkins to E. Rutherford
_____ Adam B. Sexton vs James D. Miller debt
_____ Phillip Bumgardner (who sues for the use of B.R. Johnston) vs William Wintz
_____ Parker Adkins vs Jeremiah Witcher (adm of Daniel Witcher, decd)

pg 142 Allen McClung vs William McComas G.W. Summers for tax
_____ Rachael Donathen vs James Wilson debt $30
_____ P. Blake vs Beuhring debt
_____ J.B. & W. Hite vs Mathers Rutherford & Co. debt
September 1st Term 1838
_____ James Haskell & Wakemon Fowler (partners trading under the name of
Haskell & Fowler) vs Luke Reynolds debt
_____ Frederick G.L. Beuhring vs James Webb Jr. debt

pg 143 Appearances to November Term 1838
_____ Edmund Newhouse vs William Hermon
_____ F.G.L. Beuhring assee vs William --------------- tax, H. Shelton
_____ James Webb vs Walker J.L. Sansford
_____ Moses Beckett vs Wm.R. Heath, Richard B. Heath, James Heath

pg 144 Frederick G.L. Beuhring vs William Mather debt
_____ Federick G.L. Beuhring & Co. vs Wm. Davis
_____ Absolum Holderby & Solomon Thornburg (merchants trading under
the name of A. Holderby & Co.) vs James Cox debt
_____ G.W. Shelton vs John McKeand
_____ A.W. Handley & Co. vs Willis McKeand
_____ John Bellamy vs Wade Hampton & Joseph Fulkerson debt

pg 145 John Campbell & Lewis Dod vs John Samuels (adm John Carter decd) and
Hiram Carter, Aneas Carter, Calvery Carter, Weslly Carter, ------ Hicks and
wife Angeline all devises of John Carter
_____ Henry Miller vs Benjamin Brown (adm John Hisey, decd)
_____ Anthony Lawson vs Jacob Douglas debt
_____ Leonard B. Sharp (who sues for the use of John Laidley) vs Larken Warren
and Wade Hampton

pg 146 1838 Nov 29th Absolum Holdbery & Wm.C. Hite D
_____ William Mather, Joseph Rutherford, Henry Maupin (merchants trading under

the name of Mather, Rutherford & Co.who sue for the use of Wayne McMahan) vs Isom Hall debt

_____ Hensley vs Witcher suppeonas: John Everett Jr. & Ralph Smith

_____ Jacob Baumgardner vs John W. Griffin, Abraham Trout, Henry Walker, Benjamin Swan and wife ________, David Smith and wife Sina, Elijah Ray and wife_______, William Sexton and wife Polly, William Jarrett and Matilda Jarrett and James Jarrett (all children and heirs of David Jarrett, decd)

pg 147 Andrew D. Henderson & William C. Miller (partners trading under name of Henderson & Miller) vs John S. Chapman debt

_____ same vs Josiah Swan debt for tax James M. Laidley

_____ Thomas J. Jeans(?) (who sues for the use A.W. Ferguson) vs Willis McKeand

_____ Wayne McMahon & Wilson Moore (merchants trading under the name of Wayne McMahon & Co.) vs George W. Collins debt

pg 148 Philemon Cha(pman) vs James Miller debt Levi Hampton - tax

_____ Jas. Beckett vs H.B. Hughart debt

_____ Horatio Catlett & William Williams (merchants trading under the name of Catlett & Williams) vs John Dean debt

_____ Horatio Catlett vs Woodson Hensley debt

_____ John Everett Jr. vs Richard Brown debt

pg 149 Henry W. Shelton (assee of Bussey & Rigg) vs John L. Chapman

_____ Henry & Bussey (for the use of H.W. Shelton) vs Josiah Swann

_____ John Laidley vs John Tony debt

_____ Stephen Wilson & J. Frampton (merchants trading under the name Wilson & Frampton) vs Joseph Lett debt

_____ Martin Hull vs Richard Brown debt

_____ James McLane, Wm. King & Joseph McCord (merchants trading under the name McLane, King & McCord) vs Thos.T. France & Robt. Brubaker (merchants trading under the name France & Brubaker (Frame not France ?)

pg 150 James Newman (assee of Stephen Moore) vs Overton White debt

_____ Isaac McCallister vs James Becket and wife Matilda caps

_____ Fredk.G.L. Beuhring vs Peter Newman debt

_____ (crossed out) J.H. Miller vs J.R. & L.P. Bail Lee Richards PV

pg 151 Wilson & Frampton vs Wade Hampton debt

_____ David Harshbarger vs Jacob Bumgardner

_____ David Harshbarger (assee of Jas. Kinsolving) vs Anthony Rigg debt

_____ same vs Charles Peyton debt

_____ James Kinsolving (who sues for the benefit of David Harshbarger)

vs John Peyton debt
_____ same vs Willis McKeand

pg 152 James Pinnel vs John McKeand
_____ Wm. Spurlock vs Saml. Dean debt
_____ Wayne McMahan vs John Sarten & Juda Loar
_____ William G. Henderson (assee of Chapman Maupin) vs James Heath
& Frederick G.L. Beuhring debt

pg 153 Appearances June Term 1839
_____ Samuel Kyle to Patrick H. Hensley debt
_____ Peter Grass (for use of F.G.L. Beuhring) vs Robert Alford debt
_____ Hensley vs Witcher suppeonas: Ralph Smith, Edward Elmore, John Everett Jr.
_____ David Harshbarger (assee of James Kinsolving vs Elijah G. Seamonds
_____ James Stewart vs Henry S. Bussey, Joseph Rigg & Bushrod W. Kinsolving

pg 154 James Kinsolving (who sues for the benefit of David Harshbarger)
vs Samuel Rigg debt
_____ David Harshbarger (assee of Js. Kinsolving) vs Charles Rigg debt
_____ Roland Bias vs Greenville Rigg chy
_____ Jeremiah Witcher vs Daniel Witcher & al
_____ Elizabeth Knight (adm of esate of Abner Knight, decd) vs Phillip Wintz
_____ D.J. Watts (for use of W.C. (Miller - Rucker ??) vs P. Newman

pg 155 Melchur Merritt vs Lewis D. Love(?) & Lewis Love
_____ Joseph W. Roffe vs Elijah G. Seamonds & Elijah G. Seamonds Jr.
_____ 1839 May 28th John G. & S. Miller D deed Seahol to Church(?)
_____ G.W. Shelton (assee of A.S. Hatfield) vs Morris(?) J. Swan caps
_____ William Wheeler vs Alexander Wheeler-witness: James Wheeler
& Joseph Wheeler

pg 156 Jacob Pinson vs William Lowe trespass
_____ Chas. Conner vs Geo. Calvert debt
_____ (crossed out) Joseph J. Mansfield vs Michael Laidley vs Martin Moore caps
C.L. Richard for tax
_____ John Johnston -witness for Johnston Sites
_____ John Plymale vs John Wilson(?) damage

pg 157 Deatley D 1839 Aug 6th to John Samuels D copy of Deatley's answer
_____ 1839 Aug 6th Richard McCallister copy deed of Man--- to R. Bias
_____ 1839 Aug 6th John Samuels D copy deed S.B. Sharp to W. Hampton
_____ H.B. Maupin D copy deed Mathers to White

_____ John W. Hite D copy deed P. Ray to L. Ray
_____ H.B. Maupin D copy of------ deed of trust to Hite
_____ Calvary Stephenson to Edmund McGinnis debt
_____ Wayne McMahan & Wilson Moore (merchants trading under the of Wayne McMahan & Co.) vs Kirk (?)
_____ Martin Moore vs Michael Scales(?) debt

pg 158 William T. Nicholls & Frederick More (merchants trading under the name of J.W. Nicholls & Co.) vs David Fry
_____ John Samuels D seal on Wm. Morris deed, same Cameron's deed(Conners) ditto Sites naturalization
_____ Alex.W. Handley & John W. Griffin (merchants trading under the name A.W. Handley & Co.) vs Bosoaster Scales debt
_____ Edward Stephenson & A. Stephenson vs comth suppeonas: William Ray, Benjamin Ray, Isaiah Ray, Wm. Zeaulds(?) 27 Jul 1839
_____ John D. Cameron vs J.N. Hammer(?)

pg 159 J. & S. Miller vs James Plymale case
_____ Daniel Lovejoy vs Edmund McGinnis & John W. Hite debt
_____ Edmund McGinnis (who sues for the use of Joseph Gardner) vs Overton White & John W. Hite
_____ (crossed out) Wm. Hatton vs John Lacy(?) and wife Dicy trespass
_____ James Stone vs John Frasehur debt

pg 160 George W. Chadwick vs Shockly Johnston caps
_____ G.W. Shelton vs Edwd.W. Billups debt
_____ Henderson & Miller vs Moses F. Nappier debt
_____ John Samuels D seal Miller's deed $1

pg 161 (crossed out) Thomas Beckett vs Alexander Wheeler & James Wheeler chy
_____ (crossed out) Edmund McGinnis vs Allen A. McGinnis chy

pg 162 Jospeh J. Mansfield vs John Misett damage
_____ John G. Perkins vs Isaac Ong AB
_____ Absolum Holderby vs Joseph Rigg & Philip Wintz caps
_____ (crossed out) Thomas Hatfield vs John G. Miller

pg 163 John G. Miller vs Wm.G. Miller caps
_____ Samuel Porter, Theodore M. Collins & George Evanes vs William Burkett
_____ Elizabeth Deatly (infant under 21 by Roland Bias her guardian) vs John Deatly & Frederick G.L. Beuhring
_____ J. Laidley vs Wade Hampton -suppeona: J. Wellman

_____ Elizabeth Spears vs John Brumfield McComas for tax
_____ Wade Hampton vs George P. Brumfield caps

pg 164 Superior Court Appearances July Term 1839
_____ Samuel Watson vs Shawther & Yates trespass
_____ Henry K. Terrlee vs William Turner trespass
_____ 1839 Jun 25th Solm. Thornburg copy Kilgore record
_____ James Ferguson vs George Merritt covenant

pg 165 James McGinnis vs Samuel Hensly chy
_____ Abraham Duncan McKee vs William Turner, Elijah H. Morgan, Peter Everett and Levi J. Hampton trespass
_____ John Miller vs William R. Seamons
_____ same vs Thomas Hatfield case
_____ same vs George W. Shelton
_____ Henry B. Maupin vs William Mather, Joseph Rutherford, Overton White, ------- Poor and John W. Hite chy

pg 166 Thornburg vs Saunders- make out copies of case- your copy omits sections etc
_____ Wm.R. Seamonds vs Edmd. McGinnis chy
_____ William Vaughan vs John Gilkerson damage
_____ Horatio Catlett vs Scott Ward damage

pg 167 Jeremiah Witcher vs Henry Peyton trespass - AB
_____ Fredk.G.L. Beuhring vs Jesse Toney and John Laidley chy
_____ Lewis Dodd vs Carter heirs & al chy
_____ John Gilkerson vs Andrew M. Love (?)
_____ Thomas R. Terry vs James C. Terry debt Summers for tax
_____ Clifton H. Rucker (who sues fot the use of Thos.R. Terry) vs James C. Terry

pg 168 Isaac N. Hamner vs John D. Cameron caps witness: George Zirkle, Charles Mays and old man Cameron
_____ Vincent Newman vs Frederick G.L. Beuhring damage
_____ (crossed out) Jacob Penson vs William Lowe
_____ Richard McCallister vs Rowland Bias
_____ Kirby vs Gilkerson

pg 169 Thomas A. Hereford (adm of James Wilson decd) vs Horatio Catlett suppeona H. Shelton
_____ James Webb vs W.J.L. Sanford debt
_____ Moses Beckett vs William R. Heath, Richard B. Heath, James Heath
_____ Susan Druillard vs Levi Hampton slander

_____ John W. Hite vs Peter Ray & Levina Ray chy

pg 170 Marcus L. Kibbe vs John Gilkerson case
_____ Wm. Joy vs Jos. Files case
_____ David Johnston (infant under 21 & Benjamin Johnston his father and next friend) vs Thomas Turner slander
_____ Joseph Files vs William Joy case

pg 171 Adam S. Hatfield vs Henry Peyton caps
_____ Robert Holderby vs William Peters & Moses McCormack
_____ John Morgan vs Bennett Bellemy case
_____ John Morgan vs David McCormack

pg 172 William Perry vs James Knight slander
_____ Preston Guthrie vs James Knight case
_____ Mathew L. Billemy vs Wade Hampton & William William trespass
_____ David Trobridge vs Joseph Files trespass for killing cattle

pg 173 Mary Blankenship vs John Plymale trespass
_____ Thomas G. Holland (alias Thomas T. Holland) vs Horatio Catlett
_____ Marcus S. Kibbs vs John Gilkerson case. R. Brown will give bail

pg 174 Roland Bias (adm of James Deatly) vs John Deatly & F.G.L. Beuhring debt
_____ John (Peact-Pratt)(?) vs Comth suppeonas Samuel McGinnis, Allen Christian, John Morgan & James McGinnis
_____ James Poteet vs comth suppeonas: Robert Holderby, William Poteet, Moses Varnum
_____ Ancil Varnum vs Comth suppeonas: William Stone & Augustus Woolcot
_____ William Poteat vs comth suppeonas: William Stone & Augustus Woolcot
_____ 1838 Aug 7th (S. Herrenkohl)(?) D copy Kelly's bill
_____ H. Catlett vs Seth Ward caps

pg 175 Frederick G.L. Beuhring vs Richard B. Heath, Burk McComas & David Heath
_____ William C. Terry vs John & Henry Hannon debt
_____ John W. Hite assee of W. McKeand (who sues for the use of F. Tiernan) vs Wm.B. Renick caps
_____ Isaac Crumb (infant under the age of 21 by James Crumb his father and next friend) vs Henry Night and wife Margaret slander

pg 176 Edmd. McGinnis vs Allen A. McGinnis caps
_____ Martin Moore vs Daniel Tappan caps
_____ Belden Walker & Co. vs Edmund McGinnis case

_____ Wayne McMahan (assee of Thomas Hatfield) vs William Massinger caps
_____ (crossed out) P.S. Smith vs Henry Clark debt

pg 177 September 1st 1837
_____ Eli F. Hannon and wife Margaret vs John H.Brumfield debt
_____ James Ford vs Elliott Rutherford & wife Vesta, George Adkins, (Thomas ?) Booth & wife Jane, Elizabeth Adkins, Anderson Adkins, Henry Adkins, William Adkins, Agnes Adkins
_____ Dryden Donnally, John Lewis and Crockett Lisslis(?) (late merchants trading under name of D. Donnally & Co.) vs Enoch Meadows debt
_____ issued county court 26th March 1838

pg 178 Hiram Haskins vs William Cox Sr., Madison McComas, Benjamin Cornwall
_____ Jacob Grass vs William R. Heath, Richard Heath, Stephen Heath, Burke McComas, David Heath
_____ Hannan vs comth suppeonas: David Hicks, Anthony Rigg, Jacob Merritt

pg 179 Jas. McCallister vs R.B. Heath & al chy
_____ (crossed out) Samuels make out and send to me declaration in case of Emmons vs Davis James M. Laidley
_____ (crossed out) : Lantz Richmond (who sues for the use of William and Absolum Queen) vs William Thompson
_____ Frederick G.L. Beuhring vs William R. Heath, Stephen Heath
_____ Wm.R. Heath vs Richard B. Heath, Stephen P. Heath, Burk McComas, and David Heath

pg 180 Fredk.G.L. Beuhring vs William Blue, John Heath, John Porter Jr., David Heath
_____ Absolum Holderby vs Frederick G.L. Beuhring and Patrick Collins
_____ Phil. Chapman D copy of Cundiff bill, F.G.L. Beuhring 3 copies Blue case & Wm.R. Heath case, Jesse Toney 4 copies Stafford case

pg 181 Ephram Lockwood vs William Snidow and Daniel B. Viers
_____ Joseph Fulkerson vs John Gilkerson chy
_____ Jospeh J. Mansfield vs Pellington Merritt & Obadiah Merritt debt
_____ 1837 Jun 13th F.G.L. Beuhring copy Jenkins & Davis
_____ John P.B. Maxwell vs Richd.B. Heath chy

pg 182 Ferguson vs Watts suppeonas: William Belcher & Hiram Polly
_____ John Toney vs Wm. Peters caps
_____ F.G.L. Beuhring vs Samuel Blankenship caps
_____ John Meadows vs Allen Christian

_____ Richard Damron vs Aly Watts (otherwise named Elias Watts), William Adams, William Watts, Ambrose Watts, Edmond Nappier, & Carr Noe

pg 183 William Hull vs John Peattes trespass & slander
_____ John Samuels D 1836 Sep 29th letter of adm of John Smith decd
_____ Sally Thompson vs James Ferguson debt
_____ Elizabeth Deatly (an infant by her guardian Roland Bias) vs John Deatly and Frederick G.L. Beuhring
_____ Absolum Holderby & Alexander H. Gardner (merchants trading under the name of A. Holderby & Co.) vs Richard Heath

pg 184 Ambrose Watts vs Kelley Ferguson trespass
_____ Garrett Kelly vs Henry S. Gardner caps
_____ (crossed out) Warren B. Mahone vs George W. Shelton caps
_____ (crossed out) James Crowford vs John G. Wright damage
_____ Ruel Daggs vs John Vincent debt & damage

pg 185 John Gilkerson vs Samuel Dean slander, trespass, AB
_____ Jacob Adkins Jr. vs Patrick Nappier
_____ John Toney vs Lewis Russell slander
_____ September 1st 1836
_____ Nimrod Farley vs Roland Bias and Daniel Witcher Jr. to recover 2 horses, 2 mares 1 sadle, birdle & goods & merchandise

pg 186 John Plymale vs Burwell Spurlock & Stephen ----(Spurlock ?)
_____ same vs Robert Holderby
_____ Robt. Holderby vs Ben Brown
_____ George Hudson vs Pennell Blake
_____ Bellemy & Perry vs (ink spot) Ruffner & Wm. Spurlock

pg 187 1835 Oct 1st John Hall, Anthony Lawson D, copy Bowen & Gallaher bill
_____ 1835 Oct 13th David & John ----- D, copy of decree Wilson vs Kouns
_____ 1835 Oct 23rd Thos. McComas D record- R. Bias vs D. McComas
_____ Miller's heirs (name them) by ------Miller the guardian and next friend vs James R. Clark (adm of estate of Wm. Clark) & Philip Baumgardner,& -------Knight for tax Joseph Gardner
_____ John Toney vs James Wilson

pg 188 Joseph Rutherford & Luther Richey (late partners trading under the name of Rutherford & Richey) vs Frederick G.L. Beuhring
_____ Henry Miller vs John Hizey chy
_____ Ezekiel Stone vs Van Swearingen, David Garrett, John Swearingen

vs Lewis Wellman chy
_____ James Richards (who sues for the use of John Richards) vs Philemon Chapman

pg 189 Alexander Pine vs William Poage case
_____ Henry Miller vs William Poage case
_____ Robert Holderby vs Jas. Emmons clerks fees printers fees
_____ Rhoda Miller vs Jefferson Bowen trespass
_____ Lucinda Vincent vs Benjamin Vincent chy

pg 190 Jacob Bragg & wife vs Bartlett Adkins & wife & al chy
_____ John Laidley (adm of C.W. Smith) vs John Rodgers
_____ comth vs O.L. Murray suppeonas for Prisoner Edwd.G. Wright, James Barbour, Richard Walden
_____ May 1835 Hiram McComas D copy order on Rodger heirs
_____ Ephriam Lockwood D copy Spurlock record
_____ 1835 May 16th C.W. Smith, adm D copy Davis file
_____ 1835 Jun 11th John A. Robinston D copy comth vs P.S. Murray
_____ 1835 June 19th James G. Perry & Henry Perry D, copy record B.H. White
_____ 1835 Jun 23rd A.S. Doolittle D copy Waldron(?) record

pg 191 Samuel T. Craig vs Garnett Leonard & William Poage
concerns negro boy Jacob in Poage hands
_____ 1834 Dec 26th Jas. McGinnis D copy Cookus bill
_____ Wm. Holten vs John Adkins
_____ 1835 Jan 26th Geo. Hatfield D copy of trust deed on F.G.L.Beuhring
_____ 1835 Jul 30 John Gilkerson D copy of John A.______
_____ Wm. Newman vs A. Syrus
_____ Wm. Ellington vs A. Syers

pg 192 David Ellington & wife Mary vs A.Syrus
_____ (crossed out) William Ballard (who sues for the benefit of Robert Holderby) vs John C. Kouns and Jacob Kouns merchants trading under the name of JC & J Kouns
_____ (crossed out) James Buffington vs Jacob Kouns and John C. Kouns and George Poague and Thomas Poague (merchants trading under the name of Kouns, Poague & Co.)
_____ (crossed out) John Russell vs (same firm)
_____ Joseph Rigg vs Thomas Rigg case

pg 193 1834 Oct 28th Joel Ferguson D. copy of record ----------wife
_____ Patrick Keenan (who sues for the use of Absolum Holderby) vs John Lucas, Jesse Toney, Henry Eplin and Richard Adkins

_____ 1834 Nov 13th John C. & Jacob Kouns D, copy of Wilson 's bill
_____ 1834 Nov 19th Jas. McGinnis D copy of Kookus record $8.22
copy of plat of Savage Grant $5.94
_____ H.J. Harvey (who sues for the use of William Ward) vs John C.Kouns, Jacob Kouns and George Poage trespass
_____ Jeremiah Roberts (who sues for the benefit of George Carr) vs David R. Lacy atty James M. Laidley

pg 194 Robert Holderby vs James Emmons, Adamena Smith, George Huchons & wife Mary, Elizabeth Smith & John Smith
_____ (crossed out) Samuel T. Craig vs Thomas Syrus reguarding two slaves Sarah & Amos
_____ (crossed out) Samuel T. Craig vs Garnett Lee & Philip Hizey chy reguarding negro boy Jacob
_____ September 1st 1834
_____ John Turman vs Allen A. McGinnis covenant
_____ John T. Cookus & al vs James McGinnis chy

pg 195 Jas. Holderby & Co. vs Brice Stokes debt
_____ Ohio Iron Co. vs David McCormick case
_____ Wesley Ferguson vs John H. Brumfield, John Hatfield & wife Hannah, Henderson P. Brumfield, Allen T. Brumfield, Manos B. Brumfield, Jorden Brumfield, Margaret Ann Brumfield, Kitty Ann M. Brumfield, Milton D. Brumfield, William W. Brumfield
_____ 1834 Jun 18th Wm. Hite D
_____ make copy of bill Reynolds vs Lunsford, Martha Toney & al-James M. Laidley

pg 196 John Grant vs John Bias debt & damage
_____ John Laidley (agent for John P.B. Maxwell) vs James Wheeler debt
_____ John Grant vs Roland Bias debt
_____ John Laidley (agent for P.B. Maxwell) vs Thomas Denison debt
_____ George W. Stribbling vs Henry Clark

pg 197 Jno. Jorden & Maxwell vs Jno. Porter suppeonas: Wm. Buffington, Andrew Barrett, Jas. Barrett for def
_____ John Toney vs Wm. Peter, Joseph Lett, Lewis Russell trespass, destroying timber
_____ Jacob Dean vs Heirs of Wm. Spurlock
_____ Ephram Lockwood vs ----------(?)(Gilkerson & Wm. Spurlock's heirs)?
_____ Joseph Lett vs John Toney trespass & slander

pg 198 James T. Watson vs David McCormick debt

_____ Joseph Ewing vs Origical Young & John Gilkerson caps
_____ 1834 Feb 25th John Porter D copy of case Shelton & Porter
vs J.P.B. Maxwell
_____ 1834 Feb 28th Jacob Kouns D copy of Wilson bill
_____ Kilgore (for the use of Bias) vs Deatly & Beuhring
_____ John Gilkerson vs the heirs of Wm. Spurlock

pg 199 Siles Smith (infant under 21 by Ralph Smith his father)
vs Sampson Saunders trespass
_____ Martin Moore vs Jeremiah Witcher damage trespass & slander
_____ B. Thomas Watson, Andrew Wood, Wm. M. Wood, Luther Davis Wood,
Joseph and Perry Wood vs John Preston Johnson & Eliza Mary Johnson
_____ Percivil S. Smith & Joseph Holden (merchants trading under the name of
P.S. Smith & Co.) (assee of Edmund McGinnis) vs Willis McKeand debt

pg 200 John Poteat vs Burwell Spurlock(adm of estate of Leroy Garrett)
_____ Edmund Ferguson vs Covington Ross trespass & AB
_____ Charles W. Smith vs Burwell Spurlock (adm of estate of Leroy Garrett)
& Robert Clendenan
_____ Chas. Ruffner vs Jo Fulkerson damage

pg 201 John Morris vs Stephen Spurlock (adm of Wm. Spurlock)
_____ Thomas S. Spurlock vs William Spurlock's adm
_____ Percival S. Smith & Joseph Holden(merchants trading under the
name P.S. Smith & Co.) vs Stephen Spurlock (adm of Wm. Spurlock)
_____ James Holderby & Co. vs Wm. Spurlock adm
_____ Burwell Spurlock (adm of Reuben Adkins) vs Stephen Spurlock
(adm William Spurlock)

pg 202 Frederick G.L. Beuhring (assee of James Deatley) vs Bostick Mansfield
and wife Ann(late Ann Rodgers)
_____ Burwell Johnston, Francis Johnston and Squire Johnston (assee of Sampson
Sanders) vs Willis McKeand debt McComas & Smith tax
_____ 1833 Jun F. Moore & Wellman D copy David Thomas file
_____ Benjamin Davis vs David Hogan, William Brumley & Christopher Toler
_____ September 1st 1833
_____ 1833 Sep 1st Jas. McGinnis escheator of Cabell County)
copy record Wm. Hite $4.00
_____ 1813 Sep 11th Doolittle spa. .18

pg 203 (crossed out) John Smith vs Stephen Spurlock (adm of Wm. Spurlock)
_____ (crossed out) John Scales vs William Mails damage

_____ Elizabeth Turley(by Arthur F. Turley her guardian and next friend)
vs William Mails slander Absolum Holderby damage

pg 204 John M. McConnell vs Samuel Short debt
_____ John Vaughan & Charles Vaughan vs Samuel Short caps
_____ John Porter Jr. vs Samuel Stephenson chy
_____ 1833 Jan 8th Peter Blake D abstract Beuhring's record
_____ 1833 Jul 8th Jas. McGinnis D Cookus bill
_____ Henry Peyton & wife vs Wm. Mails

pg 205 Elizabeth Deatly (infant under 21 by Roland Bias her next friend)
vs John Deatley
_____ Benjamin T. Clemons & Lewis Hazen (who sues for the use & benefit of
John Gilkerson & Benjamin Turman) vs Samuel Dean & John Dean covenant
_____ Wm. Conner vs Ruel Porter
_____ same vs Alex. Porter
_____ Robt.D. Callihan (who sues for the benefit of A. Bierne, Martin Mims, John H.
Allison & Chas. Tiernan-trading as firm A. Bierne & Co.) vs John H. Allison
_____ 1833 May 2nd Peter Dingess D copy Elkins record
_____ J.T. Cookus & al vs Jas. McGinnis (escheater)

pg 206 Thomas McComas vs Robert G. Scott & wife Susanah R. Scott,
and Elisha McComas
_____ John Merritt vs James Newman caps
_____ Joseph Malcom vs Ambrose L. Doolittle covenant
_____ Thomas H. Roberts (by Gabriel Roberts his father and next friend)
vs John McClasky trespass AB
_____ Wm. Beckett, Pleasant Roberts, John ------- witness for plf
_____ George Hatfield vs Frederick G.L. Beuhring case

pg 207 Martin Moor vs Joseph Gardner
_____ Ezekiel Lambert vs Hiram Pauly damage slander: witness Carbut William
Lucen, William Nelson
_____ comth vs John Toney suppeonas: James Russell, John Hutcherson, James
Fuller
_____ Landon vs Hatfield Suppeonas: Roland Bias, Asa Booten, Thomas
McComas Jr., Richard B. Heath

pg 208 justices vs Adam Black debt
September 1st 1832
_____ make out copy of bill McComas & Ward
_____ William Peters vs John Toney case

_____ 1832 Oct James McGinnis D copy McComas bill
_____ Andrew Roberts vs Thomas Harmon debt
_____ Peter Blake vs Frederick G.L. Beuhring debt

pg 209 April 1830
_____ comth vs William Hite McConnell PV
_____ James Ferguson vs Joseph Roberston debt Hy Clark for tax
_____ Andrew Hatfield vs James M. Condon case
_____ Tabitha Russell vs Jess McComas AB

pg 210 Lewis Russell (who sues for the use of Henry Russell) vs George W. Kouns & Jacob Kouns debt
_____ Hiram McComas vs James Deatley & wife Elizabeth (late Elizabeth Rodgers), Williams Rodgers, Madison Rodgers, Matilda Rodgers, (Tsean ?) Rodgers, Ann Rodgers & Julian Rodgers (heirs of George Rodgers, decd)
_____ 1832 Mar Jesse Blankenship & John Stafford D. copy of Toney adm
_____ Samuel Damrell vs John Dean damage

pg 211 Samuel Littler vs Ezekiel Graham caps Stribbling for tax
_____ John H. Allison vs Henry Maddy debt
September 1st 1831
_____ Andrew McComas, John Ray, Benjamin Johnston vs Sampson Sanders case
_____ Wm. Hite vs Pellington Merritt & Isaac Handley caps
_____ Wm. Jorden vs John Morris (of John), Joseph Hilyard & wife Elizabeth (late Elizabeth Morris), Calvary Morris, Levi Morris, Thomas A.Morris, William Morris, Roan Morris, and Actona Morris,___Harris & wife Eloisa

p212 (late Eloisa Morris), Thomas Spurlock & wife Manerva (late Manerva Hannan), Eliza Hannan, Thomas Hannan, Zachariah Cox & wife Elizabeth(late Elizabeth Hannan), Edmund Hannan (crossed out Esom Hannan), Esom Hannan Jr.
(added to side of page-"You are the goddamdest in this country of goddamed Virginia".)
_____ 1831 Oct 15th Robt. Wilson D copy of John Toney bill
_____ Jacob Dean vs James Butcher & John Plymale. debt
_____ D.& J. Trimble vs Stephen Wilson
_____ Catlett for the use of Ellington vs Shortridge
_____ The clerk of Cabell County and the Superior Court will issue executions in all cases in which I am for the succesful party unless otherwise specially directed as well as those which have already been had as those which may hereafter be had. Jno.M. McConnell.

pg 213 James Ball & Wm. Brumley caps

_____ John McComas vs Rowland Bias trespass AB
_____ Benja.Dean vs John C. Kouns & Jacob Kouns trespass
_____ Frederidk Moore vs John Gilkerson
_____ Jesse Toney (adm of Ruth Range) vs Jesse Blankenship & John Stafford

pg 214 George A. Bicknell vs Fredk. Moore debt
_____ Samuel Withrow vs James White & Overton White & John Hannan
September 1st 1830
_____ F.G.L. Beuhring vs Joseph Gardner caps
_____ same vs A. Holderby
_____ Jo Gardner & wife vs John Briant caps

pg 215 September 1st 1829
_____ Jeremiah Witcher vs Martin Moore
_____ Joseph Gardner vs Stephen Wilson
_____ William Jenkins of Greenbottom D county seal
_____ John Samuels D. seal Jenkins certificate
_____ John Toney vs G.W. Kouns
_____ D & J Trimble vs G.W. Kouns & al
_____ Leven L. Sherve & Thomas T. Sherve (Iron manufactures under name of Sherve & Co.) vs Geo.W. Kouns

pg 216 Josiah Jackson vs John Smith
_____ Edward W.H. Winfield vs John Plymale damage
_____ Frederick Moore vs Samuel Short & William Davis debt
_____ J. Myers & al vs Chas.C. Johnson & al

pg 217 (crossed out) Edwd. Barrett vs Byrd Brumfield caps
September 1st 1827
_____ Richard Kezer vs Samuel Short trespass
_____ Benjamin Martin vs Samuel Short damage
_____ John Talbot vs William L. Thompson, Patterson W. Thompson debt

pg 218 Byrd Brumfield vs Jno. Gardner & al debt
_____ Wm. Stowers vs Jesse Blankenship
_____ Alexander(?) M. Cooper(infant under 21 by his father Thomas Cooper) vs Edmund McGinnis - one bay horse

pg 219 John Hatfield & al vs F.G.L. Beuhring
_____ Hy Ersken vs Saml. Wilson debt
_____ Elezh. B. Grant & al vs Elisha McComas
_____ 1826 Apr 14th John Samuels D seal to Blodget certificate

_____ Elizabeth Grant vs John Porter writ
_____ John Wellman vs John Everett Jr., F.G.L. Beuhring & John Hannan
September 1st 1826
____ Jan 1827 John Samuels D. seal on Dr. Sharah certificate
ditto for Blankenship END

DEATHS FROM " FEE BOOK"

all would be prior to date listed

1826 William Merritt
William McComas
Thomas Morris
Levi Spangler
Samuel Hinch
Joseph Gardner
John Emrath

1827 David Jarrett

1828 Steven Teays

1829 -----Preston
James Alford
Ratt Rainy

1832 George Rodgers

1833 John Deatley
Keith Rains
William Spurlock
James Wilson
Leroy Garrett
Reuben Adkins
Nancy Gilkerson

1834 Ester Russell
William Brumfield
Henry Loar
Charles Smith
Charles A. Johnson
Charles T. Johnston
William Brown

1835 William Fullerton

1836 G. Spears
John M. McConnell
Elias Humphrey
Samuel Ferguson
Ralph Blankenship
Henry Rodgers

1838 Daniel Witcher
John Carter
John Hisey
Abner Knight

1857 - 1859

(RULE BOOK)

CABELL COUNTY, VA/WV

1857 - 1859 (RULE BOOK)

(The book has no title.)

The book is a list names of prosecuted parties, amount paid court with date (some payments quite lengthy) and approval by clerk and (probably) lawyer. The clerk side (right) is included only if information is different.

This book has been damaged. The first 86 pages are missing as are later pages. Its materials adds information on Cabell residents of that time.

The information in the book is usually just a list of names, but many entries show companies and partnerships of the time period.

CABELL COUNTY RULE BOOK 1857-1859

First surviving page
page 87 1857

p87 satisfied--
March Rules 1857 (lawyers)

FiFa costs $9.86
debt $125.00 with legal interest from Dec 1854 - W.B. Moore CC
(Cabell Clerk)

----

p88 - 1857 July Rules 1857
Isaac Frampton & Jeremiah Wellman
(trading under firm Frampton & Wellman) W.B. Moore CC
vs Fred.G.L. Beuhring & John G. Miller G.F. Miller

James & William Clark G.F. Miller
vs Robert M. Adam, N.S. Adam,
Henry Carter & Hugo Dietz W.B. Moore CC

Robert M. Adam G.F. Miller
vs N.S. Adam, Henry Carter, Hugo Dietz, Rudolph Dietz W.B. Moore CC

Commonwealth not satisfied
vs Price Adkins & Ambrose Smith W.B. Moore CC

William B. Fowler who sues for use of William Adkins
vs Rowland Bias, Chas. Lattin & Geo. Killgore

Commonwealth
1) vs Rowland Bias, Chas. Lattin & Geo. Killgore
2) vs Jefferson McComas & Isaac McComas
3) vs Wm. Barkenstoe
4) vs John Keller
5) vs Henry W. Shelton
6) vs David Shelton
7) vs William Doran

Richard S. Ellis
vs Charles Burks

--------- 1857

E.M. Underwood, Henry Barrett, Andrew McComas,
Absolum Holderby, Dd. Harshbarger & Rowland Bias
vs Edwd. Meneger

William Knight
vs Benjamin F. Hannon

William Dickinson & Joel Shrewsberry
(partners of Dickson & Shrewsberry)
vs Augustus S. Wolcott

----

p89 Enoch D. Blankenship (assee) of Jerome Shelton
vs William Peyton & Alexander Peyton

Enoch D. Blankenship (who sues for use of) G.A. Holten
vs Samuel Adkins

Enoch D. Blankenship (who sues for use of) G.A. Holten
vs Robert M. Adam

Francis M. Ferrell (assee) of Isaac Blake
vs Elisha McComas & John Chapman

Frank Wiger (who sues for the use of) E.H. Walton
vs Henry Carter & Hugo Dietz

Henry Adkins (who sues for the use of) V.D. Latulle
vs Robert M. Adam & N.S. Adam

Enoch D. Blankenship (who sues for the use of) George A. Holten
vs Alexander Peyton

Jacob Adkins
vs Aaron F. McKendree

St. Mark Russell (who sues for the use of)---gon Dinisson
vs William Hite

Jesse Hudson
vs John J. Nash

--------- 1857

John Collins (who sues for the use of) W.C. Miller & Co.
vs Charles H. Harless & Charles Tooley

William C. Miller & Thomas Thornburg
(trading under name of W.C. Miller & Co.)
vs Samuel Mitchell

William C. Miller & Thomas Thornburg
(trading under name of W.C. Miller & Co.)
vs Henry W. Shelton

William C. Miller & Thomas Thornburg
(trading under name of W.C. Miller & Co.)
vs William C. Mahon

William C. Miller & Thomas Thornburg one gray mare & colt
(trading under name of W.C. Miller & Co.) J.S. Wilkinson for W.B. Moore
vs James Nicely

William C. Miller & Thomas Thornburg (trading under name W.C. Miller & Co.)
vs Samuel Hensley

----

p90 James McComas (who sues for the use of) Wm. C. Miller & Co.
vs Zachariah Nicely

James Duncan (who sues for the use of) Hy. B. Maupin
vs George Killgore, Conwelsey Simmons & Chas. K. Morris

Thomas C. Wallace
vs George Killgore

Geo.W. Hensley (who sues for the use of) Thomas Merritt
vs Samuel Hensley

Jerome Shelton(who sues for the use of) Thos.C. Buffington
vs John W. Vaughan

James Parish (who sues for the use of) - Gwin
vs Henry W. Shelton

--------- 1857

Henderson Drake (adm for estate of James Hatfield, decd)
vs Orren Moore, Henry L. Webb, V.D. Letulle

Harrison Collins
vs George Killgore & Horatio H. Wood

Henry J. Samuels (special commission)
vs George Killgore & George Gallaher

Mathew Thompson (who sues for use of Sidney Bowden)
vs Alex. Peyton & William Peyton

Mathew Thompson (who sues for use of Sidney Bowden)
vs William Merritt

Henderson Drake
vs V.D. LeTulle & Henry L. Webb

Mathew Thompson (who sues for the use of) H.H. Wood
vs Richard Lunsford

Greenville Harris
vs Henry W. Shelton

James Syrus (Exec of Jas. Syrus, decd)
vs Jas. M. Thompson & Allen Madberry 2 wagons, 1 horse cart, 1 clock

----

p91 Henry H. Miller
vs Burgess Stuart

John Laidley commission
vs George Killgore, John G. Willson & C. Simmons

John Laidley commission
vs James H. Walker

John Laidley (exec of will of James Holderby, decd)
vs Silas M. Clark

G.H. Lanfman
vs John Morris

-------- 1857

William Hinchman
vs Fredk. G.L. Beuhring

John Racy
vs Olliver A. & Edmund McGinnis

H.H. Wood (who sues for the use of) Godfrey Scites
vs Rowland Bias

John Ross
vs Samuel & Richard Harris

----

p92 Samuel Wellman (adm James Russell, decd)
vs William Peters

James King
vs Henry Ashworth & others

John Loyd
vs John Alford & Thomas Hatfield (partners of Alford & Co.)

Aenas Carter
vs Henry W. Shelton

Commonwealth
vs Ephraim Spotts

John Collins (who sues for the use of Wm.C. Miller & Co.)
vs Charles H. Harless & Charles Tooley

William C. Miller & Thomas Thornburg (trading under name of W.C. Miller & Co.)
vs Samuel Mitchell

Commonwealth
vs Adolphus A. Newley

Benjamin Rigs satisfied Wm. Adkins
vs Millington Adkins for L. Adkins

Commonwealth
Price Adkins & Ambrose Smith 1857

----

p93 John S. Ross levied Wm. Adkins for L. Adkins
vs Samuel Harris & Reuben Harris

Henderson Drake
vs Victor D. Letulle & Henry L. Webb

Henderson Drake (adm of estate of James Hatfield, decd)
vs Orren Moore, Herny L. Webb & Jerome Shelton

Thomas Hatfield
vs John Alford

Francis M. Farrell (assee) of Isaac Blake money pd to T.M. Feral,
vs Elisha McComas & John Chapman J.S. Wilkins

William C. Miller & Thomas Thornburg (trading under name of W.C. Miller & Co.)
vs Henry W. Shelton & Thomas C. Buffington

James Parish (who sues for the use of) Gwinn
vs Henry W. Shelton & Thomas C. Buffington

Mathew Thompson (who sues for the use of) H.H. Wood
vs Richard Lunsford & William Peyton

Harrison Collins
vs George Killgore & Horatio H. Wood, & William Kilgore

William Hinchman
vs Fredrick G.L. Beuhring & John Alford

----

p94 Enoch D. Blankenship (who sues for the use of) George S. Holten
vs Samuel Adkins & John Alford

Washington Gwinn
vs James Parish, James Gwinn, William Killgore

Frank Weger (who sues for the use of) Eli H. Walton
vs Henry Carter & Hugo Dietz

Jerome Shelton (who sues for the use of) Thomas C. Buffington
vs John W. Vaughan & John Alford

-------- 1857

James Duncan (who sues for the use of) Henry B. Maupin
vs George Killgore, Conwelsey Simmons, Charles K. Morris, John L. Hatfield

----

Greenville Harrison
vs Henry W. Shelton & Thomas C. Buffington

William C. Miller
vs John Ward Jr. & John Ward Sr.

C.H. Hoffman
vs John W. Baumgardner

John Laidley
vs George Killgore & James Parish

H. Densmore & S.W. Surry merchants (trading under name of H. Densmore & Co.)
vs William Merritt

----

p95 Wm. R. Seamonds (who sues for the use of) Thomas M. Shelton
vs George Killgore & H.H. Wood

Merritt Johnson
vs Emmerson Turley & P.H. McCullough

Henry J. Fisher
vs Preston Hodge

John S. Ross
vs Samuel Harris & Reuben Harris

Ruffner & Donlly & Co.
vs E.D. Blankenship

James Foils
vs Henry Carter, Hugo Dietz, (partners of Carter & Dietz)

John & William Lucas (who sues for the use of) Henry I. Fisher
vs Irwin Lusher & William E. Feazle

John Alford
vs Isaac Blake

-------- 1857

A. Daniels & B.F. Swann (merchants of A. Daniels & Co.)
(who sue for the use of J.L.Keller)
vs Richard Lunsford

William M. Franklin (who sues for the use of) John Laidley
vs John W. Vaughan

James F. Hansford (President of the Guyandotte Bridge Co. ?)
vs Guyandotte Bridge Co.

James Lawson & Anthony Lawson (exec. of Anthony Lawson, decd)
vs Harvey Elkins

----

p96 W.T. Cutter
vs William Merritt

W.T. Cutter & W.L. Brown (partners of Cutter & Brown)
vs William Merritt

John V. Robbins, Ralph M. Pomeroy, Samuel L. Robbins
(trading under name of Robins & Pomeroy)
vs Mathew Thompson

James Alford
vs James Parish

John V. Robbins, Ralph M. Pomeroy, Samuel L. Robbins
(trading under name of Robins & Pomeroy)
vs William Eggers

Charles L. Roffe
vs Wilson B. Moore (Sherriff of Cabell & adm of estate of John Hill, decd.)

Aeneas Carter
vs Henry W. Shelton

John Vaughan
vs The Guyandotte Navigation Co.

Arnold Kraus(Krans)
vs Julius Freutel (next friend of Wm. Myers)

-------- 1857

James F. Davis
vs John Cook

----

p97 Commonwealth
1) vs Adolphus A. Newley
2) vs Price Adkins & Ambrose Smith

Samuel A. Childers & Alexander McComas
(adm of estate of Michael Wintz who sues for the use of Thomas Merritt)
vs John Samuels & Joseph Gill

John Collins (who sues from the use of Wm.C. Miller & Co.)
vs Charles H. Harless & Charles Tooley

William C. Miller & Thomas Thornburg (trading name of W.C. Miller & Co.)
vs James Nicely

William C. Miller & Thomas Thornburg (trading under name of W.C. Miller & Co.)
vs Samuel Mitchell

Elijah Syrus (exec of James Syrus, decd)
vs James M. Thompson & Allen Medberry

Commonwealth
1) vs John Dundas
2) vs Thomas A. Childers
p98 3) vs James Adkins
4) vs Grissom L. Bates
5) vs James Smith
6) vs Charles Paine
7) John Shelton & O.L.C. Hinesman

Mathew Thompson (who sues for the use of H.H. Wood)
vs Richard Lunsford & William Peyton

Charles L. Roffe
vs Wilson B. Moore (sheriff of Cabell) adm of estate for John Hill, decd)

John S. Ross
vs Samuel Harris & Reuben Harris

-------- 1858

Commonwealth
vs James Adkins

Henry J. Fisher
vs Preston Hodges

Cynthia Chapman
vs Elisha E. McComas

Washington Conner
vs George Proctor

----

p99 John Vaughan
vs the Guyandotte Navigation Co.

Commonwealth
vs Price Adkins & Ambrose Smith

William C. Miller
vs John Ward Jr. & John Ward Sr.

John C. Baker (who sues for the use of E.A. Smith)
vs Wm. R. Boyers

Aeneas Carter
vs Henry W. Shelton -- Allen McGinnis to pay

D.B. Scott (assee) of John Taylor
vs Philip Blum

Greatman Anderson, James Gates & William P. Wright
(partners of Anderson, Gates & Wright
vs William Boyers

----

p100 Lucian M. Wolcott & H.C. Everett (partners of Wolcott & Everett)
vs W.R. Boyers

Ruffer & Danley & Co.
vs E.D. Blankenship & James A. Holley

-------- 1858

Samuel A. Childers & Alexander McComas (adm of Michael Wintz)
(who sues for the use of Thomas Merritt)
vs John Samuels, Joseph Gill & Conwelsey Simmons

Merritt Johnson
vs Emberson Turley, P.H. McCullough & George W. Williams

William R. Seamonds (who sues for the use of Thomas M. Shelton)
vs George Killgore, H.H. Wood, & William Killgore

John Loyd
vs John Alford, Thomas Hatfield & Henry B. Maupin

John V. Robbins, Ralph M. Pomeroy & L. Robbins (partners of Robbins & Pomeroy)
vs Mathew Thompson & Alexander Samuel

James Foils (Fails)
vs Henry Carter & Hugo Dietz (partners of Cater, Deitz & H.C.Flowers)

Henry M. Johnson
vs William Beckett

----

p101 Conwelsey Simmons (who sues for the use of George Gallaher)
vs Jacob Harshbarger

John Scites
vs Richard McCallister & Benjamin Perry

P.H. McCullough
vs O. Moore

P.H. McCullough & W.C. Miller (partners of P.H. McCullough & Co.)
vs James Nicely

P.H. McCullough & W.C. Miller (partners of P.H. McCullough & Co.)
vs Ephraim Keezer

Rowland S. Bias (who sues for the use of George F. Miller)
vs Harrison Peyton

------- 1858

John Martin
vs C.S. Roffe

Joseph M. Cowell, Joseph Ford, Edward C. Miller (partners of Cowell & Co.)
vs Enoch D. Blankenship

John W. Dick
vs Anderson Johnson

Percival S. Smith (assee) of Levi Topping
vs John Allen

James A. Holley
vs Alexander B. Roberts

----

p102 John Laidley
vs David Keezer & M.M. Childers

John B. Baumgardner (who sues for the use of H.J. Samuels)
vs Henry Carter & Hugo Dietz (partners of Carter & Dietz)

Wm. Y. Joy (who sues for the use of Wm. Black)
vs H.W. Shelton & J.M. Shelton

John B. Hite & William Hite (partners of Hite & Co.)
vs Enoch D. Blankenship

Philip R. Champson
vs Charles L. Roffe

George W. Julian & Thomas T. Mason (partners of Julian & Mason)
vs Mathew Thompson

John Scites (adm of Library Johnson, decd)
vs Zachariah Nicely

William T. Nichols
vs owners of the steamboat Louisa No. 2

John Oswald
vs Alexander Davidson

-------- 1858

Thomas C. Buffington (assee) of John Grant & Co.
vs Robert Reynolds

----

p103 William J. Dillon
vs John McMahon & Wayne McMahon

Charles O. Everett (guardian of E.M. Moore)
vs Albert Laidley & W.C. Miller

Robert Fletcher
vs Albert Laidley & Wm. Hite

George Gallaher
vs David Keezer & Mathew Thompson

John Keek
vs Allen McGinnis

John Laidley
vs John Morris & Ira H. McConihay

Henry W. Shelton (who sues for the use of John Alford)
vs Thomas Belcher

Jeremiah Witcher, Thomas Chandler & Edward Webb
vs James Webb

Jerome Shelton (who sues for the use of Thomas C. Buffington)
vs John W. Vaughan & John Alford

James A. Holley
vs Alexander --

----

p104 James A. Holley
vs Aley Belcher, William Turner & Thomas Thornburg

James A. Holley
vs James C. Black

William M. Franklin (who sues for the use of) John Laidley
vs John Vaughan

-------- 1858

James H. & David Q. Guthrie (trading under of J.H. & D.Q. Guthire)
vs Charles E. Rigg

Winston Nowell
vs Christopher Scites

James Johnson
vs Christopher Scites

Ed Blankenship
vs Christopher Scites

Commonwealth
1) vs Thomas Roberts
2) vs Samuel Jordan
3) vs Charles Lawrence
4) vs John Shelton
5) vs William McWorther
6) vs Enoch M. Underwood
7) vs Washington Hensley
8) vs John Dundas
9) vs Charles Johnson
10) vs Alexander B. Roberts

James Duncan (who sues for the use of) Henry B. Maupin
vs George Killgore, Conwelsey Simmons, Charles Morris & John Hatfield

----

p105 Commonwealth
vs John Thompson

George W. Hensley
vs Elisha Hensley & F.G.L. Beuhring

Commonwealth
1) vs Clementine Poteet
2) vs Melville M. Childers
3) vs Price Adkins & Ambrose Smith
4) vs James Adkins

George Gallaher
vs David Keezer & Mathew Thompson

-------- 1858

D.B. Scott (assee) of John Taylor
vs Philip Blume

Merritt Johnson
vs Emberson Turley, P.H. McCollough & George W. Williams

Washington Gwinn
vs James Parrish & al

----

p106 James Lawson (exec) & al
vs Harvey Elkins

James A. Holley
vs Aley Belcher, William Turner, Thomas Thornburg

John Vaughan
vs Guyandotte Navigation Co.

Commonwealth
vs Wm. Doran

John Dicks
vs Alex. Johnson

John W. Hite (assee) of Benja. L. Perry
vs Harrison Peyton

John W. Hite (assee) of Wm. E. Feazle (assee of David Shelton)
vs Alexander Peyton

F.N. Roberts (assee) of James A. Holley
vs William Turner

W.C. Miller & Thomas Thornburg (trading under the name of W.C. Miller & Co.)
vs Alexander McCallister

James A. Holley
vs Irvin Lusher

----

p107 James A. Holley
vs Zacheriah Nicely, A.F. McKendree & James Bias

--------- 1858

Rowland S. Bias
vs Alexander McCallister

Thomas Roberts & Thomas Spurlock (partners of Roberts & Spurlock)
vs John R. Bell & James C. Black

Commonwealth
Myrom (Mysam) Bias

James A. Holley
vs James B. Carrol

W.T. Cutter (surviving partner of Cutter & Brown)
vs George W. Davis

O.P. Smith
vs William Woodward

James Ballard (for the use of Miller Salmon & Miller)
vs James C. Black & James Webb

Mary Newlee
vs John Morris

W.C. Miller & Thomas Thornburg (partners of W.C. Miller & Co.)
vs George W. Sheff

John Laidley (exec of James Holderby, decd)
vs Enoch D. Blankenship

----

p108 Henry M. Johnson
vs William Beckett & Seaton Rousey

James A. Holley
vs A.B. Roberts

James Ballard (who sues for the use of Perry & Presley)
vs John Lykins

Jeremiah Witcher
vs James Webb & J.C. Webb

-------- 1858

Conwelsey Simmons (who sues for the use of George Gallaher)
vs Jacob Harshbarger & David Harshbarger

James A. Holley
vs James C. Black & M. Sandford

Commonwealth
vs Thomas A. Childers & David Keezer

R. Bell & Co.
vs Eggers & Church

Solomon Midkiff
vs Guyandotte Navigation Co.

----

p109 Jas. C. Butler & Co.
vs E.H. Walton

M. Thompson for H.J. Samuels
vs Thomas Scales

W.S. Cutter & W.S. Brown
vs John P. Hatfield

P.H. McCullough
Conwelsey Simmons

Wolcott & Everett
vs John P. Hatfield

E.W. McComas
vs Irvin Lusher

Oakes & Tracey
vs Wm. Eggers

Oakes & Tracey
vs Eggers & Church

W.S. Brown & Son
vs William Merritt

-------- 1858

p110 M. Thompson (for the use of H.J. Saumels)
vs William E. Jones

Joseph W. Black & John Simpson (partners of Black & Simpson)
vs Fredrick G.L. Beuhring

W.C. Miller & Thomas Thornburg (partners of W.C. Miller & Co.)
vs Samuel A. Childers & H.B. Maupin

Charles Y. Everett (guardian of E.N. Moore)
vs Albert Laidley, John Laidley & W.C. Miller

W.C. Miller & Thomas Thornburg (partners of W.C. Miller & Co.)
vs Allen A. McGinnis

Weiler Frost & Co.
vs W.A. Holley

Philip R. Thompson
vs C.L. Roffe & John Alford

D.B. Scott (assee) of John Taylor
vs Nimrod Bryan

W.S. Cutter
vs A.S. Wolcott

John B. Baumgradner (who sues for the use of H.J. Samuels)
vs Henry Carter & Hugo Dietz & Rodoplh Dietz

Wm. F. Joy (who sues for the use of Wm. Black)
vs Henry W. Shelton, James M. Shelton & George W. William

----

p111 John Martin
vs C.L. Roffe & John Alford

Richard Lloyd & Wm. Gracy (partners of R. Lloyd & Co.)
vs William Hite.

Isaac Hatfield
vs C.L. Roffe

-------- 1858

A.S. Wolcott & W.B. Wolcott
vs Wm. H. Richards

Commonwealth
vs John Dundas & Virginia Watson

Thomas C. Buffington (assee) of John Grant & Co.
vs Robert Reynolds

R.S. Holderby (assee) of Absolum Holderby
vs W.C. Miller

Robbins & Pomeroy
vs Mathew Thompson & al

----

p112 Merritt Johnson
vs Emberson Turley , P.H. McCullough & George W. Williams

Robert Alford
vs John Alford

P.H. McCullough & W.C. Miller (partners of P.H. McCullough & Co.)
vs James Nicely

John Vaughan
vs Guyandotte Navigation Co.

John L. Keller
vs David Keyser

George F. Miller
vs David Keyser

E.H. Walton
vs John Chapman & Francis M. Farrell

William M. Franklin (for the use of J. Laidley)
vs John W. Vaughan

----

p112a Commonwealth
1) vs John Thompson
2) vs Ch----- Poteet
3) vs Harvey Black

-------- 1858

Samuel H. Childers and Alex McComas (Adminstators of Michael Wintz)
(who sues for the use of Thomas Merritt)
vs John Samuels, Joseph Gills, and C. Stewart

Jerome Shelton (who sues for the use of Thomas C. Buffington)
vs John W. Vaughan and John Alford

William C. Miller and Thomas Thornburgh (partners of Wm. C. Miller & Company)
vs Samuel Mitchel

John Laidley
vs John Morrison and Ira S. McConihay

----

p113 P.H. McCullough and William C. Miller (partners of P.H. McCullough & Co.)
vs James Nicely

W.C. Miller & Thomas Thornburg (partners of W.C. Miller & Co.)
vs Allen A. McGinnis

R. Bell & Co.
vs Wm. Eggers, O. Church (partners of Eggers & Church)

Solomon Midkiff
vs Guyandotte Navigation Co.

Elisha McComas
vs Henry Carter & Hugo Dietz partners of Carter & Dietz

Thomas C. Buffington (assee) of John Grant & Co.
vs Robert Reynolds,

Joseph C. Butler, Peter S. Brown & Henry S. Stewart (partners of J.C. Butler & Co.)
vs E.H. Walton

W.S. Cutter
vs A.S. Wolcott

W.S.Cutter & W.S. Brown (partners of Cutter & Brown)
vs John Y. Hatfield

-------- 1858

p114 Lucien M. Wolcott & Henry C. Everett (partners of Wolcott & Everett)
vs John Y. Hatfield

Commonwealth
1) vs Francis Roberts
2) vs Charles Ship
3) vs Charles W. Johnson
4) vs Franklin Johnson

W.C. Miller & Co.
vs George W. Sheff

Hiram J. Lynch (adm John Ray, decd)
vs Olliver A. McGinnis & Edmund McGinnis

Solomon Midkiff
vs Guyandotte Navigation Co.

W.S. Cutter (surviving partner of Cutter & Brown)
vs George W. Davis

Edward Webb
vs James Webb

----

p115 Jerome Shelton (who sues for the use of Thomas C. Buffington) 1859
vs John W. Vaughan & John Alford

C. McCallister (assee) of H.H. Wood
vs James M. Shelton

John S. Ross
vs Samuel & Reuben Harris

George W. Hensley
vs Elisha Hensley & F.G.L.Beuhring

James Duncan (who sues for the use of Henry B. Maupin)
vs George Killgore, Conwelsey Simmons, Charles K. Morris & John T.H. Hatfield

----

Thomas C. Buffington (who sues for the use of H.J. Samuels)
vs Guyandotte Navigation Co.

-------- 1859

John W. Hite
vs Guyandotte Navigation Co.

L.M. Wolcott & H.C. Everett (partners of Wolcott & Everett)
vs Guyandotte Navigation Co.

Mathew Thompson
vs George W. Sheff

----

p116 John B. Hite & Wm. Hite (partners of Hite & Co.)
vs Enoch D. Blankenship

Commonwealth
vs James Adkins

Robert N.B. Thompson (adm of Francis Morris, decd)
vs John Morris & Charles K. Morris

Robert N.B. Thompson (adm of Francis Morris, decd)
vs John Morris

L.M. Wolcott & H.C. Everett (partners of Wolcott & Everett)
vs John L. Hatfield

Allen McGinnis
vs Rufus P. Drown (exec of Benjamin Drown, decd)

Alexander H. Chapman
vs James M. Shelton & David Harshbarger

----

p117 John W. Eggers (who sues for the use of Baker & Westoff)
vs James M. Shelton

James A. Holley
vs Irvin Lusher & Wm. E. Feazel

George F. Miller
vs David Keyser & Levin Swann

John W. Hite (assee) of Wm. E. Feazel (who sues for the use of David Shelton)
vs Alexander Peyton

-------- 1859

John W. Hite (assee) of B.L. Perry
vs Harrison Peyton & A.F. McKendree

John S. Keller
vs David Keyser & Levin Swann

E.W. McComas (who sues for the use of R.S. Holderby)
vs Irvin Lusher & Wm. E. Feazel

James A. Holley
vs Zachariah Nicely & J. Morrison

----

p118 Richard Lloyd & Wm. Tracey (partners of R. Lloyd & Co.)
vs William Hite, John B. Hite & P.L. Beekman

P.S. Smith
vs Frederick G.L. Beuhring
Joseph W. Blackly & John Simpson (partners of Blackly & Simpson)
vs Frederick G.L. Beuhring

George Gallaher
vs David Keezer & Thomas A. Childers

William C. Miller & Thomas Thornburg (partners of Wm. C. Miller & Co.)
vs S.A. Childers, Henry B. Maupin & Chapman W. Maupin

James Ballard (who sues for the use of Miller, Salmon & Miller)
vs James C. Black & William Lawrence

O.P. Smith
vs William Woodward & E.W. Beckett

John Scites (adm of Library Johnson, decd)
vs Zachariah Nicely, James Nicely & Harrison Peyton

Thomas Roberts & Thomas Spurlock (partners of Roberts & Spurlock)
vs John R. Bell, James C. Black & William H. Lawrence

James A. Holley
vs James T. Carroll and Samuel Carroll

-------- 1859

Robert Fletcher
vs Albert Laidley & Wm. Hite

----

p119 Himewell Hill & Co.
vs William Hite & A. Laidley

Robert S. Holderby (assee) of Absolum Holderby
vs William C. Miller

Charles Conner
vs Thomas C. Buffington & Thomas J. Jenkins(partners of Thomas C. Buffington)

Henry W. Shelton (who sues for the use of W.B. Moore)
vs William J. Dillon

Jacob Gwinn (who sues for the use of James Baumgardner)
vs Rowland S. Bias

C. McCallister (assee) of H.H. Wood
vs Sidney Bowden

James A. Holley
vs Alexander B. Roberts

C. McCallister (assee) H.H. Wood
vs William Killgore

W.B. Moore (assee) Lindsey Gue (Gno)
vs William E. Feazel & John T. Hatfield

Henry Gwinn (who sues for the use of W. B. Moore)
vs E.B. Malcom

Rachel Brumfield
vs R.B. Allen & John B. Baumgardner(partners of Allen & Baumgardner)

A. Daniels (who sues for the use of P.H. McCullough)
vs Joseph W. Roffe

W.B. Moore
vs Irvin Lusher

1859

Wilson B. Moore
vs Benjamin S. Davis

William C. Miller & Thomas Thornburg (partners of Wm.C. Miller & Co.)
vs Irvin Lusher

John Lloyd (assee) of Robert Ross
vs Irvin Lusher

C. McCallister (assee) W. B. Moore
vs John Dundas & Thomas Dundas

----

p121 John W. Hite (assee) of David Keezer
vs Lewis W. Lusher, William Feazel & Irwin Lusher

William C. Miller & Thomas Thornburg partners of (Wm.C. Miller & Co.)
vs Benjamin F. Smallridge

C. McCallister (assee) W.B. Moore
vs Alexander McClary

William C. Miller & Thomas Thornburg (partners of Wm.C. Miller & Co.)
vs John Wintz

William C. Miller & Thomas Thornburg (partners of Wm.C. Miller & Co.)
vs William Turner

Peter Everett
vs William E. Feazel & John T. Hatfield

Wayne McMahone (trustee of Susan Walton)
vs Sidney Bowden

Thomas Scales (who sues for the use of W.C. Miller & Co.)
vs Lewis Lusher & David Keezer

William C. Miller & Thomas Thornburg (partners of Wm.C. Miller & Co.)
vs George W. Summers

A.N. Williams (who sues for the use of John Wheeler & H.G. Ashworth)
vs Elisha McComas

-------- 1859

F.P. Roberts
vs Perry Ballard & James Ballard

----

p122 P.H. McCullough
vs William C. Bias

William C. Miller & Thomas Thornburg (partners of Wm.C. Miller & Co.)
vs Charles Tooley

W.H. Bryan
vs Jacob Suiter

W.B. Moore
vs John Y. Hatfield & A.P. Williams

P.H. McCullough
vs Joseph W. Roffe

Wilson B. Moore
vs A.P. Williams

Robert B. Allen (assee) of George Killogre
vs Samuel Smith

Stephen Wilson
vs Jacob Suiter

Jonathan Davis
vs Jacob Suiter

W.B. Moore
vs John W. Vaughan

----

p123 James Ballard (who sues for the use of Perry & Presley Ballard)
vs John Lykins & James A. Holley

R. P. Drown (adm of Benjamin Drown decd)
vs Frederick G.L. Beuhring & Wm. Ray

C. Conner (surviving partner of C. Conner & Co.),
Thomas McCallister & Elisha Wheeler partners of McCallister & Wheeler,
Fanny & William (Curtty), Joseph Faster & A.J. Conner
vs William Killgore & William Grass

-------- 1859

Guyandotte Navigation Co.
vs Samuel A. Childers

Horatio Newberger
vs James Felix

Henrietta Newberger
vs Henry Houchins & Jesse Templeton

John Alford
vs Thomas Hatfield

----

p124 Jonathan Davis
vs Joseph Toney

Jonathan Davis
vs Caleb Stephenson

Jonathan Davis
vs William Arthur

Jonathan Davis
vs Alexander Porter

Jonathan Davis
vs James McCorkle

Jonathan Davis
vs Robinson Patton

Jonathan Davis
vs Addison Newman

Joseph Mansfield (assee) of George A. Holton
vs William C. Mahone

H.H. Wood (for use of Wm. Killgore)
vs George Killgore

-------- 1859

William Kilgore & James Gwinn
vs James Parish

William Killgore
vs James Gwinn

Joseph C. Butler, Peter S. Brown & Henry H. Stewart (partners of J.C. Butler & Co)
vs Eli. H. Walton

----

p125 commonwealth
1) vs Enoch M. Underwood
2) vs Henry Harris
3) vs Charles W. Johnson
4) vs Andrew Cremeans
5) vs Peter Smith
6) vs Mathew Butcher
7) vs Thomas Belcher
8(vs David Black
9) vs David Shelton
10) vs Calvin F. Dyer
11) vs Sampson Wines
12) vs Isaac M. Blake
13) vs Sims Childers
14) vs Zachariah Nicely
15) vs John Peyton
16) vs Thomas Carroll

----

p126 Spencer Midkiff
vs Elisha McComas & James McComas

P.H. McCullough & W.C. Miller (partners of P.H. McCullough & Co.)
vs James Nicely

W.C. Miller
vs James Nicely

John Laidley
vs John Morris & others

Linsey Gue
vs Millington Adkins

-------- 1859

Alexander H. Chapman
vs James M. Shelton

John O. Eggers (who sues for the use of Baker & Westhoff)
vs James M. Shelton

Lucian M. Wolcott & Henry C. Everett (partners of Wolcott & Everett)
vs John T. Hatfield

----

p127 W.C. Miller & Thomas Thornburg (partners of W.C.Miller & Co.)
vs William Turner

R.N.B. Thompson (adm of Frances Morris, decd)
vs John Morris & C.K. Morris

C. McCallister (assee of H.H. Wood)
vs Sidney Bowden

----

commonwealth
1) vs Haney Clark
2) vs Isaac M. Blake

Moses Frank
vs Peter Grass 1858

----

p228 Jonathan David
vs William Arthur

William Yates
vs H.A. Mealy

James Baumgardner
vs George W. Williams & John Alford

----

commonwealth
vs Enoch M. Underwood

Peter Everett
vs William E. Feazel, John T. Hatfield, Irvin Lusher

--------- 1859

Wm.C. Miller & Thomas Thornburg (partners of W.C. Miller & Co.)
Charles Tooley & Charles Tooley Jr.

Thomas Scales (who sues for the use of W.C. Miller & Co.)
vs Lewis Lusher, David Keezer & John Derton

John W. Hite (assee) of David Keezer
vs Lewis Lusher, Wm. E. Feazel, Irvin Lusher & John Derton

----

p229 W.B. Moore
vs Irvin Lusher & William E. Feazel

William C. Miller & Thomas Thornburg (partners of Wm.C. Miller & Co.)
vs G.W. Summers & S.A. Summers

John Laidley
vs John Morris & Jo W. Morris

C. McCallister (assee) H.H. Wood
vs William Killgore & William J. Forth

C. Conner (surviving partner of C. Conner & Co.), Thos. McCallister, Elias Wheeler, (partners McCallister, Wheeler), Fanny & Wm. Curttey, James Foster & A. J. Conner
vs William Killgore & Wm. J. Forth

Jonathan Davis
vs Robinson Patton & Thomas Roberts

Jonathan Davis
vs Alexander Porter & Charles Lattin

Wm.C. Miller & Thomas Thornburg (partners of W.C. Miller & Co.)
vs Irvin Lusher & William E. Feazel

----

p230 John Loyd (assee) of Robert Ross
vs Levin Swann & Wm. C. Feazel

W.B. Moore
vs John W. Vaughan & Richard Vaughan

-------- 1859

James A. Holley
vs William Turner & James M. McComas

Henrietta Newberger
vs James Felix & Isaac Blake

Henrietta Newberger
vs Henry Houchins, Jesse Templeton, Thomas Arthur

William C. Miller & Thomas Thornburg (partners of Wm.C. Miller & Co.)
vs Benjamin F. Sandridge & Asa L. Miller

C. McCallister (assee W.B. Moore)
Thomas Dundas, John Dundas, & Morris Newman

William C. Miller & Thomas Thornburg (partners of Wm.C. Miller & Co.)
vs John Wentz & William Wentz

----

p231 Jonathan Davis
vs James McCorkle & Caleb Stephenson

W.B. Moore (assee) of Lindsey Gue
vs William E. Feazel, John T. Hatfield, & John Alford

Henry W. Shelton (who sues for the use of W.B. Moore)
William J. Dillon & Martin Dillon

William R. Seamonds (who sues for the use of David Harshbarger)
vs John Morris

A. Berkey & Eveline his wife (late Eveline S. Cox)
vs C.W. Maupin & H.B. Maupin

Charles L. Roffe
vs Thomas C. Buffington

John Samuels
vs Thomas Roberts

----

p232 Christopher Scites
vs Wm. M. Franklin, John W. Vaughan & Parker Lucas

-------- 1859

Kendal Hazelton
vs Charles Lattin

George H. Summers (exec will of Adam Black)
vs John Samuels & C. L. Roffe

James H. Holley
vs John Ashworth & Henry Ashworth

Margaret Lusher
vs John Derton , Malchor Merritt, James M. Shelton & Isaac Blake

----

Henry Barrett (adm of estate John Hill, decd)
vs John Morris

John B. Hite & William Hite (partners of Hite & Co.)
vs Burgess Stuart

George W. Summers (exec of will of Adam Black, decd)
vs James R. Morris & C.L. Roffe

C.L. Roffe
vs Harvey Barrett (adm of John Hill, decd)

END

DEATHS MENTIONED IN "1857-1859 RULE BOOK"

1857	James Hatfield	1858	Library Johnson	1859	Francis Morris
	James Holderby		John Ray		Benjamin Drown
	James Russell		Michael Wintz		Adam Black
	Anthony Lawson				
	John Hill				
	James Syrus				

CABELL COUNTY,

VIRGINIA/WEST VIRGINIA

LANDS FOR TAX PURPOSES

1861-1865

Major streams and watersheds on Cabell County 1860.

#Note: Lincoln County was not separated until 1872.

Ohio River - northern boundary of the county.

All other county streams flow into the Ohio.

Named from west to east.

1. 4 Pole
2. Guyandotte
3. Little 7 Mile
4. 7 Mile
6. 9 Mile
7. Little Guyan

4 Pole - a stream measured by the surveyors as 4 poles wide.

Western boundary of the county.

Several branches - Beech Fork flows from Cabell county.

Guyandotte - over 100 miles long, heading near the Virginia line just west of Bluefield.

From north to south:

Cabell County

1. Russell Ck
2. Mud River
3. Davis Ck
4. Booten Ck
5. Swamp Br
6. Heath Ck
7. Toms Ck
8. Trace Ck
9. Merritts Ck of Guy

Little 7 Mile - connected the Ohio to Barboursville by Merritts Ck of Mud.
7 Mile - connected to Howells Mill and Teays Valley.
9 Mile - connected to Teays Valley near Mud Bridge (Milton).
Little Guyan - forms eastern boundary of county, several branches.

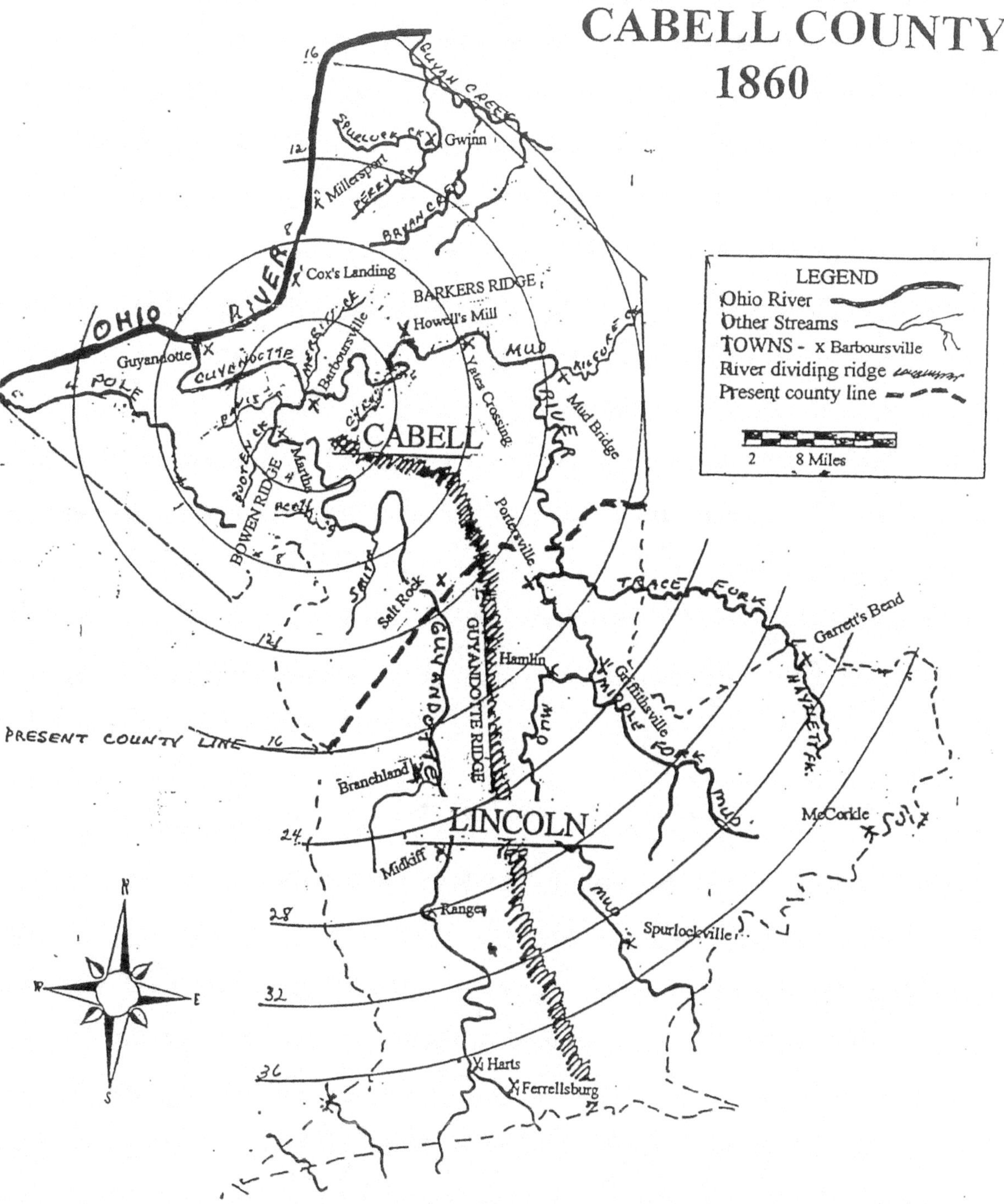
CABELL COUNTY
1860
LEGEND
Ohio River
Other Streams
TOWNS - x Barboursville
River dividing ridge
Present county line
2 8 Miles
OHIO RIVER
Guyan Creek
Gwinn
Millersport
Cox's Landing
Barkers Ridge
Howell's Mill
Guyandotte
Barboursville
Mud
Yates Crossing
Mud Bridge
Mud River
CABELL
Bowen Ridge
Martha
Salt Rock
Porterville
Trace Fork
Garrett's Bend
Hamlin
Griffithsville
Middle Fork
Guyandotte Ridge
Present County Line
Branchland
LINCOLN
McCorkle
Midkiff
Ranger
Spurlockville
Harts
Ferrellsburg
N
S
E
W

1861-1865 Assessor - Greenville Harrison

Multiple tracts with the same location and at $1 per acre value have been combined.

Please note:

(1) Like most tax lists, listings for 1861-1865 are not in true alphabetical order, just by letter. The original list is for 1861, and continuing in the same order for 1862 through 1865 unless additions where necessary. (Added date.)

I have alphabetized the entire list and added dates where changes were made. The index is names that were in addition to the property holder or from whom property was obtained or transferred.

(2) Town lots were recorded separately and has been retained.

(3) After evaluation, tax was 40% of value plus 25% of the 40%.

ABBREVIATIONS:

N-north S-south E-east W-west NE, NW, SE, SW
adj-adjacent Ck- Creek, Fk -Fork, Br - Branch

Guy - Guyandotte River, Guy'tte-Guyandotte town,
Little Guy - Lit Guy Barboursville - B'ville

(A's for 1865 are missing.)

CABELL COUNTY, VIRGINIA/WEST VIRGINIA
LAND FOR TAX PURPOSES 1861-1865

PERSON TAXED	ACRES	VALUE	LOCATION	DISTANCE TO COURT HOUSE	COUNTY RESIDES
Abbott, Legrand	17,500	$17,500	Robt. Morris tract Guyandotte		NY
deed from James Todd)					
Adams, Nancy	40	$160	Lower Ck	East-16 miles	Cabell
Adams, N.S.	1/2	$1600	Guyandotte River	West-7 miles	Missouri
Adams, William	300	$600	Big Cabell of Mud	East- 8 miles	Cabell
Adkins, Anderson	32	$525	Main Mud	South- 25 miles	Boone
" "	88	$110	East side Main Mud River	SE-22 miles	B
" "	64	$ 80	West side Main Mud	S-22 miles	B
Adkins, Anderson Jr.	80	$220	Trace FK of 4 Mile	S- 15 miles	Cabell
Adkins, David	1000	$1000	Upper Big Ck Guyandotte	S-25 miles	C
& E.W. McComas					Illinois
Adkins, Edward Estate	94	$188	Raccoon of Beech Fork	S-13 miles	Cabell
" "	100	$200	Raccoon of Beech Fork	S-13 miles	C
Adkins, Elijah M.	200	$100	Guyandotte River	S-10 miles	Wain
" "	100	$200	Head Merritts Ck of Guy	S-7 miles	Wain
(deed from McFarland)					
Adkins, Elliot	53	$ 53	Trace Fk of 4 Mile	S-18 miles	Cabell
Adkins, Green L.	100	$200	Raccoon of Beech Fork	S-13 miles	C
" "	61	$ 61	10 Mile	SE-25 miles	C
Adkins, Greenville	77	$154	Raccoon of Beech Fk	S-13 miles	C
Adkins, Hiram	325	$325	Upper Big Creek of Mud	SE-24 miles	C
" "	315	$315	Upper Big Ck of Mud	SE-24 miles	C
Adkins, Jacob Estate	136	$1088	Guyandotte	S-21 miles	Wayne
" "	25	$ 25	Guy	S-21 miles	Wain
Adkins, John	300	$300	Raccoon of Beech Fk	S-15 miles	Wain
Adkins, John C.	60	$ 60	Trace Fk of 4 Mile	S-17 miles	Cabell
" " (2 entries)	60	$150	Fall Creek	S-14 miles	C
" "	135	$270	Fall Ck	S-14 miles	C
Adkins, John T.	100	$125	Falls Branch of 4 Mile	SW-20 miles	C
" "	37	$ 37	Falls Br of 4 Mile	SW-20 miles	C
Adkins, Joseph	50	$ 50	Mud	S-25 miles	Boon
Adkins, Levi (6 tracts)	995	$995	West side Guy	S-27 miles	Cabell
" " (7 tracts)	1775	$1775	14 Mile CK	S-27 miles	C
" "	25	$ 25	Sulphur Spring Ck/14 Mile	S-27 miles	C
Adkins, Lewis					
& C. Latin	325	$325	head 14 Mile	S-36 miles	C

PERSON TAXED	ACRES	VALUE	LOCATION	DISTANCE TO COURT HOUSE	COUNTY RESIDES
Adkins, Price	141	$352.50	Falls Ck of Guy	S-14 miles	C
Adkins, Randolph	150	$375	Jackson Br/Beech Fk/12 Pole	SW-13 miles	C
" "	60	$240	Jackson Br of Beech-	SW-13 miles	C
Adkins, Richard	300	$300	Stout Ck of Guy	S-20 miles	C
" "	86	$107.50	Stout Ck of Guy	S-24 miles	C
" "	12	$180	Guy	S-23 miles	C
" "	150	$450	10 Mile Ck of Guy	S-24 miles	C
" "	25	$375	Stout Ck of Guy	S-23 miles	C
Adkins, Roffe	48	$ 48	4 Mile	S-20 miles	C
Adkins, Samuel	230	$230	10 Mile of Guy	S-24 miles	C
" "	25	$ 25	Left side Guy	S-24 miles	C
" "	48	$ 48	Head 4 Mile	S-20 miles	C
Adkins, Sylvester	50	$ 50	Left Fk 4 Mile	S-16 miles	Wain
Alford, George Estate & Thomas Roberts	100	$1000	Middle Fk of Mud	SE-25 miles	Cabell
Alford, George & Robt. Alford	116 2/3	$116.66	Middle Fk of Mud	SE-16 miles	C
Alford, James	35	$105	Middle Fk Mud	SE-25 miles	C
" "	187	$1696	Middle Fk Mud	SE-25 miles	C
" "	70	$87.50	Middle Fk Mud	SE-25 miles	C
Alford, John	150	$150	Merritts Ck of Mud	S-25 miles	C
" "	30	$37.50	Mud	SE-18 miles	C
" "	112	$846	Merritts Ck of Mud	S-20 miles	C
Alford, Robert	25	$250	Middle Fk of Mud	S-33 miles	C
Alford, William Estate	79	$79	Merritts Ck	S-26 miles	C
Allen, B.	65 ft.	$60.94	Barboursville	town	C
Allen, Robt. B.	19.5	$60	adj B'ville	town	C
Andrews, Horace	550	$550	Guyandotte	S-27 miles	NY
Angel, Washington	90	$135	Mill Fk of Swan	E-11 miles	Cabell
Ansell, Michael, Martin John & Leonard	150	$4711	Ohio	W-6 miles	C
Ansell, Martin Jr.	137	$274	9 Mile	NE-10 miles	C
Ansell, Martin Sr.	310	$3420	Ohio River	NE-10 miles	C
" "	165	$666	Goose Creek	NE-10 miles	C
Arthur, James	50	$250	Mud River	E-9 miles	C
Arthur, John	93	$139.50	Big Cabell of Mud	E-6 miles	C
Arthur, Thomas	50	$250	Mud River	E-9 miles	C
Ashworth, Andrew	100	$150	Mud River	S-25 miles	C

PERSON TAXED	ACRES	VALUE	LOCATION	DISTANCE TO COURT HOUSE	COUNTY RESIDES
Ashworth, Isaac Estate					
& William Beckett	47	$282	Trace Fk of Mud	SE-20 miles	C
Ashworth, John	192	$960	Trace Fk of Mud	SE-20 miles	C
Ashworth, Jonathan (Jinatha)Estate					
& Robert Thompson	91	$318.50	Trace Fk	SE-20 miles	C
Ashworth, M, I, & H	385	$962.50	Haney Fk of Big Creek	S-21 miles	C
Ashworth, Susan	137.5	$137.50	Big Buffalo	SE-12 miles	C
-B-					
B--met, C.J.					NY
& W. Weed	4167	$6250	Little Guy	NE-14 miles	NY
B-- , James	481	$962	Mill Ck of Mud	E-17 miles	Cabell
deeds from G. Killgore, H.J. Samuels, H.B. Maupin					
B--on, George W.	88 1/4	$529.50	Mud	SE-17 miles	C
B--oen, Ann F.	18	$18	School House Br	SW- 8 miles	Wayne
" "	5	$7.50	Buck Fk	W-10 miles	W
Ball, Henry	140	$1260	Mud	SE-16 miles	Cabell
Ball, Hettie Ann	120	$1500	Mud	E-9 miles	C
Ball, James	285	$1140	Killgore Ck	E-16 miles	C
" "	40	$160	Killgore Ck	E-16 miles	C
Ball, Layfayette	124	$1550	Mud	E-9 miles	C
Ball, Martha	122	$1525	Mud	E-9 miles	C
Baker, Henry	50	$50	Hopkins Tract Little Guy	NE-14 miles	C
" "	50	$50	Hopkins tract Little Guy	NE- 14 miles	C
Baker, John L.	186	$1488	Both sides Guy	S-23 miles	C
" "	20	$120	Guy	S-23 miles	C
" "	20	$20	West side Guy	SE-23 miles	C
Baker, John L.					
& J. McComas	173	$173	Guy	S-24 miles	C
Baker, John L.					C
& Henry McFarland	135	$135	10 Mile Ck of Guy	S-20 miles	NY
Baker & Hayden & Lattin	556	$556	Cangers Br of 10 Mile	S-25 miles	Cabell
Ballard, James					
& J.W. Ballard	700	$700	Middle Fk of Mud	SE-24 miles	C
Ballard, Samuel					
& J.W. Ballard	80	$240	Trace Ck	SE-20 miles	C
same " "	140	$280	Middle Fk of Mud	SE-20 miles	C
same " "	200	$600	Big Creek	SE-20 miles	C
same " "	25	$50	Mud	SE-25 miles	C
same " "	161	$161	Merritts Ck of Mid Fk Mud	SE-25 miles	C

PERSON TAXED	ACRES	VALUE	LOCATION	DISTANCE TO COURT HOUSE	COUNTY RESIDES
Barnett, Andrew-Estate	50	$100	Mud	SE-20 miles	C
" "	100	$200	Left hand Fk of Mud	SE-20 miles	C
" "	100	$350	Mud	SE-20 miles	C
" "	72 1/2	$145	Guy	S-16 miles	C
" "	245	$2021.25	Mouth of Mid Fk Mud	SE-20 miles	C
Barrett, Andrew & James Barrett	40	$160	Between forks of Mud	SE-20 miles	C
same " "	50	$100	Sycamore Fk of Mud	SE-25 miles	C
Barrett, Andrew & Joseph Barrett	79	$98.75	Merritt's Fk of Mid Mud	SE-22 miles	C
Barrett, Andrew J.	608	$1924.24	Mud	SE-26 miles	C
deed from J.A. Holley					
Barrett, B.E. & S. Ballard		----	-----	---	----
Barrett, Edward-Estate	43 1/2	$43.50	Main Fork of Mud	SE-22 miles	C
Barrett, H. (torn)	522	$522	Middle Fk of Mud	SE-24 miles	Boone
" "	667 1/3	$667.33	Middle Fk of Mud	SE-24 miles	B
reduced by deeds to R. & G. Alford and D.M. Roberts					
(Barrett) (torn) & A.J. Holten	1400	$1400	Middle Fk of Mud	SE-24 miles	B
Barrett, Joseph	72 1/2	$145	West side Guy	S-16 miles	B
" "	45	$270	Trace Fk of Mud	SE-25	B
" "(2 tracts)	1590	$1590	Middle Fk of Mud	SE-26 miles	B
Baumgardner, James	493	$1745	Merritt's Ck of Mud	N- 2 miles	C
" "	5	$60	Mud	E- 1 mile	C
" "	200	$1000	Ohio	NW- 3 miles	C
Baumgardner, John	158.4	$2057.25	Guyandotte	W-2 miles	C
Bays, Henry	25	$25	Parsons Fk of Mud	SE-25 miles	C
Bays, John	50	$50	Sycamore Fk/Sugar Tree/Mud	SE-25m	C
deed from William L. Draper					
Bays, Riley	65	$81.25	Sycamore Fk/Sugartree/Mud	SE-25m	C
deed from William F. Draper					
Beaver, William H.	151	$188.75	Middle Fk of Mud	SE-30 miles	C
" "	510	$765	Sugar Tree Fk of Mud	SE-30 miles	C
Becker, John A.	1 1/2	$1200	adj Barboursville	W side	C
" "	1/4	$25	adj Barboursville	W side	C
Becker & Westhoff	1	$1500	Mud at Barboursville	E side	C
Beckett, Andrew L.	55	$110	Fudges Ck	SE-8 miles	C
Beckett, Charles W., Sr.	75	$225	Fudges Ck	SE-7 miles	C
deed from James Beckett					

PERSON TAXED	ACRES	VALUE	LOCATION	DISTANCE TO COURT HOUSE	COUNTY RESIDES
Beckett, Leander	320	$800	10 Mile Ck	S-20 miles	C
Beckett, Moses	140	$840	Charley's Ck of Mud	E-14 miles	C
Beckett, William	100	$100	Trace Fk of Mud	SE-18 miles	Putnam
" "	100	$600	Trace Fk of Mud	SE-20 miles	P
Beckett, William & C. Lattin			---- ---- -----		----
Bellomy, Lewis & David Steamburger	100	$100	Little Guyandotte	NE-15 miles	Cabell
Bernard, Jacques Misseler Harvey Cashod-----			-----	-----	
Beuhring, F.G.L. (Estate)	1	$800	Mud	SW 1/2	C ('65)
" "	400	$5000	Ohio	W-10 miles	C
" "	1/2	$762	adj. Guy'tte	W-7 miles	C
Beuhring, F.R.D	100	$400	Morris Ck of 4 Pole	W-9 miles	C
Bexfield, Richard	150	$375	Little Guy	NE-15 miles	C
Bias, Absolum	70	$437.50	Tylers Ck	SE-9 miles	Putnam
Bias, Anderson	100	$300	Buffalo of Mud	SE-13 miles	Cabell
" "(2 tracts)	133 3/4	$133.75	Buffalo of Mud	SE-16 miles	C
Bias, Anderson	111	$111	Buffalo of Mud	SE-16 miles	C
Bias, Berry	78	$415.84	Merritt's Ck-Mud	W-2 miles	C
Bias, Daniel	280	$700	Merritt's Ck of Guy	S-7 miles	C
Bias, David H.	268	$1340	Guy	S-6 miles	C
Bias, James	100	$300	Falls Ck of Guy	S-14 miles	C
Bias, James, Jr.	100	$650	Tylers Ck	S-10 miles	C
Bias, James B.	77 3/4	$77.75	Between Buffalo & Bear Ck.	SE-12	C
Bias, James H.	213	$319.50	Head of Trace Ck	SE-12 miles	C
Bias, John	58	$377	Tyler Ck	SE-9 miles	C
Bias, Larkin	200	$500	Lower 2 Mile	S-12 miles	C
Bilger, William A.	31,000	$31,000	Mud	S-25 miles	PA
Billups, Peter	100	$100	Trace Fk of Mud	SE-20 miles	Putnam
Black, -- . C.	1970	$1970	Trace Fk	SE-16 miles	Cabell
Black, Adam-Estate	212	$1778.68	Mud	E-7 miles	C
Black, James C.	100	$200	Rt Fk of Trace Ck	SE-25 miles	C
" "	6 1/2	$6.50	Mud	SE-22 miles	C
" "	27	$27	E side Main Fk of Mud	SE-24 miles	C
Black, James C. 1/2 to C. Lattin	754	$754	E side Main Fk of Mud	SE-23 miles	C
Black, William	240	$1560	Mud	E-7 miles	C
Blake, Isaac deed from James Pinnell	8	$260	Mud	SE 1/2 mile	C
Blake, Jeremiah	50	$450	Big Cabell Ck	E- 9 miles	C

PERSON TAXED	ACRES	VALUE	LOCATION	DISTANCE TO COURT HOUSE	COUNTY RESIDES
Blake, Peter - Estate	100	$200	9 Mile of Ohio	NE-7 miles	C
Blake, Peter - Estate & Sarah Blake	242 1/2	$2910	Esler Ck	SE-1 mile	C
Blake, Sarah	169	$253.50	Reces Ck	E-21 miles	C
Blankenship, E.D.	400	$2000	Main Fk Mud	SE-17 miles	C
Blankenship, Margaret-Est.	25	$125.50	4 Pole	W-6 miles	Wayne
Bledsoe, W. L.	65	$162.50	Trace Ck of Guy	S-11 miles	Cabell
" "	85	$85	Trace Ck of Guy	S-10 miles	C
Booten, Morris	90	$90	4 Pole	SW-7 miles	C ('65)
Bowden, Sidney	3/4	$1500	adj Barboursville	E side	C
Bowen, Abner, Estate	26	$156	Cow Fk of Little Guy	NE-15 miles	C
Bowen, Ann F.	18	$18	School House Br	SW- 8 miles	W ('65)
" "	5	$7.50	Beech Fk	W-10 miles	W ('63)
Bowen, Davis(David)	55	$55	Head waters Madison Ck	SW-10 miles	Wayne
Bowen, Ezekiel	30	$60	Little Guy	NE-14 miles	Cabell
Bowen, French	75	$187.50	Raccoon Fk of Beech	SW-12 miles	C
" "	100	$100	Luke Br of Raccoon	SW-14 miles	C
Bowen, Jefferson, Jr.	57	$57	Beech Fk of 12 Pole	SW-12 miles	Wayne
" "	8	$8	School House Br	SW-10 miles	W
Bowen, Jefferson B.	422	$1477	Long Branch	SW-8 miles	W
" "	20	$30	Long Branch	W-7 miles	W
" "	4	$6	Long Branch	W-7 miles	W
" "	8	$12	Long Branch	W-7 miles	W
" "	20	$30	School House Br	SW-10 miles	W
" "	125	$125	Francis Br & Faling Br	SW-10 miles	W
" "	152	$304	Camp Br of Long Br	SW-10 miles	W
" "	190	$264.10	Beech Fk	SW-10 miles	W
Bowen, John L.	312	$312	Long Br	SW-8 miles	W
Bowen, Samuel	600	$600	Hopkins Tract Little Guy	NE-13 miles	Cabell
Brady, Edward(3 tracts)	10,000	$10,000	Mud	SE-23 miles	PA
" " (2 tracts)	18000	$18,000	Mud	SE-25 miles	PA
Browdowski, Stanislow-Est	100	$300	Little Guy	E-16 miles	Cabell
Brown, James	4	$4	Mouth of Heath Ck	SE-17 miles	C
" "	101.75	$610.5	Mud	SE-17 miles	C
Brown, James H.	2000	$2500	Middle Fk of Mud	SE-24 miles	Kanawha
" "(3 tracts)	4055	$4055	Mud, Coal & Davis	SE-35 miles	K
Brown, Thomas	72	$72	Trace Fk of Mud	SE-20 miles	Cabell
" "	40	$240	Mud	SE-20 miles	C

PERSON TAXED	ACRES	VALUE	LOCATION	DISTANCE TO COURT HOUSE	COUNTY RESIDES
Brown, Thomas					
& S. Reynolds	240	$240	Mud	SE-16 miles	C
Brown, Thomas S.	101 3/4	$610.50	Mud	SE-17 miles	C
deed from James Brown					
Brumfield, John-Estate	330	$1980	Guy	S-32 miles	C
" "	100	$100	Ugly Ck	S-32 miles	C
" "	115	$115	Guy	S-30 miles	C
Brumfield, John Estate					C
& C. Lattin	696	$696	Hamilton & Ugly Ck	S-29 miles	Logan
same " "	525	$525	14 Mile	S-29 miles	C & L
& L.A. Childers & M. Harris					
Brumfield, William	50	$250	W side Guy	S-27 miles	Cabell
Bryan, Jacob	410	$900	Lower Ck of Mud	E-9 miles	C
Bryan, Lawrence	514	$1398	Little Guy	NE-16 miles	C
" "	18	$54	Little Guy	NE-16 miles	C
Bryan, Nimrod	25	$50	Trace Fk of Little Guy	NE-15 miles	C
Bryant, Nimrod	560	$1540	Little Guy	NE-15 miles	C
" "	100	$100	Hopkins Tract	NE-15 miles	C
Buffington, James	1/2	$800	adj Guy'tte	W-7 miles	C
Buffington, James H.	250	$312	Raccoon Fk of Beech Fk	SW-13 miles	C
Buffington, James R.	354	$6372	Ohio	NW-5 miles	C
Buffington, John	258 1/2	$9030	Wm. Buffington Tract/OH	W-8 miles	C
Buffington, Peter C.	428	$16,050	Ohio	W-10 miles	C
" "	2173.5	$7,607	Davis Ck & 4 Pole	SW-6 miles	C
" "	35	$35	Long Branch	SW-8 miles	C
Buffington, Thomas J.	235	$4332	Guy	SW-12 miles	-Louisana('65)
Buffington, Thomas C.	1/2	$7.50	adj Guy'tte	W-7 miles	Cabell
Buffington, William-Estate	49	$98	Sulphur Spring of Mud	E-4 miles	C
" "	825 1/2	$22,526.70	Ohio	W-8 miles	C
" "	140.1	$6444.60	Ohio	W-7 miles	C
" "	235	$4232	Ohio	SW-12 miles	C
" "	152	$6750	Ohio	SW-9 miles	C
" "	1	$5	Sulphur Spring of Mud	E-4 miles	C
Buffington, W. H.	150	$3000	Ohio	W-8 miles	C
Burns, Andrew	50	$62.50	West side Big Ck	SE-25 miles	C
Burns, Andrew, Jr.	40	$160	West side Big Ck	SE-25 miles	C
Burns, David	138	$207	Mud	SE-20 miles	C
Burns, Isiah	88	$88	Trace Fk	SE-20 miles	C
" "	35	$52.50	Trace Fk of Mud	SE-18 miles	C

PERSON TAXED	ACRES	VALUE	LOCATION	DISTANCE TO COURT HOUSE	COUNTY RESIDES
Burns, James	235	$2115	Trace Fk of Mud	SE-17 miles	C
Burns, Job	130	$650	Big Ck of Trace Fk	SE-20 miles	C
" "	70	$87.50	Trace Fk of Mud	SE-20 miles	C
- C -					
Capet, John E.	3250	$3250	Robt. Morris Tract on Guy	S-20 miles	NJ
deed from Chas. K. Whitney and John W. Porter					
Campbell, John-Estate	148	$222	Fernatts Ck	S-24 miles	Cabell
Carpenter, Alexander	220	$330	Main Fk of Sugartree	SE-35 miles	C
Carpenter, Anderson	135	$135	Middle Fk of Mud	SE-22 miles	C
Carpenter, Elisha	690	$690	Mud	E-17 miles	C
Carpenter, Lewis	150	$750	E side Mud	SE-20 miles	C
Carpenter, William	50	$50	Little Guy	NE-14 miles	C
Carrol, James T.	100	$400	Mud	SE-20 miles	C
" "	1000	$6000	Mud	SE-20 miles	C
Carrol, Samuel	300	450	Head of Mill Ck of Mud	NE-12 miles	C
Carson, William A.	450	$900	Merritts Ck of Guy	S-8 miles	C
Carter, Hiram	180	$720	4 Pole	W-6 miles	C
Chandler, Andrew J.	168	$168	Trace Fk of Mud	SE-25 miles	C
Chapman, German	195	$292.50	Carters Ck	E-10 miles	C
" "	60	$60	Mud	E-12 miles	C
Chapman, John & James B. Chapman	75	$150	Guy	S-18 miles	C
Chapman, John, Jr.	75	$300	Mud	E-14 miles	C
Chapman, Martha	25	$175	Mud	E-14 miles	C
" "	9	$9	Carter Ck of Mud	SE-13 miles	C
Chapman, Philemon-Est.	213	$2769	Guy	S-18 miles	C
Chapman, William	200	$300	Kilgore Ck	E-17 miles	C
Chatterton, George	105	$525	4 Pole	W-7 miles	C
Cheevis, Daniel	666 1/3	$1333.33	Cabell Ck of Mud	NE-6 miles	OH
Childers, Abraham M.	105	$577.50	Lf Fk Heath Ck	S-6 miles	Cabell
Childers, Benjamin	310	$818.48	Madison Ck	S-11 miles	Wayne
Childers, Greenville	100	$275	Merritts Ck of Guy	S-6 miles	Cabell
Childers, M. & C. Lattin	37	$37	14 Mile Ck	S-30 miles	C
Childers, Nancy	50	$500	Smith Ck	S-7 miles	C
Childers, Thomas-Estate	155	$775	Merritts Ck of Guy	S-6 miles	C
Childers, Thomas-Estate & C. Lattin	350	$350	E Fk of 14 Mile Ck	S-33 miles	C
Church, Octavius	1/2	$1100	adj Barboursville	E-side	C('65)

PERSON TAXED	ACRES	VALUE	LOCATION	DISTANCE TO COURT HOUSE	COUNTY RESIDES
Church, Octavius	1/2	$183.75	adj Barboursville	E-side	C(MN)
Cincinnati Coal & Mining	24	$2400	Guy	SE-24 miles	C
Clarke, Getty	200	$200	Big Cabell Ck	NE-17 miles	OH
Clarke, Charles R.	316	$316	4 Pole	W-5 miles	Cabell
Clarke, Peter	1/10	$206.31	adj Guy'tte	W-7 miles	NY
" "	120	$240	Lit Guy	NE-17 miles	NY
Clarke, Silas	2/10	$1500	adj Guy'tte	W-7 miles	Cabell
Collins, Charles	273	$2184	Merritts Ck of Mud	N-2 miles	C
Collins, Jane & A. Reed	2560	$5120	Guy	SE-25 miles	C
Collins, William	47	$470	Head Merritts & Lit 7 Mil	N-2 miles	C
Connell, Priscilla	136	$408	9 Mile Ck of Ohio	NE-7 miles	C
Connely, Bailey	15	$15	E side Guy	S-25 miles	C
Conner, Andrew	22	$110	Mouth of Charleys Ck	E-12 miles	C
Conner, Andrew deed from George Kilgore	225	$1575	Charleys Ck	E-12 miles	C
Conner, Charles	50	$100	Charleys Ck	S-14 miles	Putnam
Conner, James	63	$63	2 Mile Ck of Mud	SE-12 miles	Cabell
Conner, John	115	$143.75	Cow Br of Mill Ck	E-16 miles	C
" "	316	$395	Cow Br of Mill Ck	E-16 miles	C
Conner, William	25	$25	West side Mud	SE-10 miles	C
Conner, William-Estate	50	$400	Mud	E-12 miles	C
" " (3 tracts)	166	$166	Mud	SE-14 miles	C
" "	25	$25	upper side Mud	SE-14 miles	C
" "	25	$25	Camp Ck of Mud	SE-14 miles	C
" "	43	$43	Mill Br of Mud	SE-13 miles	C
" " & R. Keaton	190	$190	2 Mile Ck of Mud	E-12 miles	C
Conner, William, Sr.	50	$600	Mud	E-12 miles	C
" " & George Kilgore	100	$100	Mud	E-12 miles	C
Conner & Kilgore & R. Keaton	26	$52	Mud	E-12 miles	C
Cook, John	113	$425	Davis Ck	W-3 miles	KY
Cooper, Silas	50	$350	Mud	SE-20 miles	Cabell
Cooper, Thomas	95	$380	Mud	SE-27 miles	C
Cox, James O.	2 1/2	$587.5	Mud	E-6 miles	C

PERSON TAXED	ACRES	VALUE	LOCATION	DISTANCE TO COURT HOUSE	COUNTY RESIDES
Cox, John A., William, Theadon, Alphonso, Adeline, Sarah	4	$360	Ohio	N-5 miles	C
Cox, William	200	$8000	Ohio	NW-5 miles	C
Cremeans, Bailey	175	262.5	Mill Ck of Mud	E-13 miles	C
Cremeans, H. & J.M. Cremeans	75	$75	Branch of Lit Guy	NE-16 miles	C
Cremeans, Higgins	50	$75	Lit Guy	NE-16 miles	C
Cremeans, Moses-Estate	685	$1370	Mud	SE-20 miles	C
Cremeans, Noah & Thomas Holley	105	$157	Mill Fk of Lower Ck	NE-11 miles	C
Cremeans, Sanders	51	$153	Merritts Ck of Guy	SE-3 miles	C
" "	50	$100	Rt Fk of Indian Ck	S-11 miles	C
" "	35	$35	Madison Ck	SW-12 miles	C
Crouse, Joseph	120	$360	Fudges Ck	E-8 miles	C
" "	50	$75	Fudges Ck	E-8 miles	C
Crum, Daniel	150	$375	Rt Fk 4 Mile	S-20 miles	C
Crump, George W. deed from Thomas H. Woods	118	$472	Lewis Dodd's Tract on Russell Ck	W-6 miles	C
Crump, Isaac	199	$796	Guy	W-6 miles	C
" "	300	$1200	4 Pole	SW-6 miles	C
Curry, A. N. & R. N. McCallister	457	$457	Trace Fk of Mud	SE-20 miles	C
Curry, Hiram	270	$1080	Buffalo Ck of Mud	SE-18 miles	C
Curry, William	5	$30	Main Fk of Mud	SE-20 miles	C
" "	50	$50	Little Laurel Ck	SE-25 miles	C
" "	3	$18	Main Fk of Mud	SE-20 miles	C
" "	150	$1800	Mud	SE-20 miles	C
" "	35	$157.50	Mud	SE-20 miles	C
Curry, " & C. Lattin	26	$26	Lf Fk 9 Mile Ck of OH	N-5 miles	C
Cushing, Charles C.	160	$400	Big Cabell Ck of Mud	E-7 miles	CA
Cyrus, Elijah	81	$486	Thoms Ck	E-3 miles	C
Cyrus, Elizabeth	100	400	Thoms Ck	E-3 miles	C
Cyrus, James-Estate	75	$450	ThomsCk	E-3 miles	C
" "	39	$214.50	Thoms Ck	E-3 miles	C
" "	40	$100	Thoms Ck	E-3 miles	C
- D -					
Daniels, Anthony	1/4	$7.60	Mud adj Barboursville	E-side	C
Davis, Alvin	256	$544	Toms Ck & Trace Ck	S-8 miles	C

PERSON TAXED	ACRES	VALUE	LOCATION	DISTANCE TO COURT HOUSE	COUNTY RESIDES
Davis, Calvin, heirs	63	$282	9 Mile Ck	N-9 miles	C
Davis, Daniel	300	$300	Beech Fk	SW-12 miles	Wayne
" "	152	$304	Camp Ck	SW-10 miles	W
Davis, James M.J.	91.6	$91.67	4 Mile Ck	S-18 miles	C
Davis, James MC	355	$1331.25	Rt Fk 4 Mile Ck	S-20 miles	Cabell
" "	169	$211.25	Rt Fk 4 Mile Ck	S-20 miles	C
" "	83	$83	Davis Fk 4 Mile	S-20 miles	C
" "	116	$116	KY Fk 4 Mile	S-18 miles	C
Davis, Mary	1	$400	Guy	W-8 miles	C
" "	2	$40	Guy	W-8 miles	C
Davis, Sterlling G.	23	$115	Lower Ck	E-9 miles	C
Davis, William G.	50	$75	Lf Fk Davis Ck	W-2 miles	C
" "	100	$125	Lf Fk Davis Ck	W-5 miles	C
" "	26	$78	Davis Ck	SW-3 miles	C
Dawson, Thomas	100	$100	Mud	E-10 miles	C
Deal, Henry	291	$1373.52	Mill Ck of Mud	E-12 miles	C
" "	69	$103.50	Johns Ck	NE-14 miles	C
Deal, Lewis	60	$300	Lit Guy & 7 Mile	NE-10 miles	C
DeBoy, John	372	$650	Long Branch	SW-7 miles	C
Dennison, John	150	$225	Big Cabell	E-8 miles	C
Derton, Elizabeth	6/10	$1921.68	Guy & Mud adj B'ville	N-side	C
Derton, Harrison	5/10	$280	adj Barboursville	E-side	C
Derton, William	5/10	$250	adj Barboursville	E-side	C
Dial, Elisha	25	$250	E side Guy	S-6 miles	C
" "	200	$200	Trace Fk of 4 Mile	S-6 miles	C
Dial, John & Elisha Dial	220	$1650	W side Guy	S-6 miles	C
Dial, John M.	1425	$3919.25	4 Mile Ck of Guy	S-14 miles	C
Dial, Polly	82	$184.50	Raccoon Fk of Beech Fk	SW-13 miles	MO
Dietz, Rodulphus	1/2	$600	adj Guy	town	C('65)
Dillon, Marlin	60	$360	4 Pole	SW-6 miles	C
Dillon, William J.	50	$200	4 Pole	SW-6 miles	C
Dodd, James	141	$211.50	Trace Fk of Mud	SE-30 miles	C
" "	751	$1126.50	Climers & Big Ck	SE-30 miles	C
" "	2700	$2700	Trace Fk & Mud Fk-Mud	SE-28 miiles	C
Dodd, Mary	50	$100	OH	W-7 miles	KY
Dodd, Rebecca	100	$200	OH	W-7 miles	KY
" "	50	100	Hopkins Tract on OH	E-16 miles	KY
Douthit, William	1/10	$1400	adj Guy'tte	W-7 miles	Cabell

PERSON TAXED	ACRES	VALUE	LOCATION	DISTANCE TO COURT HOUSE	COUNTY RESIDES
Drake, Henderson	125	$815	Guy	S-22 miles	C
" "	150	$375	French Br of Guy	S-25 miles	C
" "	412.5	$515.62	Laurel Ck & Fernatt Br	S-25 miles	C
" "	445	$1100	Fernatt Ck	S-25 miles	C
" "	17.5	$17.5	Btw Baileys Br & 9 Mile	S-25 miles	C
" "	80	$480	Btw Baileys Br & 9 Mile	S-25 miles	C
" "	242	$1210	Guy	S-23 miles	C
Draper, William F.	89	$111	Sugartree Fk of Mud	E-25 miles	C
" "	100	$125	" " "	E-25 miles	C
" "	85	$106.25	" " "	E-25 miles	C
" "	70	$70	" " "	E-25 miles	C
Drowgoth, Nuger	114.5	$143.20	Hopkins Tract	E-10 miles	OH
Dudley, Ambrose	345	$345	Mud	E-10 miles	OH
" " (Cincinnati)	210	$210	4 Pole	W-10 miles	OH
Dundass, Ann	1/2	$1050	adj Barboursville	E-side	Cabell
Dundass, Thomas	135	$270	Mud	E-3 miles	C
Dunkle, David	210	$2100	Guy	S-1 mile	C('65)
Dusenberry, Wm C. Estate	856	$14,532	Guy	S-3 miles	C
" "					C
& W. Thompson	180	$1080	Guy	S-2 miles	C
Dusenberry, Wm. F.	45	$56.25	Head Smith Ck	S-10 miles	C
Dyes, Henry	67	$67	Lf Fk of 14 Mile Ck	S-24 miles	C
- E -					
Eagleston, Thomas	165	$830	Middle Fk Mud	SE-20 miles	C
deed from ~~Benjamin~~(Jerymine) Witcher					
Eden, James E.	50	$75	Middle Fk of Davis Ck	SW-5 miles	C
deed from Wm.G. Davis					
Eden, Edward	150	$600	Davis Ck	SW-3 miles	C
Egan, Edward	470	$587.50	Lit Guy	NE-12 miles	KY
Egner, William G.	130	$130	Sugartree Fk of Mud	SE-27 miles	Cabell
Egnor, Archibald	234	$234	Sugartree Fk of Mud	SW-27 miles	C
" "	150	$450	Sugartree Fk of Mud	SW-27 miles	C
Elmore, Edward	105	$236.25	Prices Ck	SW-7 miles	C
" "	32	$32	Prices Ck	SW-7 miles	C
" "	7	$13	Prices Ck	SW-7 miles	C
deed from Samuel Sanders					
Elkins, Harvey	105	$262.50	Little Hart	S-30 miles	C
Elkins, Joel	50	$50	E Fk of 14 Mile	S-28 miles	C
Elkins, Patterson	50	$75	Sycamore Fk of Sugartree	SE-25 miles	C

PERSON TAXED	ACRES	VALUE	LOCATION	DISTANCE TO COURT HOUSE	COUNTY RESIDES
Elkins, Reece W.	37	$37	9 Mile Ck	S-25 miles	C
" "	125	$156.25	E Fk of 14 Mile	S-28 miles	C
Eplin, Henry	100	$650	4 Mile Ck	S-20 miles	C
" "	40	$40	Wolf Pen of 9 Miles	S-22 miles	C
Eplin, Julia Ann	77	$173.25	Raccoon of Beech	S-11 miles	C
Eplin, Randolph	160	$160	Mill Br of Raccoon/Beech	W-18 miles	C
" "	75	$187.50	4 Mile Ck	S-20 miles	C
Eplin, William	100	$250	4 Mile Ck	S-20 miles	C
" "	65	$65	4 Mile Ck	S-20 miles	C
Emmerson, Benjamin	34	$136	Lit Guy	NE-16 miles	C
Espee, Augustus(Pittsburgh)	50	$62.50	Lit Guy	NE-12 miles	PA
" "	78	$98.14	Lit Guy	NE-12 miles	PA
Estes, James H.	200	$300	Mud	E-12 miles	Cabell
Everett, Charles T.	1000	$12,500	OH	W-10 miles	C
deed from F.G.L. Beuhring (Ex.)					
Everett, Henry C.	4 1/2	$407	near Guy'tte	W-7 miles	C
Everett, John	45	$1575	Guy	NW-6 miles	C
Everett, John S.	90	$2070	Guy	NW-6 miles	C
Everett, Mathew & C.T. Everett	711	$3910.50	Mud	E-6 miles	C
" same & same	90	$315	Big Cabell	E-6 miles	C
Everett, Peter	133	$665	Mud	NE-1 mile	C
Everett, Talton W.	60	$2100	Guy	NW-6 miles	C
Everett, Talton W. & J.S. Everett	120	$4200	Guy	NW-6 miles	C
Eves, Thomas	165	$448.15	4 Pole	SW-11 miles	C
- F -					
Farrel, Francis M.	50	$50	Mud	E-8 miles	C
Farrier, John B.	56	$112	Heath Ck	S-5 miles	C
Feazel, William E.	110	$110	4 Mile	S-20 miles	C
" "	100	$100	Between 9 Mile & Guy	S-25 miles	C
" "	15	$15	mouth of Camp Ck	S-21 miles	C
Ferguson, Jesse	20	$80	7 Mile Ck of OH	NE-5 miles	C
Ferguson, Joseph	70	$70	7 Mile Ck of OH	NE-9 miles	C
Fernatter, S. & J. Dempsey	100	$400	Between 10 Mile & 4 Mile	S-26 miles	C
Felix, James	200	$500	Lit Guy	E-14 miles	C
Forth, John & H. Barrett	28	$28	Mud	SE-20 miles	C

PERSON TAXED	ACRES	VALUE	LOCATION	DISTANCE TO COURT HOUSE	COUNTY RESIDES
Frampton, Isaac-Estate	200	$900	OH	W-11 miles	C
" "	15	$150	4 Pole	W-11 miles	C
" "	10	$100	4 Pole	W-11 miles	C
" "	200	$800	4 Pole	W-11 miles	C
" "	455	$18,200	OH	W-11 miles	C
" "	450	$12,150	OH	W-11 miles	C
" "	140	$945	OH	W-11 miles	C
Franklin, Edward	37	$243.75	Upper 2 Mile Ck of Guy	S-16 miles	C
" "	100	$700	Upper 2 Mile Ck	S-16 miles	C
" "	465	$465	Upper 2 Mile Ck	S-16 miles	C
" "	50	$325	Upper 2 Mile Ck	S-16 miles	C
Franklin, John L.	10	$150	Guy	S-20 miles	C
Freeman, William S.	17,119	$17,119	SE side Mud	E-10 miles	PA
" "	25,000	$25,000	SE side Mud	SE-8 miles	PA
Freutel, Julius	1/10	$38	adj Barboursville	E-side	C
" "	85	$255	9 Mile of OH	N-9 miles	C
" "	405	$405	Little 2 Mile of Mud	E-13 miles	C
" "	75	$75	9 Mile of OH	N-12 miles	C
one deed from John W. Jefferson, 3 deeds reduced by sale to C. Lattin					
Frutell, Julius	1/4	$250	adj Barboursville	E side	C
Fuller, Sylvester	294	$3528	Russell Ck of Guy	W-4 miles	C
" "	3 1/2	$301	Guy	W- 4 miles	C
- G -					
Gallaher, Edward	100	$300	4 Pole	W-12 miles	Cabell
Gallaher, John	193	$965	Heath Ck of Guy	S-3 miles	C
" "	241	$1205	Heath Ck of Guy	S-3 miles	C
Gardner, Benjamin (Est.)	227	$1362	Guy	W-1 mile	KY ('65)
" "	1	$1100	adj Barboursville	W-side	KY
Gardner, James	240	$360	Mill Ck of Lit Guyan	NE-14 miles	NY
Garrett, James	6	$36	Trace Fk of Mud	SE-20 miles	Cabell
" "	97	$97	Trace Fk of Mud	SE-20 miles	C
" "	1124	$4496	Trace Fk of Mud	SE-20 miles	C
" "	98 3/4	$987.50	Trace Fk of Mud	SE-20 miles	C
" "	61	$940	Mud	E-4 miles	C
" "	453	$6364.65	Mud	E-5 miles	C
" "	25	$4200	Falls of Mud	E-5 miles	C
Gibheart, John Jr.	50	$50	Mill & Lower Cks	NE-10 miles	C
Gibheart, John Sr.	50	$50	Mill & Lower Cks	NE-10 miles	C
Gilkerson, Morris	82	$82	Both sides Guy	S-20 miles	Wayne

PERSON TAXED	ACRES	VALUE	LOCATION	DISTANCE TO COURT HOUSE	COUNTY RESIDES
Gilkerson, Morris	39	$39	McClarity Fk of 4 Mile	SW-16 miles	W
" "	30	$30	both sides of 4 Mile	SW-16 miles	W
Gill, Joseph	120	$600	Cow Fk of Little Guyan	N-16 miles	Cabell
" "	740	$1850	Madison Ck	S-10 miles	C
" "	871	$2179.50	Mill Ck	S-8 miles	C
" "	30	$30	Falter Smith Ck (Walter ?)	S-12 miles	C
" " (2 tracts)	356	$356	Fall Ck	S-14 miles	C
Goff, Leonard-Estate	181 1/2	$907.50	Lit Guy	N-16 miles	C
Good, Thomas	50	$199	Middle Fk of Mud	SE-30 miles	C
" "	85	$338.30	Mid Fk Mud	SE-30 miles	C
" "	75	$298.50	Mid Fk Mud	SE-30 miles	C
" "	50	$199	Mid Fk Mud	SE-30 miles	C
all deeds from Michael Rogers					
Good, Samuel	188	$235	Sugartree Fk of Mud	SE-22 miles	C
" "	33	$41.25	Sugartree Fk of Mud	SE-22 miles	C
Gordon, Jacquis	984	$984	Robt. Morris Tract of Guy	S-20 miles	NJ
Gotlick, Henrick	100	$100	Lit Guy	NE-14 miles	Cabell
Graham, Jonas	310	$1240	4 Pole	W-10 miles	C
" "	2	$24	4 Pole	W-8 miles	C
deed from Mark Stephenson					
Grass, Peter	275	$275	Trace Ck near Wolf Pen Fk	SE-30 miles	C
Grass, Peter	150	$150	Climers Ck	SE-25 miles	C
Gries, Phillip	19,500	$19,500	Robt. Morris Tract/Guy	S-20 miles	NY
Griffith, Ephram	155	$465	Sycamore Fk of Sugartree	SE-25 miles	Cabell
" "	445	$1068	Middle Fk of Mud	SE-30 miles	C
reduced with deed to James H. Roberts					
Griffith, James M.	70	$350	Trace Fk of Mud	SE-26 miles	C
Griffith, Lafayette	220	$440	Straight Fk of Mid Fk Mud	SE-30 miles	C
" "	130	$130	Middle Fk of Mud	SE-22 miles	C
Griffith, Lorenzo D.	100	$100	Road Fk of Mud	SE-25 miles	C
Griffith, W.M.	120	$300	Wolf Pen Fk/Trace Fk/ Mud	SE-25 miles	C
Griffon, John W.-Estate	173 1/2	$2949.50	Guy	W-4 miles	C
" "	36	$612	Pea Ridge	W-3 miles	C
" "	53 1/4	$913.75	Guy	W-4 miles	C
" "	155	$775	4 Pole	W-7 miles	C
Gue, Lindsey (Est.)	244	$244	Madison Ck	S-12 miles	C ('63)
" "	100	$100	Lf Fk Fall Ck	S-15 miles	C
" "	72 3/4	$72.75	Madison Ck	S-12 miles	C
deed from Millington Adkins					

PERSON TAXED	ACRES	VALUE	LOCATION	DISTANCE TO COURT HOUSE	COUNTY RESIDES
Gunnoe, Ralph	280 1/2	$561	Sugartree	SE-30 miles	C
Guthrie, James H.	289	$289	Lit Guy	NE-16 miles	OH
Guthrie, William	100	$125	Between OH & 9 Mile	N-10 miles	OH
Guyandotte Land Co.	160	320	Guy	S-16 miles	Cabell
" "	467 1/2	$2337.50	4 Mile of Guy	S-18 miles	C
" " & Whitney	1	10	9 Mile of Guy	S-24 miles	C
Guyandotte Navigation Co.	4	$200	Guy	W-6 miles	C
" "	5	$250	Guy	W-6 miles	C
" "	3	$30	adj Guy'tte	W-7 miles	C
Gwinn, Andrew S.	280	$2520	Mud	E-9 miles	C
" "	120	$840	Mill Ck of Mud	E-11 miles	C
Gwinn, Henry	200	$1600	Mud	E-10 miles	C
Gwinn, John	99 1/2	$12.45.75	Mud	E-9 miles	C
" "	91 1/2	$1143.75	Mud	E-8 miles	C
" "	6	$78	Mud	E-9 miles	C
Gwinn, Marietta	139	$1737.50	Mud	E-9 miles	C
Gwinn, Washington	128	$1000	Mud	E-9 miles	C
- H -					
Hagan, William	19	$695	OH	W-7 miles	C
Hagan, William H.	256	$5394	OH	W-8 miles	C
" " & P.C. Buffington	146	$292	Long Branch	W-8 miles	C
Hagar, George (3 tracts)	895	$895	14 Mile Ck	S-30 miles	C
" "	250	$250	Sulphur Spring Fk/14 Mile	S-30 miles	C
" "	105	$210	14 Mile	S-30 miles	C
" "	25	$50	14 Mile	S-30 miles	C
Hager, Andrew	128	$704	Middle Fk of Mud	SE-25 miles	C
Hager, James	150	$900	Middle Fk of Mud	SE-25 miles	C
Hager, Joseph	50	$400	Mid Fk Mud	SE-25 miles	C
" "	20	$20	Mid Fk Mud	SE-30 miles	C
" "	74	$222	Mid Fk Mud	SE-30 miles	C
" "	111	$138.75	Straight Fk/Mid Fk/Mud	SE-30 miles	C
" "	18	$22.50	Straight Fk/Mid Fk/Mud	SE-30 miles	C
" "	150	$750	Straight Fk/Mid Fk/Mud	SE-30 miles	C
Hager, Lewis (Cincinnati)	100	$100	Mid Fk Mud	SE-20 miles	OH
Hagley, George-Estate	70	$280	7 Mile Ck of OH	N-6 miles	Cabell
Hagley, Peter	50	$100	Merritts Ck & Long Bottom	N-7 miles	C
" "	19	$95	9 Mile Ck of OH	N-7 miles	C

PERSON TAXED	ACRES	VALUE	LOCATION	DISTANCE TO COURT HOUSE	COUNTY RESIDES
Hale, Robert	846	$846	Lit Guy	NE-10 miles	Putnam
Handley, A. W.	110	$1799.60	Mud	E-6 miles	Putnam
Handley, Augustus H.	50	$600	Teays Valley	E-15 miles	Putnam
Handley, Thomas-Estate	225	$2700	Teays Valley	E-16 miles	Cabell
" " & John Morris	2222	$2222	Mud	E-15 miles	C
Handley, Sampson	50	$1250	Turnpike Rd	E-5 miles	C
Hannan, Joseph	243	$7291.50	OH	N-17 miles	C
" "	400	$1600	Lit Guy	N-17 miles	C
Hannan, Lucinda J. deed from Alexander Griffith	75	$375	Mid Fk of Mud	S-35 miles	C
Hannan, Thomas	150	$2497.50	West side of Mud	SE-20 miles	C
Hannan, Thomas A.	300	$1200	Mud	SE-18 miles	C
" "	200	$200	Mud	SE-22 miles	C
Harbar, Jesse	500	$1250	Mud	SE-20 miles	C
Harber, Joseph deed from Harrison Roberts	50	$150	Ropes Run of Mud	S-19 miles	C
Harless, William R.	65	$390	Locust Rough Fk of 4 Mile	S-18 miles	C
" "	215	$430	Locust Rough Fk of 4 Mile	S-18 miles	C
" "	66	$82	4 Mile Ck	S-20 miles	C
" " (2 tracts)	80	$80	Locust Rough	S-16 miles	C
Harris, Greenville (son/Sam)	160	$200	10 Mile Ck	S-25 miles	C
Harris, John	108	$108	McClardeys Fk of 14 Mile	S-20 miles	C
" "	54 1/2	$54.50	4 Mile	S-20 Miles	C
Harrison, Greenville	235	$235	W side Guy	S-30 miles	C
" "	1/4	$720	adj Barboursville	W-side	C
" "	90	$90	14 Mile Ck	S-30 miles	C
Hashberger, Jacob	505 1/2	$4549.50	Mud	E-12 Miles	C
" "	77 1/2	$624.75	Mud	E-5 miles	C
" "	175	$3500	Mud	E-6 miles	C
" "	100	$1200	Mud	E-6 miles	C
Hatfield, Andrew L.	50	$300	Guy	S-6 miles	C
Hatfield, Farmandy F.	300	$450	Guy	S-28 miles	C
" "	217	$271.25	10 Mile Ck	S-25 miles	C
" "	40	$40	14 Mile of Guy	S-25 miles	C
" "	40	$40	Lick Fk of 14 Mile	S-30 miles	C
Hatfield, George	120	$1800	Guy	S-7 miles	C
Hatfield, Henry	207	$621	Guy	S-6 miles	C
Hatfield, Moses	195	$975	Guy	S-6 miles	C

PERSON TAXED	ACRES	VALUE	LOCATION	DISTANCE TO COURT HOUSE	COUNTY RESIDES
Hatfield, Moses	7	$105	Charley's Low Gap	S-4 1/2 miles	C
Hatton, Solomon	150	$1012	Rt Fk 4 Pole	SW-12 Miles	C
Hawkins, Thomas	100	$200	Mud	SE-18 miles	C
Hayden, Alphaus	112	$112	Trace Fk of Mid Fk of Mud	SE-25 miles	C
deed from Kilgore & Lattin					
Hayden, A. & C. Lattin	158	$197.50	Big Ck of Trace Fk	SE-22 miles	C
Hayden, A., C. Lattin, & C. Black	3350	$3350	9 Mile Ck of Guy	SE-25 miles	C
Hayden, Lattin & Black	650	$812.50	Big Ck of Trace Fk	SE-22 miles	C
Hayden, A., C. Lattin, C. Black, H.B. More, J.A. Becker, C.K. Morris , G.F. Miller & H.B. Maupin	830	$1037	Lit Cabell & 9 Mile	N-3 miles	C
Heath, Nelson B.-Estate	200	$900	Tylers Ck	S-9 miles	C
Hearst, Arnold(Hiert)	200	$200	Lit Guy	NE-10 miles	NY('62)
Helmick, Alex(Helsmick)	30	$30	Lower Ck of Mud	E-11 miles	Taylor
Henderson, James	49	$784	Mud	E-5 miles	Cabell
" "	64	$872	Mud	E-6 miles	C
" "	60	$510	Mud	E-5 miles	C
Hensley, Andrew J.	75	$600	Guy	SW-2 miles	C
Herrenkohl, Albert	1/10	$375	Barboursville	W-side	C
Herrenkohl, Charles	100	$100	Lit Guy	NE-14 miles	C
Hinchman, William	200	$1600	Hinchman Bend of Guy	S-7 miles	C
Hinckle, George	90	$90	10 Mile	S-25 miles	C
Hite, John B. & William Hite	1/3	$2844.50	adj Guy'tte	W-7 miles	C
" "	1/10	$9.60	adj Guy'tte	W-7 miles	C
Hite, John W.	4	$400	adj Guy'tte	W-7 miles	C
Hoback, Lorenzo	2	$120	Turnpike	W-5 miles	C
Hohenberger, Joseph	50	$50	Hopkins Tract Mud & Guy	NE-14 miles	C
deed from G. & W. Porter					
Holderby, George	184	$5,520	OH	N-4 miles	C
" "	1/10	$1,034.25	Guy'tte	W-7 miles	C
" "	1/8	$697.50	Guy'tte	W-7 miles	C
Holderby, Elizabeth	360	$6, 840	OH	N-6 miles	C
" "	1/4	$2,629.50	adj Guy'tte	W-7 miles	C
Holderby, Sarah	270 1/2	$5,000	OH above Guy'tte	W-7 miles	C
Holderby, Susan	456	$14,400	Guy	W-5 miles	C
" "	30	$600	Guy	W-5 miles	C

PERSON TAXED	ACRES	VALUE	LOCATION	DISTANCE TO COURT HOUSE	COUNTY RESIDES
Holderby, William					
& Edward & Henry	382 1/2	$17,210.50	OH	W-9 miles	C
" "	160	$640	4 Pole	W-10 miles	C
Holderby, Wm., Ed. & Hy	500	$5000	above Guy'tte	W-7 miles	C
" "	100	$1200	Guy & OH	W-5 miles	C
" "	102.5	$1230	Guy & OH	W-5 miles	C
" "	127	$1590.40	mouth of Guy	W-7 miles	C
" "	46.75	$781.33	mouth of Guy	W-7 miles	C
" "	205	$3280	OH	N-4 miles	C
" "	25	$125	Russell Ck	N-4 miles	C
" "	144	$1125	Guy	NW-4 miles	C
" "	2 1/2	$250	adj Guy'tte	W-7 miles	C
" "	1/4	$289.25	Guy'tte	W-7 miles	C
Holdryde, Elizabeth	100	$125	Lit Cabell Ck	E-6 miles	C
Holdryde, John-Estate	305	$915	Lit Cabell Ck	E-6 miles	C
Holdryde, Olivia	125	$156.25	Lit Cabell Ck	E-6 miles	C
Hollenback, John	100	$400	4 Pole	W-10 miles	C
Hollenback, Martin					
& Henry Hollenback	75	$300	4 Pole	W-10 miles	C
Holly, William	50	$275	Rt Fk Mud	SE-20 miles	C
Holton, Allen	65	$325	Mud	SE-25 miles	C
Holton, George A.	20	$140	East side Mud	SE-20 miles	C
" "	100	$150	East side Mud	SE-20 miles	C
" "	20	$110	East side Mud	SE-20 miles	C
" "	20	$60	Rt Fk Mud	SE-20 miles	C
" "	192	$2491	Mud	SE-20 miles	C
" "	130	$1950	Guy	S-12 miles	C
" "	244	$732	Coleman Ck	S-12 miles	C
" "	195	$195	Trace Ck of Mid Fk Mud	SE-25 miles	C
deed from Kilgore, Lattin & Hayden					
Holton, James	150	$150	Sugartree	SE-25 miles	C
Holton, Joseph	130	$1560	Middle Fk Mud	SE-22 miles	C
" "	60	$120	Middle Fk Mud	SE-20 miles	C
Holston, Peter	48	$150	Sycamore of Sugartree	SE-25 miles	Kanawha
Holston, William A. (2trac)	153	$153	Sugartree of Mud	SE-25 miles	Cabell
" "	50	$300	Sugartree	SE-22 miles	C
" "	230	$230	Rt Fk Climers Fk	SE-30 miles	C
" "	62	$77.50	Sycamore of Sugartree Fk	SE-22 miles	C
" "	235	$935.30	Sugartree	SE-30 miles	C

PERSON TAXED	ACRES	VALUE	LOCATION	DISTANCE TO COURT HOUSE	COUNTY RESIDES
Howe, Elias	10,000	$10,000	Cabell Co.	E-12 miles	NY
Howell, Armstead	165	$990	Trace Ck	S-6 miles	Cabell
Hudson, Lewis-Estate	44 1/2	$445	Teays Valley	E-13 miles	C
Hughes, Spottswood	213	$479.25	Davis Ck	W-4 miles	C
Hull, Martin	110	$4510	OH	W-14 miles	C
" "	198	$1191	4 Pole	W-14 miles	C
Hulett, Alexander	182	$273	Hopkins Tract	N-12 miles	NY
deed from Charles McClasky					
Hunter, Charles	100	$100	Hopkins Tract	NE-11 miles	Cabell
Hunter, Samuel	60	$120	Bowan Br	SW-10 miles	C
" "	120	$120	Falls Ck of 4 Mile	S-20 miles	C
" " & Porter	160	$440	Falls Ck of 4 Mile	S-18 miles	C
- I -					
Irby, William (Staunton)	16	$43.36	OH	W-11 miles	VA
- J -					
James River & Kanawha Turnpike	1/2	$350	Guy at Barboursville	NW side	C
Janion, Paul	100	$100	Hopkins Tract	E-9 miles	NY
Jenkins, Albert G.	1465	$35,687.50	Greenbottom	N-14 miles	Cabell
" "	90 3/4	$363	Lit Guy(will/Wm. Jenkins)	N-16 miles	C
Jenkins, Anderson	25	$100	Trace Fk Lit Guy	NE-16 miles	C
Jenkins, Cary-Estate & James McWharter	190	$570	Trace Fk Lit Guy	NE-16 miles	C
Jenkins, Thomas J.	1465	$35,687.50	Greenbottom	N-14 miles	C
" "	256	$6400	OH	N-4 miles	C
" "	2/10	$385.68	adj Guy'tte	W-7 miles	C
" "	2	$200	adj Guy'tte	W-7 miles	C
Jenkins, William A.	1465	$35,687.50	Greenbottom	N-14 miles	C
all from will of William Jenkins					
Jewell, Benjamin R.	100	$100	Hopkins Tract Big Cabell	NE-12 miles	Cabell
Jewell, Sarah	300	$300	Hopkins Tract Big Cabell	NE-12 miles	C
Jolliffe, John (Cincinnati)	282 1/2	$282.50	4 Mile Ck of Guy	S-20 miles	Ohio
Jones, William E.	3/4	$108.33	Mud at B'ville	E side	Cabell
Johnson, Andrew	110	$577.50	Bear Ck	S-12 miles	C
Johnson, Elizabeth	104	$208	Raccoon Ck	S-14 miles	C
Johnson, Franklin	130	$1770	Mud	SE-23 miles	C
Johnson, Harvey	50	$125	Bear Ck	S-12 miles	C
" " (2 tracts)	100	$700	Mud	E-13 miles	C
same & Wm. Conner Sr.	16	$16	Mud	E-13 miles	C

PERSON TAXED	ACRES	VALUE	LOCATION	DISTANCE TO COURT HOUSE	COUNTY RESIDES
Johnson, John	220	$440	Raccoon Ck of Beech Ck	S-14 miles	C
" "	117	$117	Raccoon Ck of Beech Ck	S-18 miles	C
" "	62	$62	S side of Raccoon Ck	S-18 miles	C
Johnson, John					
& James Johnson	100	$350	Reas Ck (Rece)	S-12 miles	C
Johnson, Madison	200	$1600	Mud	E-12 miles	C
Johnson, Manivett (2 tract)	170	$170	Raccoon Ck	S-14 miles	C
" "	45	$270	Raccoon Ck	S-13 miles	C
" "	200	$600	Raccoon Ck	S-13 miles	C
Johnson, Perry	100	$300	Bear Ck	S-12 miles	C
Johnson, Smoot-Estate	100	$250	Bear Ck	S-12 miles	C
Johnson, W.					Fayette
& C. Lattin	248	$248	Mud	SE-24 miles	Cabell
Johnson, W.					Fayette
& J. Black	100	$100	Mud	SE-24 miles	Cabell
Johnson, Wesley	15	$60	Bear	S-12 miles	C
Johnson, William	260	$260	Main Fk of Mud	SE-24 miles	Fayette
Johnson, William	50	$175	Bear Ck	S-12 miles	Cabell
Johnson, William					Fayette
& H. Holten	662	$662	Mud	SE-24 miles	Cabell
Johnston, James	203	$9135	OH	W-10 miles	C
Johnston, Merritt	192	$567	Raccoon Ck	S-13 miles	C
" "	300	$900	Raccoon Ck	S-14 miles	C
" " (2 tracts)	136	$136	Raccoon Ck	S-14 miles	C
Jordon, Andrew	203	$994.70	Mud	E-11 miles	C
" "	125	$125	Kilgore Ck	E-12 miles	C
Joy, Thomas	21	$147	OH	N-8 miles	C
" "	140	$315	9 Mile	N-8 miles	C
" "	30	$150	9 Mile	N-8 miles	C
Joyce, Thomas	15,000	$15,000	Robt. Morris Tract	S-20 miles	NY
deed by Lignana Abbott					
- K -					
Kaus, Krauski (Wellman)	100	100	Hopkins Tract	NE-9 miles	WA
('63-Krous, Krowski, Walden)					
Keenan, A.					
& S. Scott	1/4	$420	adj Guy'tte	W-7 miles	Cabell
Keenan, D.M.F.	25	$25	Bear Ck of Guy	S-12 miles	C
Keenan, Patrick	100	$100	4 Mile Ck	S-22 miles	C
Keller, John L.	195a	$427.50	4 Pole	W-7 miles	MO

PERSON TAXED	ACRES	VALUE	LOCATION	DISTANCE TO COURT HOUSE	COUNTY RESIDES
Keller, John L.(Killer)	40	$600	Mud	E-1/2 mile	MO
" " (?)('63)	95	$427.50	4 Pole	W-7 miles	MO
Kelly, Hiram (Keller)	100	$125	head of Mill Ck & Lit Guy	E-20 miles	C
" "	51 3/4	$51.75	Mill Ck of Mud	E-20 miles	C
Kessinger, Wilson	100	$100	Straight Fk of Mud	SE-25 miles	Boone
Keyser, David	410	$1845	Guy	SE-20 miles	Cabell
" "	330	$1650	Guy	SE-20 miles	C
Keyton, Reuben	175	$600	2 Mile Ck	SE-14 miles	C
" "	25	$300	Mud	SE-10 miles	C
" "	175	$1097	Mud	SE-10 miles	C
Keyton, Richard	50	50	Carter Ck of Mud	SE-10 miles	C
Keyton, Ryland	63	$63	Mud	SE-14 miles	C
" "	50	$50	2 Mile of Mud	SE-12 miles	C
Kile, Thomas (see Kyle)	5/8	$200	adj B'ville	W side	C
Kilgore, Thomas W.	197	$2462.50	Mud	E-10 miles	C
Kilgore, William	330	$1980	Mud	N-5 miles	C
Killgore, George (3 tracts)	772	$772	Kilgore Ck	E-12 miles	Cabell
" "	53	$66.25	Kilgore Ck	E-12 miles	C
" "	40	$80	Mud	E-9 miles	C
" "	30	$30	Mud	E-9 miles	C
Kinder, Samuel	65	$325	Mud	SE-20 miles	C
" "	10	$80	Mud	SE-20 miles	C
King, James	450	$1800	Mud	SE-10 miles	C
King, Jesse	30	$240	Mud	SE-10 miles	C
King, John-Estate					
& S. King	deed from David Payton to John Peyton				
& John Peyton	90	$180	McComas Br of Guy	N-14 miles	C
King, Sampson	47	$94	Guy	S-18 miles	C
Kirk, John	155	$465	Turkey Ck	SE-24 miles	C
Kitchum, Alonzo G.	1500	$1500	10 Mile Ck of Guy	SE-25 miles	C
Knight,Abner E.	(deed from James Knight)				
& L. Abner Knight					
& Robt. H. Knight					
& William Knight	559 1/2	$2797.50	OH	NE-9 miles	C
Knight, George	270	$2090	9 Mile of OH	N-9 miles	C
" "	70	$175	9 Mile of OH	N-9 miles	C
" "	73	$292	Lf Fk of 9 Miles	N-9 miles	C
Knight, Henry	335	$4187.50	OH	N-5 miles	C
" "	75	$375	7 Mile Ck of OH	N-5 miles	C

PERSON TAXED	ACRES	VALUE	LOCATION	DISTANCE TO COURT HOUSE	COUNTY RESIDES
Knight, Henry	101 3/4	$712.25	OH	NE-9 miles	C
Knight, Henry	126 1/4	$631.25	9 Mile of OH	N-7 miles	C
deed from Lemuel G. Connell					
Knight, James	341 1/2	$2391.50	OH	N-9 miles	C
Knight, Matthew	60	$210	Heath Ck	S-5 miles	C
deed from Thomas Spurlock					
Knight, Susanna	90	$279	Lit Guy	NE-10 miles	C
Kraus, Hergo(Hugo) ('63)					
& Walter Kraus	1040	$1305	Mud & 7 Mile	NE-4 miles	C
" "	70	$350	Merritts Ck of Mud	NE-4 miles	C
Kyle, Sam & G.F. Miller					
S. Woodyard	55	$220	7 Mile Ck of OH	N-5 miles	C
- L -					
Laidley, Albert	124	$620	Camp Ck	W-12miles	C
" "	560	$3780	Rt fk of 4 Pole	W-12 miles	C
" "	84	$462	4 Pole	W-12 miles	C
" "	80	$120	Branch of 4 Pole	W-9 miles	C
Laidley, John (Est.)	160	$6960	OH	W-9 miles	C ('65)
Lake, David	100	$200	Big Ck of Main Mud	SE-20 miles	C
Lake, Nicholas	565	$1130	Big Ck of Main Mud	SE-20 miles	C
" "	65	$130	Big Ck of Main Mud	SE-20 miles	C
Lambert, Peter	150	$150	Hopkins Tract	NE-16 miles	C
Lansford, Joshua	25	$25	Mud	SE-20 miles	C
" "	86	$602	Mill ck	E-17 miles	C
Lansford, Richard	306	$(116)	Toms Ck	S-4 Miles	C
Lapton, David B. (Lasston)	245	$245	Mud	E-10 miles	C
Latten, Charles	747	$747	Big Ck/Trace Ck/Mud	SE-20 miles	C
" " (2 tracts)	321	$321	Raccoon	S-14 miles	C
" "	181.6	$181.66	Mud	SE-20 miles	C
" " (3 tracts)	628	$628	4 Mile & 14 Mile of Guy	S-18 miles	C
" "	500	$500	Merrits/Mid Fk of Mud	SE-23 miles	C
" "	1	$231.24	adj Barboursville	E side	C
" "	1 1/4	$150	deed/W.C. Miller " "	E side	C
" "	2	$62.48	d/Julius Freutel - " "	E side	C
" "	60	$60	d/Geo. Kilgore - Mud	SE-13 miles	C
" "					
& George Kilgore	12	$24	Guy	S-25 miles	C
Latten & Kilgore	16	$32	Mud & Charley Ck	E-12 miles	C

PERSON TAXED	ACRES	VALUE	LOCATION	DISTANCE TO COURT HOUSE	COUNTY RESIDES
Latten, Charles, C.K. Morris, W.B. Moore, J.H. Becker, G.F. Miller					
& H.B. Maupin	995	$995	Btw Trace & Mid Fk/Mud	SE-23 miles	C
Lawrence, Charles Sr.	200	$200	2 Mile Ck & Mile Br	SE-14 miles	C
" "	203	$1437.26	Mud	SE-18 miles	C
" "					C
& Worden	448	$448	Big Cabell & Trace Fk	SE-22 miles	Kanawha
Lawrence, John					K
& M. Rogers	29	$29	Sugartree Fk of Mud	SE-30 miles	K
Lawrence, William H.	78	$156	head waters Trace Ck	SE-25 miles	Cabell
" " (2 tracts)	74	$74	Trace Ck/Middle Fk/Mud	SE-25 miles	C
Lawson, A.					Logan
& E. Ward	1930	$1930	E side Guy	S-30 miles	Wythe
Lawson, Joseph	60	$225	Mud	SE-25 miles	Cabell
Lawson, William	140	140	Scary Ck of Mud	SE-25 miles	Cabell
Leaning, Thomas-Estate	4000	$4000	Guy (4 tracts)	S-8 miles	PA
Legg, James	165	$825	Mill Ck	E-8 miles	Kanawha
Lesag, Julius (LeSage)	35	$126	OH	N-10 miles	Cabell
" "	81	$202	OH	N-8 miles	C
" "	100	$200	9 Mile Ck of OH	N-7 miles	C
LeTulle, Victor-Estate	13 1/2	$49.95	adj Guyandotte	W-7 miles	C
Licker, Henry	100	$100	Hopkins Tract	NE-16 miles	C
Lloyd, John	1/10	$450	adj Barboursville	E-side	C
Love, Ann	500	$2500	Rich Bottom of Guy	S-3 miles	Cabell
Love, Daniel	500	$3500	Mud	E-6 miles	C
Love, William	226	$2499.56	Mud	E-7 miles	C
" "	20	$30	Mud	E-7 miles	C
Lovejoy, John					
& Jennetta Lovejoy	229	$518.25	4 Pole	W-9 miles	C
Lucas, Calvry	80	320	head 4 Mile	S-16 miles	C
Lucas, Parker (2 tracts)	399	$399	Rock House/4 Mile Ck	S-20 miles	C
" "	150	$1125	Guy	SW-17 miles	C
" "	256	$1203	Rt fk of 4 Mile	SW-17 miles	C
" "	361	$722	4 Mile	S-18 miles	C
" "	50	$100	Guy	S-18 miles	C
" "	50	$200	Guy	S-18 miles	C
Lusher, Irvin	134	$201	Big Cabell	E-9 miles	C
" "	290	$425.40	1 Mile Ck of Guy	S-14 miles	C
" "	435	$678.60	1 Mile Ck of Guy	S-14 miles	C
" " (3 tracts)	885	$885	Guy	S-20 miles	C

PERSON TAXED	ACRES	VALUE	LOCATION	DISTANCE TO COURT HOUSE	COUNTY RESIDES
Lusher, Irvin	285	$570	Wilson Tract on Guy	S-20 miles	C
Lusher, Margaret	290	$3480	Mud	E-1 mile	C
" "	200	$500	Reece's Ck	E-2 miles	C
" "	191	$382	Mud	E-2 miles	C
Lykins, John	249	$4751.04	Mud	SE-20 miles	C
- M -					
Malcom, Edward B.	1 1/4	$900	Mud	E-8 miles	C
" "	130	$1690	Mud	E-8 miles	C
Malcom, John	85	$977.50	Mud	E-8 miles	C
Malcom, John M.	125	$1875	Mud	E-8 miles	C
" "	30	$60	Mud	E-8 miles	C
Malcolm, Robert-Estate	59	$59	Fudges Ck	E-9 miles	C
Marsden, Henry	50	$125	Hopkins Tract	NE-16 miles	C
" "	57	$85.50	Hopkins Tract	NE-16 miles	C
" "	100	$250	Hopkins Tract	NE-16 miles	C
Marsden, Jane Augustine	100	$100	Hopkins Tract	NE-16 miles	NY
Maupin, Chapman, W. & Hilderson	1298	$1622.50	Big Fudge Ck	E-7 miles	Cabell
Maupin, Henry B.	68 1/2	$556.87	Rt Fk of 9 Mile of OH	W-6 miles(?)	C
" "	1	$100	Mud adj B'ville	E-side	C
" "	75	$225	Rt Fk of 9 Mile of OH	N-5 miles	C
Maupin, Margaret & D. Love (life estate)	276	$3180	Mud	E-6 miles	C
May, Jacob W.	197	$1182	Mud Fk of Mud	SE-30 miles	C
Mays, Elish	1/10	$495.83	adj Guy'tte	W-7 miles	C
McAlister, Lucinda & Hannah & Adeline	228	$2137.50	Bear Ck	S-10 miles	C
McAlister, John	250	$625	Lf fk of Trace of Guy	S-12 miles	C
McAlister, Preston	62 1/2	$125	Fudges Ck	SE-10 miles	C
McAlister, Richard-Estate	276	$828	Trace Ck	SE-25 miles	C
McAlister, Richard	300	$750	Trace Ck of Guy	SE-10 miles	C
deed from Thomas McCowan & R.S. Bias					
McAlister, Thomas	2	$20	Teays Valley	E-13 miles	Putnam
" "	31	$77.50	Teays Valley	E-13 miles	P
McAllister, Thomas	170	$170	Charley Ck	SE-14 miles	P
McAllister, James	25	$250	Teays Valley	E-14 miles	Cabell
McAllister, Malcom	740	$1680	Teays Valley	E-15 miles	C
McAllister, Olivia	332.5	$3657.50	Teays Valley	E-15 miles	C
McAllister, Perry	103	$103	Trace Fk	SE-25 miles	C

PERSON TAXED	ACRES	VALUE	LOCATION	DISTANCE TO COURT HOUSE	COUNTY RESIDES
McAllister, Sylvester					
& John Harvey	210	$210	Rt fk of Trace Fk	SE-30 miles	C
McColough, P.H.	235	$470	Merritts Ck of Guy	S-7 miles	C
" "	57	$114	Heath Ck	S-7 miles	C
" "	110	$220	Heath Ck	S-7 miles	C
" "					
& H.J. Samuels	1025	$1025	Davis Ck	SW-4 miles	C
McColough, P.H.					
& C.L. Roffe	544	$544	14 Mile Ck	S-30 miles	C
McComas, David & Elisha McComas					
& James McComas	90	$270	Rich Knob	S-25 miles	C
" same	100	$1200	Guy	S-14 miles	C
" same	75	$300	McComas Br	S-6 miles	C
McComas, Elisha	80	$160	4 Mile	S-20 miles	C
" "	320	$3000	Lower Sulphur Br-4 Mile	S-20 miles	C
" "	50	$50	Long Br of 4 Mile	S-20 miles	C
" "	70	$140	4 Mile	S-20 miles	C
" "	60	$240	4 Mile	S-20 miles	C
" "	100	$100	McClarity/Sulphur Spring	S-20 miles	C
" "					
& T.J. McComas	70	$70	Fall Cr of 4 Mile	S-20 miles	C
" same	80	$100	4 Mile	S-20 miles	C
McComas, Elisha					
& C. Lattin	433	$433	4 Mile	S-20 miles	C
McComas, Elisha					
& A.F. Richman	225	$225	4 Mile	S-19 miles	C
McComas, Elisha-Estate	50	$100	Guuy	S-10 miles	C
McComas, Harrison	90	$270	Rich Knob	S-25 miles	C
" " (2 tracts)	110	$110	head 6 Mile-Listin Br	S-25 miles	C
" "					
& David McComas	180	$540	Btw 6 & 9 Mile creeks	S-25 miles	C
McComas, Isaac	31 1/2	$472.50	Guy	S-23 miles	C
McComas, James	25	$500	Guy	S-13 miles	C
McComas, James					
& Eisha McComas	500	$5250	Guy	S-24 miles	C
McComas, James					
& Thomas McComas-Est	139	$542	Guy	S-13 miles	C
McComas, James M.	210	$1575	McComas Br	S-15 miles	C
McComas, John	50	$75	Big Ck of Trace Fk	SE-20 miles	C

PERSON TAXED	ACRES	VALUE	LOCATION	DISTANCE TO COURT HOUSE	COUNTY RESIDES
McComas, John	35 1/2	$35.50	Big Ck of Trace Fk	SE-20 miles	C
McComas, Patrick K.	90	$112.50	Btw Chapman/McComas	S-15 miles	Logan
McComas, Thomas-Estate	24	$480	Guy	S-10 miles	Cabell
McComas, Thomas					
& William Johnston	100	100	head 10 Mile	S-25 miles	C
McComas, Thomas J.	150	$1200	Guy	S-12 miles	C
" " (2 tracts)	370	$370	4 Mile	S-21 miles	C
" "	100	$125	14 Mile	S-21 miles	C
McComas, William	442	$13,260	Guy	W-1 mile	C
" "	1/4	$500	adj Barboursville	W side	C
" "	61	$1464	Mud	NE-2miles	C
" " & West McComas					
& E.W. McComas	175	$1750	Guy	S-10 miles	C
McComas, William-Estate	87	$975	Guy	S-24 miles	C
" "	30	$195	Guy	S-24 miles	C
" "	300	$375	lf side 9 Mile	S-24 miles	C
" "					
& Irvin Lusher	250	$312.50	lf side 9 Mile	S-24 miles	C
McComas, W.W.	1/2	$50	adj Barboursville	W-side	Giles
McComas,					
McColough & Roffe	148	$444	Madison Ck	S-12 miles	Cabell
McConiha, Malinda	75	$1275	Guy	NW-3 miles	Kanawha
McCorkle, Alexander M.	25	$31.25	Fudge Ck	SE-14 miles	Cabell
" " (2 tracts)	416	$416	Porters Fk of Fudge Ck	SE-14 miles	C
McCorkle James	27	$81	4 Pole	W-8 miles	C
" "	202	$404	4 Pole	W-8 miles	C
McCrand, John	175	$2100	Guy	S-11 miles	C
McFarland, Henry & other	174,557	$174,557	Guy, Mud, 4 Pole	S-12 miles	NY
" "	500	$6000	Falls Trace of Guy	S-14 miles	NY
" "	50	$150	Falls Trace of Guy	S-14 miles	NY
" "	150	$1260	Falls Trace of Guy	S-16 miles	NY
" "	350	$700	Falls Trace of Guy	S-16 miles	NY
McFarland, H.					
& Wm. Martin	283.5	$1412.52	4 Mile Ck	S-20 miles	NY
" " same	38	$231.25	4 Mile Ck	S-20 miles	NY
" " same	220	$275	4 Mile Ck	S-20 miles	NY
McFarland &				NY	
Spencer Midkiff	811	$4330.74	Guy	S-14 miles	Cabell
McGinnis, Allen B.	66	$2310	Guy	W-5 miles	C

PERSON TAXED	ACRES	VALUE	LOCATION	DISTANCE TO COURT HOUSE	COUNTY RESIDES
McGinnis, Edmund	445	$445	Mud	E-9 miles	Texas
McGinnis, Ira J.	370	$370	4 Miles	S-20 miles	Cabell
McGinnis, John B.	50	$50	Btw Smith & Madison	S-10 miles	C
McGinnis, Oliver A.	10a	$30	Russell Ck	W-4 miles	TX ('65)
McGinnis, P.A.	10	$30	Russell Ck	W-4 miles	TX
" "	500	$500	Little Guy	NE-13 miles	TX
" "	12 1/2	$12.50	4 Pole	SW-12 miles	TX
McKee, John	64,000	$64,000	Guy & Mud	SE-16 miles	NY
McKendree, A. F. & William Johnson	185	$185	4 Mile	S-30 miles	Cabell
McKendree, Robt.-Estate & E.W.Blume	5/8	$300	adj Barboursville	W side	Cabell
McNealy, Benjamin	100	$100	McNealy's Br	S-25 miles	C
" "	100	$100	4 Mile	SE-25 miles	C
McWarter, James-Estate	285	$285	Kilgore Ck	E-11 miles	C
McWarter, Peter	100	$100	Guy	S-30 miles	C
Merritt, John	76 2/3	$2763	Mud & Guy	S-16 miles	C
" "	1 7/9	$5388.88	Lower Falls Mud/ MILL	N-1/2 mile	C
" " & Melchor Merritt	2/9	$711.11	Lower Falls Mud/MILL	N-1/2 mile	C
Merrit, John & Turley	88	$88	Lit 2 Mile	E-12 miles	C
Merritt, Malchor	194	$2328	Mud	E-1 mile	C
Merritt, Melchor	410	$410	Rece Ck/Everett Ck/Toms	E-2 miles	C
Merritt, William	1 1/2	$1048.38	2 lots B'ville on Guy	W side	C
" " & Co.	245	$245	Mud	E-9 miles	C
Midkiff, Gordon	115	$244.37	Trace & Tom's Ck	S-8 miles	C
Midkiff, Lewis	24	$36	Guy	S-14 miles	C
" "	170	$1275	Guy	S-14 miles	C
" "	100	$150	Falls Ck of Guy	S-15 miles	C
Midkiff, Solomon	420	$2205	Guy	S-8 miles	C
" "	150	$1575	Guy	S-13 miles	C
" "	30	$150	Trace Ck of Guy	S-9 miles	C
" "	100	$400	Trace Ck of Guy	S-9miles	C
" "	235	$705	Trace Ck of Guy	S-9 miles	C
" "	10	$10	Bear Ck-deed H.McFarland	S-10 miles	C
Midkiff, Spencer	191	$815.57	Guy	S-13 miles	C
" "	282	$2115	above falls of Guy	S-15 miles	C
" "	7	$21	Guy	S-13 miles	C
" "	100	$200	Guy	S-14 miles	C

PERSON TAXED	ACRES	VALUE	LOCATION	DISTANCE TO COURT HOUSE	COUNTY RESIDES
Midkiff, Spencer	1	$30	Guy	S-13 miles	C
" "	310	$1860	Guy	NW-4 miles	C
" "	350	$1750	Guy-deed from Sol Midkiff	S-14 miles	C
Midkiff, Spencer	509	$764.50	Falls Ck of Guy	S-14 miles	C
deed from Charles Tooley					
" " (2 tracts)	75 1/2	$75.50	Falls Ck/Guy-deed Poteet	S-14 miles	C
Miller, George F.	2	$680	adj Baroursville	E-side	C
" "	15	$150	Lit 7 Mile-dd/Ewing Clark	N-2 miles	C
" "	60	$225.90	7 Mile of OH	N-6 miles	C
deed from John N. Jefferson					
Miller, Henry	80	$520	4 Pole	W-8 miles	C
Miller, Henry H.	1/10	$1499.90	adj Guy'tte	W-7 miles	C
Miller, Jacob	90	$450	Middle Fk of Mud	SE-25 miles	C
Miller, James	100	$1400	Mud	E-7 miles	C
Miller, John	300	$2499	Mud	E-7 miles	C
" "	250	$500	Mud	E-7 miles	C
Miller, John G.	500	$17,700	Guy R	NW-1/4 mile	C
" "	75	$168.75	Heath Ck	S-5 miles	C
" "	140	$720	Heath Ck	S-5 miles	C
Miller, William C.	10 1/2	$313.12	Mud adj B'ville	E-side	C
" "	2	$2700	adj B'ville	E-side	C
" "	350	$350	headwaters 10&14 Mile Ck	S-27 miles	C
" "	185	$370	Merritts Ck of Guy	S-5 miles	C
" "	10	$250	adj B'ville	E-side	C
" "	71	$2059	adj B'ville	E-side	C
" "	6 1/2	$195	adj B'ville	E-side	C
" " d/HM McFarland	150	$150	4 Mile Ck of Guy	S-18 miles	C
" "	125	$125	2 Mile Ck of 10 Mile Ck	S-27 miles	C
" "part/Jas.W.Walker	180	$720	Davis Ck	SW-3 miles	C
" " d/ McFarland	30	$105	Davis Ck	SW-3 miles	C
" " (2 tracts)	120	$120	4 Mile Ck of Guy	S-18 miles	C
" "	192.5	$192.50	Scary Ck of Mud	SE-25 miles	C
" "	240	$240	Rt side of Mud Fk of Mud	SE-25 miles	C
" " (2 tracts)	312	$312	4 Mile	SE-18 miles	C
Miller, William C. & P.C. Buffington	285	$285	7 Mile & 9 Mile of OH	E-4 miles	C
Miller, William C. & H. More	1	$6023	Guy R adj Barboursville	NW-side	C
" "same	325	$1300	4 Mile of Guy	SW-18 miles	C

PERSON TAXED	ACRES	VALUE	LOCATION	DISTANCE TO COURT HOUSE	COUNTY RESIDES
" Miller & More	100	$150	4 Mile	SW-18 miles	C
" "same	50	$150	4 Mile	SW-18 miles	C
Miller, William C. & Co.	168	$168	Guy	SE-25 miles	C
" "	222	41554.88	Mud R adj B'ville	E-side	C
Miller, Wm. C., Thos. Thornburg					
& A. Lawson & E. Ward	775	$775	W side Guy	S-19 miles	C
Mitchell, James	694	$694	Lit Guy	NE-16 miles	Mason
Moore, Gradison	22 2/9	$44.45	Mud	SE-34 miles	Cabell
Moore, Mathew	100	$200	Mud Fk of Mud	SE-34 miles	C
Moore, Sarah	30	$1050	Above Guyandotte	NW-7 miles	C
Moore, William K.	180	$360	Sulphur Fk of Mud	SE-34 miles	C
Moore, Wilson B.	133	$931	Bear Ck	S-13 miles	C
" "	216	$540	Trace Ck of Guy	SE-10 miles	C
deed from R.S. Bias					
Morris, Charles K.	2117	$13,975	Guy (Martha)	S-2 miles	C
Morris, John	2300	$2300	Teays Valley	E-12 miles	C
" "	992	$11,904	Teays Valley	E-12 miles	C
" "	88 1/3	$706,66	Charley's Ck	E-12 miles	C
" "	170	$170	Teays Valley	E-12 miles	C
" "	780	$6240	Teays Valley	E-12 miles	C
" "	285	$2850	Teays Valley	E-12 miles	C
" "	1450	$14,500	Guy	S-5 miles	C
" "	400	$400	Charley's Ck	SE-14 miles	C
" "	70	$140	Charley's Ck	SE-14 miles	C
" "	200	$1200	Charley's Ck	SE-14 miles	C
" "	115	$115	Charley's Ck	E-12 miles	C
Morris, John					
& James Nelson-Estate	556	$2264	Mud & Kilgore Ck	E-12 miles	C
" same	63 1/2	$508	Teays Valley	E-14 miles	C
" same	69 3/5	$208.80	Teays Valley	E-14 miles	C
Morrison, James-Estate	163	$733.50	Heath Ck	S-5 miles	C
Morrison, John	35	$350	Guy	S-9 miles	C
" " & Wm. Rogers,					
& H.F. Draper	120	$120	Cabell Ck of Guy	SE-6 miles	C
Morrison, John F.	360	$1800	Guy	S-8 miles	C
" "	325	$2275	Guy	S-9 miles	C
" "	35	$350	Guy	S-6 miles	C
Morrison, Patrick	400	$2800	Guy	S-2 miles	C
Morrison, Thompson	175	$700	Guy	S-7 miles	C

PERSON TAXED	ACRES	VALUE	LOCATION	DISTANCE TO COURT HOUSE	COUNTY RESIDES
Morrison, Washington	8	$40	Guy	SE-8 miles	C
Moss, Virginus Randolph	14	$683.20	Tom's Ck	S-5 miles	C
Mullens, Spencer	125	$150	14 Mile Ck	S-30 miles	Logan
Mullens, Spencer A.	228	$228	E side 14 Mile	S-30 miles	L
" "	200	$250	E side 14 Mile	S-30 miles	L
" "	185	$185	Camp Br	SE-30 miles	L
Munford, James T.	50	$50	Hopkins Tract	NE-10 miles	NY
Myers, Charles	480	$720	Fudge Ck	E-6 miles	Cabell
" "	14	$14	Fudge Ck	E-6 miles	C
- N -					
Newberger, Harrietta	500	$500	Hopkins Tract	N-12 miles	NY
" "	400	$800	Hopkins Tract	N-12 miles	NY
Newberger, Joseph	100	$100	Hopkins Tract	NE-16 miles	NY
Newman, Joseph	110	$660	Toms Ck of Mud	E-4 miles	OH
Newman, Russell	199	$796	Mud	E-12 miles	OH
" "	150	$1200	Mud	E-12 miles	OH
" "	27	$33.75	Mud	E-12 miles	OH
" "	4	$60	Mud	E-10 miles	OH
Nicely, James	144	$576	Merritts Ck of Guy	S-7 miles	Cabell
Nicely, Zachariah	198.5	$198.50	Buffalo Ck	SE-16 miles	C
Nicholas, John S.	100	$700	Mud	E-16 miles	C
Noel, Winston	390	$975	Lower 2 Mile Ck of Guy	S-12 miles	C
Noell, Winston & E.J. McGinnis	100	$125	14 Mile Ck	S-30 miles	C
- O -					
Ott, Simiom	337	$337	Mud Fk of Mud	SE-30 miles	C
" "	500	$500	Porters Fk of Mud	SE-25 miles	C
Otts, William	400	$1800	Middle Fk Mud	SE-32 miles	C
Owen, Eppy	129	$516	4 Pole	SW-25 miles	C
Owen, S.	100	$271	OH	W-11 miles	C
- P -					
Page, James H.	210.5	$9057.50	OH	W-9 miles	C
Paine, William	150	$4125	OH	W-9 miles	C
Parish, James	213	$639	Johns Ck	E-14 miles	C
" "	218	$379.50	Kilgore Ck	E-14 miles	C
Parker, Greenville	13067	$13,067	Lit Guy & Mud	NE-14 miles	C
Parson, Nancy & Sylvester Adkins	97	$194	Raccoon of Beech	SW-13 miles	Logan
Parsons, John W.	75	$187.50	Rt Fk of 4 Mile	S-20 miles	Cabell

PERSON TAXED	ACRES	VALUE	LOCATION	DISTANCE TO COURT HOUSE	COUNTY RESIDES
Parsons, Thomas	24	$54	4 Mile Ck of Guy	S-20 miles	C
Patrick, H. (Porter ?)	306.5	$1072.75	Smith Ck of Guy	S-10 miles	C
Patton, Robertson-Estate	85	$599.25	Trace Fk of Mud	SE-19 miles	C
" " (2 tracts)	260	$260	Trace Fk of Mud	SE-19 miles	C
Pauley, Washington-Estate	250	$625	Mud Fk of Mud	SE-30 miles	C
" "	155	$155	Trace Fk of Mud	SE-30 miles	C
Payton/Peyton					
Payton, Alex	43	$43	Ousely Ck	-	-
Payton, Harrison	250	$625	Lf Fk of Trace Ck of Guy	S-12 miles	C
Payton, Perry	240	$300	(Mile or Mill) Ck of Guy	S-15 miles	C
Payton, Sophia M.	311	$3110	Mud	E-2 miles	C
" "	324	$3888	Mud	E-2 miles	C
" "	141	$2410	Mud-deed Thos. Dundas-ex	E-2 miles	C
Perry, Benjamin L.	93	$469.37	Tyler Ck	S-9 miles	C
Perry, Elijah	100	$212.50	Trace Fk	S-8 miles	C
Perry, John	75	$487.50	Lit Guy	NE-16 miles	C
" "	81	$162	Hopkins Tract	NE-16 miles	C
" " & William Perry	30	$30	Lit Guy	W-16 miles	C
Perry, Silas B.	150	$787.50	Guy	S-8 miles	C
Perry, William	88	$572	Lit Guy	NE-16 miles	C
" "	57 1/2	$57.50	Cow Fk of Lit Guy	NE-14 miles	C
" "	75	$75	Hopkins Tract	NE-16 miles	C
Perry, William-Estate	125	$230	Lower Ck of Mud	E-10 miles	C
Peyton/Payton					
Peyton, Henry	172	$688	Middle Ck of Guy	S-15 miles	C
" "	140	$175	Btw 1 Mile & 2 Mile Ck	S-15 miles	C
Peyton, John	157	$157	2 Mile Ck of Guy	S-14 miles	C
Pine, Alexander	220	$1100	4 Pole	W- 14 miles	C
Plybon, John	3501	$1400	Camp Ck	W-8 miles	C
Poar, Elisha	207	$699.66	Mill Ck	E-9 miles	C
Pogue, James H.	210.5	$9057	OH	W-9 miles	C ('65)
Porter, David-Estate	510	$637.50	Mud	SE-13 miles	C
" "	373	$466.25	Mud-west side	SE-13 miles	C
" "	1023	$3069	Mud-east side	SE-13 miles	C
" "	65	$520	Mud	SE-12 miles	C
" "	360	$450.75	Mud	SE-16 miles	C
" "	40	$160	Mud	SE-16 miles	C
" "	50	$125	Mud-east side	SE-13 miles	C
" "	30	60	Buffalo of Mud	SE-16 miles	C

PERSON TAXED	ACRES	VALUE	LOCATION	DISTANCE TO COURT HOUSE	COUNTY RESIDES
Porter, James	190.7	$667.62	Guy-will/John Porter	S-10 miles	C
" "	435.7	$1524.60	Madison & Smith Cks	S-11 miles	C
Porter, Jerual	625	$2187.50	Smith Ck of Guy	S-10 miles	C
" "	90	$135	Madison Ck	S-16 miles	C
" "	150	$150	Mill Br of Raccoon	SW-15 miles	C
Porter, John-Estate(2 trts)	422	$422	Raccoon of Beech Fk	SW-15 miles	C
Porter, John W.	3275	$3275	Robt. Morris Tract	S-20 miles	NY
Porter, Samuel	150	$375	Raccoon of Beech Fk	SW-13 miles	Cabell
" "	60	$60	Fernatt Br	S-12 miles	C
Porter, William	375	$1500	Trace Ck of Mud	SE-12 miles	C
" "	125	$500	Mouth of Trace Ck of Mud	SE-12 miles	C
" " & David Porter	60	$180	Mud	SE-13 miles	C
Poteet, Clermont(Clementine)	100	$1100	Guy	W-5 miles	C
Poteet, H.C.	425.5	$2998.02	Big Cabell	E-6 miles	C
" " & Preston Hodge	2	$100	Mud-deed / C.T.Everett	E-6 miles	C
Poteet, H.C. (reduced by deed to Wagoner & Hohenberger) & A.L. Wilson	225	$599.50	Edmunds Ck of Mud	E-7 miles	C
Poteet, Skelton	125	$1000	Guy	W-5 miles	C
Powell, Phillip	280	$2800	Mud	SE-20 miles	C
" "	100	$328	Mud Fk of Mud	SE-20 miles	C
" "	1	$3	S side Main Mud	SE-20 miles	C
Price, Joseph	5/8	$4175	adj Guy'tte	W-7 miles	C
- R -					
Ray, Isaac	60	$60	Dry Br of Guy	S-18 miles	C
Ray, Isaiah (Est.)	393	$1572	4 Pole	W-7 miles	C ('65)
Ray, William	226	$226	4 Pole (order S. Sanders)	W-5 miles	C
" "	145	$580	4 Pole deed/H.Barrett	W-8 miles	C
" "	50	$150	Bear Ck	SE-13 miles	C
Reardon, John	52	$130	Hopkins Tract	NE-15 miles	C
Reece. Abia	300	$5550	Mud	E-10 miles	C
Reece, A., Joseph Reece-Esate & Abia Reece	150	$10,008.50	Mud	E-4 miles	C
Reece, Edward C.	100	$200	Mud	E-11 miles	C
Reece, James H.	100	$1250	Mud	E-10 miles	C
Reece, John M.	433	$1247	Mud	E-13 miles	C
" "	316	$316	Kilgore Ck	E-14 miles	C
" "	11	$22	Headwaters of Mill Ck	E-15 miles	C

PERSON TAXED	ACRES	VALUE	LOCATION	DISTANCE TO COURT HOUSE	COUNTY RESIDES
Reese. John M.	177	$422.50	Sanders Ck	E-9 miles	C
" "	323	$323	E side Mud	SE-20 miles	C
" "	417	$834	Middle FK of Mud	SE-20 miles	C
" " (2 tracts)	36 1/2	$36.50	SE of Mud Bridge	E-11 miles	C
deed from George Kilgore & C. Lattin					
" "	220	$330	Cowhide Br of Mud	SE-20 miles	C
deed from John M. Jordan					
Reece, Joseph-Estate	50	$150	Lit Cabell	E-4 miles	C
Reece, Margaret	62 1/2	$2337.50	Guy	W-5 miles	C
Reece, Warren P.	45	$540	Mud	E-11 miles	C
" "	55	$330	Mud	E-9 miles	C
" "	50	$50	Mud	E-9 miles	C
last 2 deeds from George Gallaher & wife					
Reynolds, Archibald	100	$250	Trqce Ck	S-12 miles	C
Reynolds, James	244	$793	Dry Br of Mud	E-9 miles	C
" " (2 tracts)	483	$483	Big 2 Mile of Mud	E-9 miles	C
" " & John Black	575	$575	Dry Br of Mud	E-9 miles	C
Reynolds, John & John Black	100	$100	Lf Fk Dry Br	NE-9 miles	C
Reynolds, Simeon & T.S. Brown	240	$240	Mud	SE-12 miles	C
Ricketts, G.C.	250	$2500	4 Pole	W-8 miles	C
Rigg, Thomas H.-Estate	200	$1200	Lit Guy	N-19 miles	C
Rindye, Joseph F.	1000	$1000	Robert Morris Tract	E-20 miles	C
deed from Charles K. Whitley					
Roach, William H.	127	$127	Big 2 Mile of Mud	S-12 miles	C
deed from James Reynolds					
Roberts, Alexander B.	225	$2025	Mid Fk of Mud	SE-22 miles	C
Roberts, D.M.	66 2/3	$66.66	Scary Ck	S-22 miles	C
Roberts, Francis	150	$150	Trace Ck of Mud	S-12 miles	C
Robert, Henry & Bartholemew Roberts	66 1/2	$798	Teays Valley	E-13 miles	C
" same	150	$150	Charleys Ck	E-13 miles	C
Roberts, James J.	40	$80	Mud	SE-20 miles	C
" "	35	$70	Mud	SE-20 miles	C
" "	131	$917	Mud	SE-20 miles	C
Roberts, James M.	131	$917	Mud	SE-27 miles	C
Roberts, John L.	25	$50	Mid Fk of Mud	SE-22 miles	C

PERSON TAXED	ACRES	VALUE	LOCATION	DISTANCE TO COURT HOUSE	COUNTY RESIDES
Roberts, Jones	290	$1998.10	Trace Fk of Mud	SE-20 miles	C
Rogers, James W.	50	$150	Lick Log Br of Sugartree	SE-30 miles	C
deed from Ephraim Griffith					
Rogers, John C.	270	$270	Sugartree	SE-30 miles	Kanawha
" " & Samuel Cabell					
& William F. Draper	365	$365	Btw Sycamore & Merritts	SE-30 miles	K
" same	286	$286	Mid Fk of Mud	SE-30 miles	K
Rogers, Michael	29	$115.42	Sugartree of Mud	SE-30 miles	K
deed reduced by Thomas Good					
Rogers, William C.	1/10	$500	adj Guy'tte	W-7 miles	Cabell
deed from Lewis Sedinger					
Roffe, Charles	1034	$15,510	Guy	S-1 mile	C
" "	1000	$1000	2 Mile Ck	SE-12 miles	C
" "	1350	$2700	Guy	SE-3 miles	C
Roffe, Charles L.	1400	$2800	Guy	SE-8 miles	C
" "	170	$170	Long Br	SW-8 miles	C
" "	245	$1225	Toms Ck	SE-4 miles	C
" "	460	$1840	Toms Ck	SE-4 miles	C
" "	341	$1364	Big Fudge	E-6 miles	C
" "	280	$1120	Big Fudge	E-7 miles	C
" "	100	$200	Big Fudge	E-7 miles	C
" "	100	$100	Fudge Ck	E-7 miles	C
" "	200	$300	Guy	S-16 miles	C
" "	200	$700	Mud & Guy	S-14 miles	C
" "	97	$242.50	Guy	S-16 miles	C
" "	45	$180	Beech Fk	SW-10 miles	C
" "	25	$50	Old Falls Br	S-20 miles	C
" "	50	$250	Collins Ck	S-7 miles	C
Roffe, C. L.					
& William Miller	1700	$2550	Guy & Mud	S-14 miles	C
Roffe, C. L.					
& John Samuels-Estate	675	$1350	Guy & Mud	S-4 miles	C
Roffe, James H.	100	$600	Tylers Ck	S-9 miles	C
Ross, John S.	100	$600	4 Mile Ck	S-20 miles	Wayne
" "	600	$600	14 Mile Ck	S-30 miles	W
Ross, Robert	41	$41	Smith Ck of Guy	S-10 miles	C
" " & John Samuels,					
& James Gill	300	$300	Trace Fk of 4 Miles	S-20 miles	C
Ross, Samuel	320	$320	10 Mile Ck	S-25 miles	C

PERSON TAXED	ACRES	VALUE	LOCATION	DISTANCE TO COURT HOUSE	COUNTY RESIDES
- S -					
Samuels, H.C.	100	$400	OH	NW-6 miles	C
Samuels, John-Estate	221.6	$6650	adj B'ville	E-side	C
" "					
& John Alford	68	$68	Btw Guy & Mud	SE-25 miles	C
" same	112	$112	Btw Guy & Mud	SE-25 miles	C
" same	769	$769	Btw Guy & Mud	SE-25 miles	C
Samuels, Rebecca A.	1/5	$1060.30	adj B'ville	E-side	C
Sanders, Samuel	100	$100	4 Pole	W-5 miles	C
Sandridge, Benjamin	125	$625	Lit Cab	NE-6 miles	C
Sarten, John W.	70	$70	BtwLit Ugly & Hamilton	S-36 miles	C
Savage, John W.	750	$750	Hopkins Tract	NE-11 miles	C
Sawyer, Nathaniel	160	$200	Hopkins Tract	NE-14 miles	C
Schmes, Francis	50	$50	Hopkins Tract on Lit Guy	NE-14 miles	C
Scott, D.B.-Estate	25	$37.50	Lit Guy	NE-16 miles	C
" "	30	$120	Lit Guy	NE-14 miles	C
" "	75	$375	Lit Guy	NE-15 miles	C
" "	15	$30	Lit Guy	NE-14 miles	C
" "	68	$85	9 Mile	NE-9 miles	C
" "	100.5	$210.12	Hopkins Tract	NE-16 miles	C
Scott, Sanford (Est.)	1/10	$606.61	adj Guy'tte	W-7 miles	C ('65)
Seashols, John (3 Tracts)	560	$560	Kilgore Ck	NE-13 miles	Putnam
" "	180	$360	Teays Valley	E-13 miles	P
Sheff, Andrew	255	$1499.50	Mud	E-6 miles	Cabell
" "	33	$66	Mud	E-7 miles	C
" "	20	$20	Mud	E-7 miles	C
Shelton, Henry W. (Est.)	391.4	$5477.50	Guy	W-3 miles	C ('65)
" "	74	$1036	Guy	W-3 miles	C
Shelton, James M.	3/4	$600	adj B'ville	E-side	C
Shelton, Jerome	195	$1560	Guy	S-13 miles	C
Shelton, Susan-Life Estate	269	$2421	Guy	W-2 miles	C
Sheperd, Forest	2560	$2560	9 Mile Ck	S-26 miles	C
Shipe, Charles	3/8	$341.62	adj B'ville	W-side	C
Short, Robert	418	$2487.10	Mud	SE-22 miles	C
Shultz, Joseph	50	$200	Hopkins Tract	NE-16 miles	C
Shy, Benjamin					
& B. Drown-Estate	100	$320	Russell Ck	W-3 miles	C
Shy, Benjamin					
& William Wintz	75	$225	4Pole Ck	W-6 miles	C

PERSON TAXED	ACRES	VALUE	LOCATION	DISTANCE TO COURT HOUSE	COUNTY RESIDES
Sidebottom, Joseph	300	$300	Trace Ck	SE-12 miles	Boon
" "	160	$160	Trace Ck	SE-12 miles	Boon
Siders, Samuel	100	$350	Lower Ck	E-9 miles	Cabell
Simmons, Conwelsey	262	$262	Dry Br	E-9 miles	C
" "	400	$12,000	Frying Pan of Guy	S-4 miles	C
" "	103	$515	Guy	S-3 miles	C
" "	123	$615	Swamp Br of Guy	S-3 miles	C
" "	157.5	$456.50	Swamp Br	NW-1 mile(?)	C
" "	110	$550	Swamp Br	S-3miles	C
" "	193.75	$581.25	Guy	NW-1 mile	C
" "	123	$369	Swamp Br	S-3 miles	C
Simmons, George W. Jr.	160	$2000	Mud	E-10 miles	C
" "	110	$150	Johns Ck	E-10 miles	C
" "	18.5	$74	Mud	E-10 miles	C
" "	33	$49.50	Mud	E-10 miles	C
" "	30	$30	Br of Mud	E-10 miles	C
" "	41	$164	Mud	E-10 miles	C
" " (2 tracts)	492	$492	Kilgore Ck	NE-13 miles	C
" "	110	$839	Mud	E-7 miles	C
" "	98	$98	Johns Ck of Mud	E-11 miles	C
" "	78.3	$78.60	John & Mill Ck of Mud	E-11 miles	C
Simmons, Sampson	238	$1190	Swamp Br	S-3 miles	C
" "	195.5	$945.50	Swamp Br	S-3 miles	C
Simmons, Mary F.	434	$2170	Swamp Br.	S-3 miles	C
Sinton, David (Cincinnati)	100	$100	Hopkins Tract	NE-10 miles	OH
Sites, Christopher	150	$232.50	9 Mile of Guy	S-23 miles	Cabell
" "	270.5	$270.50	9 Mile of Guy	S-20 miles	C
" "	67	$83.75	Rt side of 9 Mile of Guy	S-25 miles	C
Sites, Christopher Jr.	70	$350	9 Mile of Guy	S-20 miles	C
" "	30	$120	9 Mile of Guy	S-24 miles	C
" " & James McComas	63	$94.50	9 Mile of Guy	S-23 miles	C
Sites, Christopher Sr.	600	$1500	Guy	S-13 miles	C
Sites, Godfrey	150	$375	Lf Fk of Trace Fk of Guy	S-12 miles	C
Smalley, George C.	300	$300	Hopkins Tract	NE-11 miles	C
Smallridge, John-Estate	137.5	$1650	Teays Valley	E-14 miles	C
" "	785	$785	Kilgore Ck	E-14 miles	C
Smith, Ballard	85	$170	Guy'tte E-side	W-7 miles	C
Smith, Jacob M.	95	$390	Beech Fk 12 Pole	SE-8 miles	C

PERSON TAXED	ACRES	VALUE	LOCATION	DISTANCE TO COURT HOUSE	COUNTY RESIDES
Smith, Jackson-Estate	325	$325	W side Guy	S-25-miles	C
Smith, James	250	$250	Buzzards Br of Trace Fk	SE-20 miles	C
" "	40	$50	Mud	E-12 miles	C
" "	272	$340	Mill Ck	E-17 miles	C
Smith, Martha	50	$337.50	Mud	SE-18 miles	C
Smith, Moses	45	$90	Long Br of Mid Fk	Sw-9 miles	C
Smith, Peter-Estate	740	$2220	Rt Fk Trace Ck	SE-18 miles	C
" "	187	$187	Rt Fk Trace Ck	SE-18 miles	C
Smith, P.S.	1/5	$1048.49	Guy'tte	W-7 miles	C
" "	1 3/4	$175	Guy'tte	W-7 miles	C
" "	1/4	$12.50	Guy'tte E-side	W-7 miles	C
Smith, Samuel	170	$170	Mud	SE-25 miles	C
Smith, Thomas	50	$200	Johns Ck of Mud	E-12 miles	C
" "	103	309	Mill Ck	E-13 miles	C
Smith, Viola	80	$1040	Heath Ck	S-4 miles	C
Smith, William	50	$300	14 Miles Ck	SW-25 miles	C
" "	50	$625	Guy	SW-25 miles	C
" " & H. Drake	62	$155	E side Guy	SW-25 miles	C
Snodgrass, James-Estate	220	$1485	Mud	SE-22 miles	C
Snodgrass, James B.	550	$882	Mud	SE-22 miles	C
" "	9	$9	Mud	SE-22 miles	C
" "	100	$150	Big Creek of Mud	SE-22 miles	C
" "	65	$9750	Mud	SE-22 miles	C
Spears, Benjamin	50	$100	9 Mile of Guy	S-26 miles	C
Spears, James	68	$68	Lf Fk 9 Mile	S-26 miles	C
Spears, Peyton	100	$150	9 Mile of Guy	S-26 miles	C
Spears, Thomas	50	$50	Sulphur Spring of 9 Mile	S-26 miles	C
Spears, William	175	$262.50	9 Mile of Guy	SW-22 miles	C
Spurlock, David	250	$2250	Lit Guy	W-16 miles	C(E not W)
" "	75	$300	Lit Guy	W-16 miles	C(E)
" "	70	$175	Lit Guy	W-16 miles	C(E)
" "	20	$40	Lit Guy	W-16 miles	C(E)
" "	680	$1360	Lit Guy	W-16 miles	C(E)
Spurlock, Harrison	150	$450	Mid Fk of Mud	SE-30 miles	C
Spurlock, Harrison R.	104	$104	Sams Br of Road Fk	SE-30 miles	C
Spurlock, James H.	100	$200	Cow Fk of Lit Guy	N-16 miles	C
Spurlock, Jesse	81	161	Hopkins Tract	NE-16 miles	C

PERSON TAXED	ACRES	VALUE	LOCATION	DISTANCE TO COURT HOUSE	COUNTY RESIDES
Spurlock, Thomas	80	$640	Mid Fk of Mud	SE-22 miles	C
" " & Alex Spurlock-Est.	121	$99.73	Road Fk of Mid Fk of Mud	SE-27 miles	C
" same	111	$111	head of Mud	SE-28 miles	C
" "	66	$66	Middle Fk Mud	SE-30 miles	C
Stanley, Robert	25	$50	head of 2 Mile of Mud	SE-11 miles	C
" "	141	$176.26	Toms Ck	SE-7 miles	C
" "	105	$157	head Fudge Ck	SE-9 miles	C
" "	50	$50	Btw Cabell & Toms Ck	SE-7 miles	C
" "	20	$30	Head Trace Ck	SE-12 miles	C
Stephenson, Anthony	170	$255	10 Mile Ck	SE-20 miles	C
Stephenson, Calvary M. Est	272	$1224	4 Pole Ck	W-8 miles	C
Stephenson, George & J.T. Adkins	160	$160	10 Mile Ck	SE-20 miles	C
Stephenson, Jackson	165	$165	10 Mile Ck	SE-25 miles	C
Stephenson, Mark	7	$28	4 Pole Ck	W-7 miles	C
Stephenson, Thomas	75	$450	10 Mile Ck	SE-24 miles	C
" " (2 tracts)	136	$136	10 Mile of Guy	SE-24 miles	C
" " & Sam Adkins	402	$402	10 Mile Ck of Guy	SE-24 miles	C
Stephenson, William	105	$315	Davis Ck	W-6 miles	C
Stowasser, Francis	70	$70	Lit Guy	NE-14 miles	C
Stuart, Robert	14.5	$4913	OH	NW-7 miles	C
Strother, Elizabeth H.(Phila)	4000	$4000	Mud & Guy	S-20 miles	C
Strupe, William	117.5	$1762.50	Mud	N-1 mile	C
" "	1 7/8	$13.12	Mud	E-1/2 miles	C
" "	77	$770	Mud	E-1 mile	C
" "	25	$50	Mud	E-1 mile	C
" "	126	$335	Rush Fk of Big Cabell	E-8 miles	C
Sullivan, James	61	$76.25	Lit Guy	NE-15 miles	C
Swann, Ballard S.	150	$487.50	Toms Ck	S-8 miles	C
Swann, Henly C.	207	$621	Guy-east side	S-7 miles	C
Swann, Hezekiah	660	$2164.54	Toms Ck	S-8 miles	C
Swann, John K.	359.5	$1797.50	Merritts Ck of Guy	S-7 miles	C
Swann, Leaven	276	$1656	Smith & Merritts Ck	S-6 miles	C
Swann, Thomas-Estate	41.5	$249	Smith & Merritts Ck	S-6 miles	C
Sweetland, J.V.	394	$3940	Mud	E-3 miles	C

PERSON TAXED	ACRES	VALUE	LOCATION	DISTANCE TO COURT HOUSE	COUNTY RESIDES
Switzer, J.					
& A.B. Howell	295.4	$997.88	W side Big Cabell	E-6 miles	C
" same (Howells Mill)	2	$5900	Mill site on Mud River	E-6 miles	C
- T -					
Taylor, Allen	100	$100	Big 2 Mile Ck of Mud	SE-12 miles	C
Taylor, John	150	$150	Lit Guy	E-15 miles	Mason
" "	275	$753.53	Big Cabell of Mud	E-8 miles	M
Templeton, James	150	$825	Mud	E-13 miles	Cabell
Templeton, Jesse	45	$180	Lower Ck	E-8 miles	C
Tessen, Andrew	100	$100	Hopkins Tract	NE-11 miles	C
Thomas, Nelson	95	$285	Mud	NE-6 miles	C
Thomas, Nelson-Estate	39	$39	Cabell Ck	E-6 miles	C
Thompson, Matthew	1/2	$250	adj B'ville	W-side	C
" "	6	$120	Mud	SE-1/2 mile	C
" "					
& A.H. Samuels	83	$83	Laurel Hill of Guy	SE-26 miles	C
Thompson, Patterson-Est.	500	$6500	Guy	S-3 miles	C
Thompson, Robert	30	$90	Trace Ck of Mud	SE-20 miles	C
Thompson, Robert Jr.	170	$170	Mud	SE-25 miles	C
" " "	1 1/4	$625	Big Ck, Trace Fk of Mud	SE-20 miles	C
Thompson, Robert S.	298	$993.33	Mouth of Raccoon/Mud	SE-20 miles	C
Thornburg, James L.	100	$4100	OH	--	C
Thornburg, John					
& James Everett	91	$1365	Guy	W-2 miles	C
Thornburg, Solomon-Est. & John Thornburg					
& J. Everett	450	$9000	Guy	W-1 mile	C
Thornburg, Thomas	41	$41	Head of Russell Ck	W-4 miles	C
Tiernan, John (Est.)	130	$5980	OH	W-8 miles	OH ('65)
Tillotson, David	819	$1028.50	Lit Guy	NE-15 miles	NY
Todd, James	39,000	$39,000	Guy-Robt. Morris Tract	S-20 miles	NY
deed from George A. Brown					
Todd, Mary(Cincinnati)	30	$90	Big Ugly	S-33 miles	OH
" "	100	$100	Guy	S-7 miles	OH
" " (3 tracts)	430	$430	Guy	SE-21 miles	OH
" "	50	$50	head 4 mile	S-24 miles	OH
" "	1280	$1280	Guy	SE-16 miles	OH
" "	57	$57	Merritts Ck	SW-7 miles	OH
" "	50	$50	Tylers Ck	S-10 miles	OH
Tooley, John	50	$50	Fall Ck of Guy	S-15 miles	Cabell

PERSON TAXED	ACRES	VALUE	LOCATION	DISTANCE TO COURT HOUSE	COUNTY RESIDES
Tooley, Tandy	40	140	Merritts Ck	S-7 miles	C
" "	7	$21	Merritts Ck	S-7 miles	C
" "	130	$325	Merritts Ck	S-7 miles	C
Toppin, John	161	$483	Head 4 Pole	W-7 miles	C
Toppin, Lewis L.	157	$471	4 Pole	W-7 miles	C
Toppin, William	195	$975	4 Pole	W-7 miles	C
Towney, David	100	$100	Sandy Fk of Sugartree/Guy	SE-30 miles	C
Trotter, Preston (Richmond)	250	$250	Raccoon Fk of Trace Fk	SE-12 miles	VA
" "	250	$250	Big Ck of Trace Fk	SE-15 miles	VA
Turley Estate					
& E. & Isiah(Turley)	200	$1000	Mud	E-4 miles	Cabell
Turley, Emberson	180	$180	Madison Ck	S-10 miles	C
" "	190	$380	Madison & Merritt Ck	S-10 miles	C
Turnan, John(see Tiernan)	776	$3840	OH	N-6 miles	OH
" "	25	$125	9 Mile of Oh	N-6 miles	OH
" "	1/20	$3000	adj Guy'tte	W-7 miles	OH
" "	7/8	$1799.87	adj Guy'tte	W-7 miles	OH
" "	1/4	$2200	adj Guy'tte	W-7 miles	OH
" "	1/10	$508.75	adj Guy'tte	W-7 miles	OH
Turner, Thomas	100	$1300	Guy	W-5 miles	Cabell
Turner, William	360	$1440	near falls of Guyandotte	S-15 miles	Wayne
" "	1/8	$150	adj Guy'tte	W-7 miles	W
" "	15	15	Long Br of Guy	S-15 miles	W
" "	57	$171	Long Br	S-15 miles	W
" "					W
& Leonard Turner	320	$320	E side Guy	S-28 miles	Cabell
Turner, Leonard	4 1/2	$33.50	Laurel Hill	S-28 miles	C
- V -					
Vanderwart, Charles	1000	$1000	Robert Morris Tract/Guy	S-20 miles	NY
" "	1225	$1225	Robt. Morris Tract	S-20 miles	NY
both deeds from Charles W. Whitney					
Vanname, Allette	750	$750	Lit Guy	NE-18 miles	Cabell
Vaughn, John W.	144	$360	2 Mile of Guy	S-17 miles	C
" "	110	$137.52	2 Mile	S-17 miles	C
" "	5	$5	2 Mile	S-17 miles	C
" "	36	$198	2 Mile	S-17 miles	C
" "	257	$514	2 Mile	S-17 miles	C
Vess, Sarah	95	$95	Lit Lawne of Mud	SE-22 miles	C
deed from James Webb Sr.					

PERSON TAXED	ACRES	VALUE	LOCATION	DISTANCE TO COURT HOUSE	COUNTY RESIDES
Vickers, Thomas	300	$600	Mud	SE-16 miles	C
- W -					
Walker, James H.	50	$175	Davis Ck	W-3 miles	C
deed William C. Miller					
Wallace, Andrew	70	$140	Lit Guy	NE-14 miles	C
Wallace, Benj.-Estate	479	$1077.75	head Mill Ck	E-17 miles	C
Wallace, Thomas	291	$653.75	head Mill Ck	E-17 miles	Mason
Walls, Anderson					
& John Cabell(2 tract)	330.5	$330.50	Scary Ck of Mud	SE-25 miles	Cabell
Ward, Evermont					
& A. Lawson	1125	$1125	Guy	SE-32 miles	Logan
Warren, George W.	111.5	$111.72	7 Mile-dd/Greenville Parker	N-6 miles	OH
Warwick, Julius	20	$20	Mid Fork of Trace Fk	SE-25 miles	Cabell
Weager, --	79.8	$759.65	Lit Guy	NE-14 miles	C
Webb, Henry L.	4	$800	adj Guy'tte	W-7 miles	TX ('65)
Webb, James-Estate	300	$2400	Mud	SE-20 miles	C
" "	75	$187.50	Charley Ck	E-16 miles	C
Webb, William	195	$799.50	Mud	SE-16 miles	C
" "	100	$150	Big Ck of Trace Fk	SE-16 miles	C
Wentz, Lewis (deed from Wm. Collins)					
& John W.	75	$375	Bobs Br of 7 Mile of OH	N-4 miles	C
Wentz, William	204	$1836	4 Pole	W-4 Miles	C
Westhoff, Arnold	26	$2210	Mud, adj B'ville	E-side	C
Wheeler, Eli	522	$1044	Porter Fk of Mud	S-35 miles	C
Wheeler, James	50	$162.50	Sugartree Fk/Mud	SE-30 miles	C
Wheeler, James-Estate	40	$120	Lf side Sugartree	SE-30 miles	C
Wheeler, John	125	$125	Wilson Br/Trace Fk	S-25 miles	C
Wheeler, Reason	218	$1199	Mud	E-12 miles	C
Wheeler, William					
& Joseph	363.3	$363.33	Mud	SE-18 miles	C
White, James H.	40	$40	West Br of Lit Guy	NE-18 miles	C
White, John F.	400	$400	Lit Guy	NE-15 miles	C
Wilkinson, Benjamin	62.5	$125	Br of Buffalo	SE-20 miles	C
" "	150	$300	Buffalo	SE-16 miles	C
" "	118	$118	Buffalo	SE-16 miles	C
Wilkinson, John S.	174	$522	Buffalo Ck	SE-16 miles	C
" "	50	$100	Buffalo Ck	SE-16 miles	C
" "	195.5	$195.50	Straight Fk of Buffalo	SE-16 miles	C
deed from H. McFarland					

PERSON TAXED	ACRES	VALUE	LOCATION	DISTANCE TO COURT HOUSE	COUNTY RESIDES
Williams, George W.	26.5	$26.50	Davis Ck	SW-4 miles	C
Williams, James Sr.	75	$150	Charley Ck	E-16 miles	C
Williams, Jonathan-Estate	180	$720	Mid Fk of Mud	SE-31 miles	C
Williams, Mourning	25	$100	Trace Ck	SE-12 miles	C
Williams, William	666	$10,656	OH	W-14 miles	C
" "	1 1/4	$25	4 Pole	W-14 miles	C
Wilson, Asa L.	140	$980	Mud	E-5 miles	C
" "	80	$400	Mud	E-4 miles	C
" "					
& Isaac (Wilson)	150	$450	Wild Cat Ck of Mud	E-2 miles	C
Wilson, James	400	$5600	Guy	W-4 miles	C
" "	125	$406	Br of Russell Ck	W-4 miles	C
" "	85	$1445	Guy	W-3 miles	C
" "	120	$1800	Guy	W-3 miles	C
" "	72	$1225	Guy	W-3 miles	C
" "	105	$1036	Guy	W-3 miles	C
" "	15	$225	Guy	E-2 miles	C
Wilson, John-Estate					
& J. Morris	63.6	$509.33	Teays Valley	E-14 miles	C
" same	69.3	$208.80	Teays Valley	E-14 miles	C
Winch, Tomas B.	358	$787.66	Lit Guy	NE-15 miles	C
Wingo, Abner	2	$1220	Mud, adj B'ville	E-side	C
Winters, Esther	14	$42	9 Mile of OH	N-9 mile	C
Witcher, Jeremiah	805	$1610	Mid Fk Mud/d Thos.Eagleston	SE-20 m	C
" "	28	$84	Falls of Guy	SE-22 miles	C
" "	4 1/2	$9	Mid Fk of Mud	SE-20 miles	C
" "	30	$236.40	Mid Fk of Mud	Se-22 miles	C
" "	500	$3545	Mud-deed James C. Black	SE-20 miles	C
Wooten, Winston	25	$50	Head of Sanders Ck	E-10 miles	OH
Woodyard, Presley	37	$185	7 Mile of OH	N-5 miles	Cabell
Woodyard, W. C.	30	$93	7 Mile of OH	N-5 miles	C
Wright, Edward D.	150	$1500	Guy	W-5 miles	C
Wright, William O.	1025	$1025	Davis Ck	W-1 mile	C ('65)
Wysong, Creed	415	$1660	Mud	SE-16 miles	C
" "	100	$200	Mud	SE-22 miles	C
" "	60	$120	Mud	SE-22 miles	C
- Y -					
Yates, William W.	200	$2000	Mud	E-16 miles	C
Young, James	50	50	Charleys Ck	E-13 miles	C

PERSONS WITH TOWN LOTS

PERSON TAXED	LOT	VALUE	LOCATION	COUNTY
Ayres, Mahlon	#21	$300	Guyandotte	C
" "	#20-part	$50	Guy	
Baker, John C.	#4	$225.39	Guy -deed fron Wm. Hite	Cabell
Baumgardner, John B.	#16-NE 1/2	$600	Barboursville	C
Beekman, Lewis	#28-1/3	$650	Guy	C
Beuhring, F.G.L.-Estate	#31-1/5	$200	B'ville	C
Brown, Vina, Sarah C. & A. J. Brown & John Brown				OH
& J.T. Dusenberry	#22	$150	Guy - 1/2 to Dusenberry	C
Buffington, James R.	#25,26,27	$9000	Guy	C
" "	#4	$2350	Guy	C
" "	#2 - 1/3	$950	Guy	C
" "	#14	$150	Guy	C
Buffington, Peter C.	#19 - 1/2	$350	Guy	C
" "	#26 - S 1/2	$2600	Guy	C
Buffington, William-Estate	#7	$250	Guy	C
" "	#8	$800	Guy	C
Campbell, John	part Pub Sq	$300	Barboursville	C
Carroll, Thomas	#34	$900	Guy	C
Carter, Henry	#11	$700	Guy	C
Chapman, A.M.	#23	$500	Guy	C
Clarke, Lyman	#33 - part	$1000	Guy	C
Clarke, S.M	#28 - 1/3	$950	Guy	C
Conner, James -Estate	#20	$2000	B'ville	C
Curry, William	#16	$125	Hamlin	C
Dietz, Hugo	#2-1/8 & #1	$2300	Guy	C
Dietz, Mary	#4	$675	Guy	C
Dietz, Rodolph	#10	$800	Guy	C
Dunkle, A.J.	#16 - 1/3	$300	Guy	OH('63)
Dusenberry, J.T.	#20	$1200	Guy	C
Everett, John S.	#7	$1375	Guy	C
Everett, J.S., Wellington & others	#10	$250	Guy	C
Everettt, Richmond-Estate	#30 - 1/3	$100	B'ville	C
Farrell, Francis M.	#33 (17ft)	$50	B'ville	C
" "	#30	$400	B'ville	C
Flowers, Alford C.	#13 (77')	$250	Guy	C
Flowers, Ezra H.	#23 - 1/4	$125	Guy	C
" "	#7 - 1/4	$350	Guy	C

PERSONS WITH TOWN LOTS

PERSON TAXED	LOT	VALUE	LOCATION	COUNTY
Fuller, Sylvester	#7	$250	Guy	C
" "	#15	$700	Guy	C
Gardner, Benjamin(Est.)	#29	$1200	B'ville	KY ('63)
" "	#19 - 1/2	$800	B'ville	KY
" "	#36	$50	B'ville	KY
" "	#20	$100	B'ville	KY
Grass, Albina	#6	$550	Guy	C
Hagan, William H.	#1	$150	B'ville	C
" "	#2	$150	B'ville	C
" "	#10	$150	B'ville	C
" "	#25	$150	B'ville	C
" "	#4	$150	B'ville	C
" "	fraction Lot B	$150	B'ville	C
Harrison, Greenville	#28	$150	B'ville	C
Hatfield, John T.	#22 - 1/2	$700	B'ville	C
Hatfield, Thomas	#12	$650	B'ville	C
" "	#11	$150	B'ville	C
Hayslip, Thomas J.	#16 - 1/3	$1000	Guy	C
Hazeltine, Kendall	#6	$250	Guy	C
Hibbens, John	#33 (55')	$340	B'ville	C
" "	#37	$185	B'ville	C
" "	#22	$50	B'ville	C
" "	#38	$250	B'ville	C
Hiltbruner, Jacob	#2 & #3 -1/2	$2500	Guy	C
Hite, Francis	#1 - 6/7	$1000	Guy	C
Hite, John B.	#31	$1600	B'ville	C
" "	#25	$1100	B'ville	C
" "	#30	$800	B'ville	C
Hite, John W.	#13 - 2/3	$3500	B'ville	C
Hohenberger, Joseph	#22 - part	$350	B'ville	C
Holderby, Robert S.	#5 -1/4	$675	B'ville	C
Holley, James A.	#13	$25	Hamlin	C
" "	#14	$25	Hamlin	C
" "	#15	$25	Hamlin	C
" "	#12	$125	Hamlin	C
Houskins, Francis	#33 (28')	$700	Guy	C
Kilgore & Seamons	#2	$200	Guy	C
" "	#10	$200	Guy	C

PERSONS WITH TOWN LOTS

PERSON TAXED	LOT	VALUE	LOCATION	COUNTY
Kyle, Thomas	#27	$500	B'ville	C
LeTulle - heirs	#5 - 2/3	$1300	Guy	C
LeTulle, Victor-Estate	#3	$1500	Guy	C
" "	#11 - 1/2	$1400	Guy	C
LeTulle, Victor-Estate	#12	$335	Guy	C
" "	#13	$2200	Guy	C
" "	#14	$250	Guy	C
" "	#15	$200	Guy	C
LeTulle, V. Lawrence	part of #1 & 2$950		Guy	TX
Lloyd, Richard				
& R. Bell	#32	$1100	Guy (deed Lewis Sedinger)	C
Lusher, Irvin	part Pub Sq	$800	B'ville (public Square)	C
" "	part Pub Sq	$400	B'ville	C
Lusher, M.				
& J. Baumgardner	#25	$150	B'ville	C
Mather, O.W.	#19 -1/2	$600	B'ville	C
Maupin, Henry B.	#18 - part	$500	B'ville	C
Mays, Elisha	#16 - 1/2	$500	Guy	C
McComas, Elisha W.	#26	$600	B'ville	IL
McCorkle, Alex M.	#12	$1800	Guy	C
McKendree, Robert-Estate	#21	$1200	B'ville	C
McMahn, Wayne	#26 - 1/2	$600	Guy	C
Merritt, John	#1	$100	B'ville	C
Miller, George F.	#6,7,8	$900	B'ville	C
Miller, H.H.	#7	$1200	Guy	C
" "	#5	$800	Guy	C
" "	#10	$3600	Guy	C
Miller, John G.				
& C.S. Miller	#14	$100	B'ville	C
" same	#15	$700	B'ville	C
" same	#24	$400	B'ville	C
" same	part Pub Sq	$4000	B'ville	C
" same	part Pub Sq	$900	B'ville	C
Miller, William C.				
& C. & Thos. Thornburg	#17	$3200	B'ville	C
" same	#4 - 1/2	$50	B'ville	C
" same	#5 - 1/2	$50	B'ville	C
Moore, Mary	#9	$400	B'ville	C

PERSONS WITH TOWN LOTS

PERSON TAXED	LOT	VALUE	LOCATION	COUNTY
Moore, Orren	#1 - 1/2	$2600	Guy	C
" "	#20 - 2/3	$1400	Guy	C
Moore, W.B.	#23	$800	B'ville	C
" "	#18 - part	$500	B'ville	C
Morris, Joseph W.	#17	$1050	Guy	C
Ricketts, G.C.-Estate	part Pub Sq	$3100	Pub Sq in Guyandotte	C
Rogers, William C.	#8	$1600	Guy	C
Russell, John-Estate	#32	$700	Guy	C
Schapdu, Charles-Estate	#14	$400	Guy (name Chapdu)	C
Sedinger, Lewis-Estate	#27 - part	$600	Guy	C
Shelton, Anthony	#2	$400	B'ville	C
" "	#3 - 1/3	$50	B'ville	C
Shelton, Thomas	#3 - 1/2	$400	B'ville	C
Shonberger, John B.	#A - 1/4	$50	Guy	C
Simmons, Mary F.	#6, part #5	$1200	Guy	C
Smith, D. D.	#11 - 1/2	$1000	Guy	C
Smith, Josephine G.	#20	$1350	Guy	C
		(deeds from John W. Hite & E.A. Smith)		
Smith, P.C.	#14	$150	Guy	C
" "	#A - 1/4	$50	Guy	C
" "	#18	$3500	Guy	C
" "	#29	$800	Guy	C
" "	#31 - part	$200	Guy	C
" "	#22 -part	$398	Guy (deed L.M. Wolcott)	C
Smith, Whitcomb	#20 -2 parts	$1015	Guy	C
Spurlock, M.J.	#19 - 1/2	$500	Guy	C
" "	#27 - 1/2	$1000	Guy	C
Stewart, Robert	#13	$1150	Guy	C
Stone, Martha & others	#13 - 1/3	$600	Guy	C
Thornburg, Thomas	#34	$600	B'ville	C
" "	#32	$100	B'ville	C
Tiernan, John	#21	$500	Guy	OH
" "	#26 - 1/2	$450	Guy	OH
Walton, Eli H.	#19 - 1/2	$450	Guy	C
Ward, Walton-Estate	#33 -1/4	$400	Guy	C
Watson, N.A.	#16 - 1/2	$300	B'ville (deed Thos.Dundas heirs)	C
Wellington, Erastus-Est.	#8, 9	$950	Guy	C
Wigner, John	#24 - 1/2	$400	Guy	C

PERSONS WITH TOWN LOTS

PERSON TAXED	LOT	VALUE	LOCATION	COUNTY
Williams, George W.	#10	$150	B'ville	C
" "	#13	$2000	B'ville	C
Witcher, Jeremiah	#18 - 1/4	$1200	B'ville (deed M.S.Thornburg)	C
Wood, Avis	#22 - part	$350	Guy	C

DEATHS INDICATED IN THESE TAX BOOKS

Adkins, Edward 1861
Adkins, Jacob 1861
Alford, George 1861
Alford, William 1861
Ashworth, Isaac 1861
Ashworth, Jonathan 1861
Barnett, Andrew 1861
Barrett, Edward 1861
Beuhring, F.G.L. 1861
Black, Adam 1859
Blake, Peter 1861
Blankenship, Margaret '61
Bowen, Abner 1861
Browdowski, Stanislow 1861
Brumfield, John 1861
Buffington, Wm. 1861
Campbell, John 1861
Chapman, Philemon 1861
Childers, Thomas 1861
Conner, James 1861
Conners, Wm. 1861
Cremeans, Moses 1861
Cyrus, James 1861
Davis, Calvin 1861
Drown, Benjamin 1858
Dusenberry, Wm. C. 1861
Everett, Richmond 1861
Frampton, Isaac 1861
Gardner, Benjamin 1861
Goff, Leonard 1861
Griffon, John W. 1861
Gue, Lindsey 1861
Hagley, George 1861
Handley,Thomas 1861
Heath, Nelson B. 1861
Holdryde, John 1861
Hudson, Lewis 1861
Jenkins, Cary 1861
Jenkins, William 1861
Johnson, Smoot 1861
King, John 1861
Laidley, John 1861
Lawson, Anthony 1857
Leanaing, Thomas 1861
LeTulle, Victor 1861
Malcom, Robert 1861
McAlister, Richard 1861
McComas, Elisha 1861
McComas, Thomas 1861
McComas, William 1861
McKendree, Robert 1861
McWarter, James 1861
Morrison, James 1861
Nelson, James 1861
Nelson, Thomas 1861
Patton, Robertson 1861
Pauley, Washington 1861
Perry, William 1861
Porter, David 1861
Porter, John 1861
Ray, Isaiah 1861
Reece, Joseph 1861
Ricketts, G.C. 1861
Rigg, Thomas H. 1861
Russell, James 1857
Samuels, John 1861
Scott, D.B. 1861
Scott, Sanford 1861
Schapdu, Charles 1861
Sedinger, Lewis 1861
Shelton, Henry W. 1861
Smallridge, John 1861
Smith, Jackson 1861
Smith, Peter 1861
Snodgrass, James 1861
Spurlock, Alex 1861
Stephenson, Calvary M.'61
Swann, Thomas 1861
Syrus, James 1857
Thompson, Patterson 1861
Thornburg, Solomon 1861
Tiernan, John 1861
Ray, John 1858
Wallace, Benjamin 1861
Ward, Walton 1861
Webb, James 1861
Wellington, Erastus 1861
Wheeler, James 1861
Williams, Jonathan 1861
Wilson, John 1861
Wintz, Michael 1858

CABELL TAX LANDS 1861-1865

LOT HOLDERS - GUYANDOTTE 1861

Public Square
G.C. Ricketts, Est.
#1 Francis Hite
Hugo Dietz
Lawrence Letulle
Orren Moore
#2 James R. Buffington
Hugo Dietz
#3 Jacob Hiltbruner
V. Letulle, Est.
#4 John C. Baker
James R. Buffington
Mary Dietz
#5 V. Letulle, Est.
H.H. Miller
Mary Simmons
#6 Albina Grass
Kendall Hazeltine
Mary Simmons
#7 Wm. C. Buffington
John S. Everett
Ezra Flowers
Sylvester Flowers
H.H. Miller
#8 William C. Buffington
William C. Rogers
Erastus Wellington, Est.
#9 Erastus Wellington, Est.
#10 Rodolph Dietz
J.S. Everett
E. Wellington
#11 Henry Carter
V. Letulle, Est.
D.D. Smith
#12 Victor Letulle, Est.
Alex McCorkle
#13 Victor Letulle, Est.
Alford C. Flowers
Robert Stewart
Martha Stone
#14 Victor Letulle, Est.
James R. Buffington
Charles Chapdu, Est.
P.C. Smith
#15 Victor Letulle, Est.
Sylvester Flowers
#16 A.J. Dunkle
Thomas J. Hayslip
Elisha Mays
#17 Joseph W. Morris
#18 P.C. Smith
#19 Peter C. Buffington
M.J. Spurlock
Eli H. Walton
#20 Orren Moore
Mahlon Ayers
T. Dusenberry
Josephine G. Smith
Whitcomb Smith
#21 Mahlon Ayers
John Tiernan
#22 Brown Heirs
T. Dusenberry
P.C. Smith
Avis Wood
#23 A.M. Chapman
Ezra H. Flowers
#24 John Wigner
#25 James R. Buffington
#26 James R. Buffington
Peter C. Buffington
Wayne McMahan
John Tiernan
#27 James R. Buffington
Lewis Sedinger, Est.
M.J. Spurlock
#28 Lewis Beekman
S.M. Clark
#29 P.C. Smith
#30
#31 P.C. Smith
#32 John Russell, Est.
Richard Boyd
R. Bell
#33 Lyman Clarke
Francis Houskins
Thomas Carroll
Walton Ward

#A John B. Shonberger
P.C. Smith

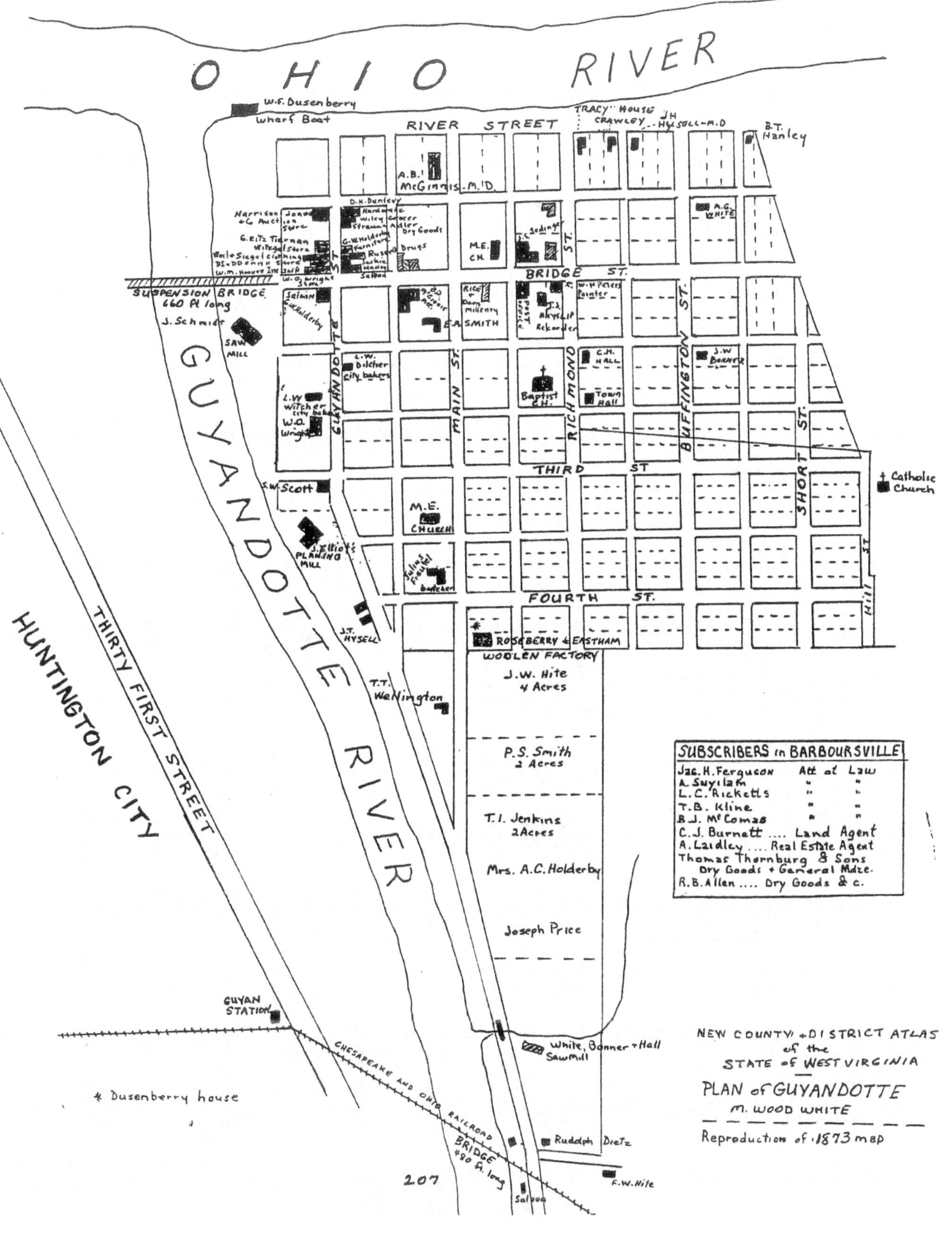
OHIO RIVER
W.F. Dusenberry
Wharf Boat
RIVER STREET
TRACY HOUSE
CRAWLEY
B.T. Hanley
A.B. McGinnis. M.D.
A.G. WHITE
M.E. CH.
BRIDGE ST.
SUSPENSION BRIDGE
660 Ft long
J. Schmidt
SAW MILL
E.A. SMITH
T.J. Hyslip Recorder
C.H. HALL
Town Hall
J.W. Bonner
L.W. Dilcher city bakery
L.W. Witcher city bakery
W.O. Wright
Baptist CH.
GUYANDOTTE
MAIN ST.
RICHMOND
BUFFINGTON ST.
SHORT ST.
THIRD ST
Catholic Church
S.W. Scott
M.E. CHURCH
J. Elliot's PLANING MILL
butcher
FOURTH ST.
Hill ST
J.T. HYSELL
ROSEBERRY & EASTHAM
WOOLEN FACTORY
J.W. Hite
4 Acres
T.T. Wellington
P.S. Smith
2 Acres
T.I. Jenkins
2 Acres
Mrs. A.C. Holderby
Joseph Price
GUYANDOTTE RIVER
THIRTY FIRST STREET
HUNTINGTON CITY
GUYAN STATION
White, Bonner + Hall
Saw Mill
CHESAPEAKE AND OHIO RAILROAD
BRIDGE
480 ft. long
Rudolph Dietz
F.W. Hite
Saloon
* Dusenberry house
SUBSCRIBERS in BARBOURSVILLE
Jas. H. Ferguson Att at Law
A. Suylam " "
L.C. Ricketts " "
T.B. Kline " "
B.J. McComas " "
C.J. Burnett .... Land Agent
A. Laidley .... Real Estate Agent
Thomas Thornburg & Sons
Dry Goods + General Mdze.
R.B. Allen .... Dry Goods &c.
NEW COUNTY + DISTRICT ATLAS
of the
STATE of WEST VIRGINIA
PLAN of GUYANDOTTE
M. WOOD WHITE
Reproduction of 1873 map

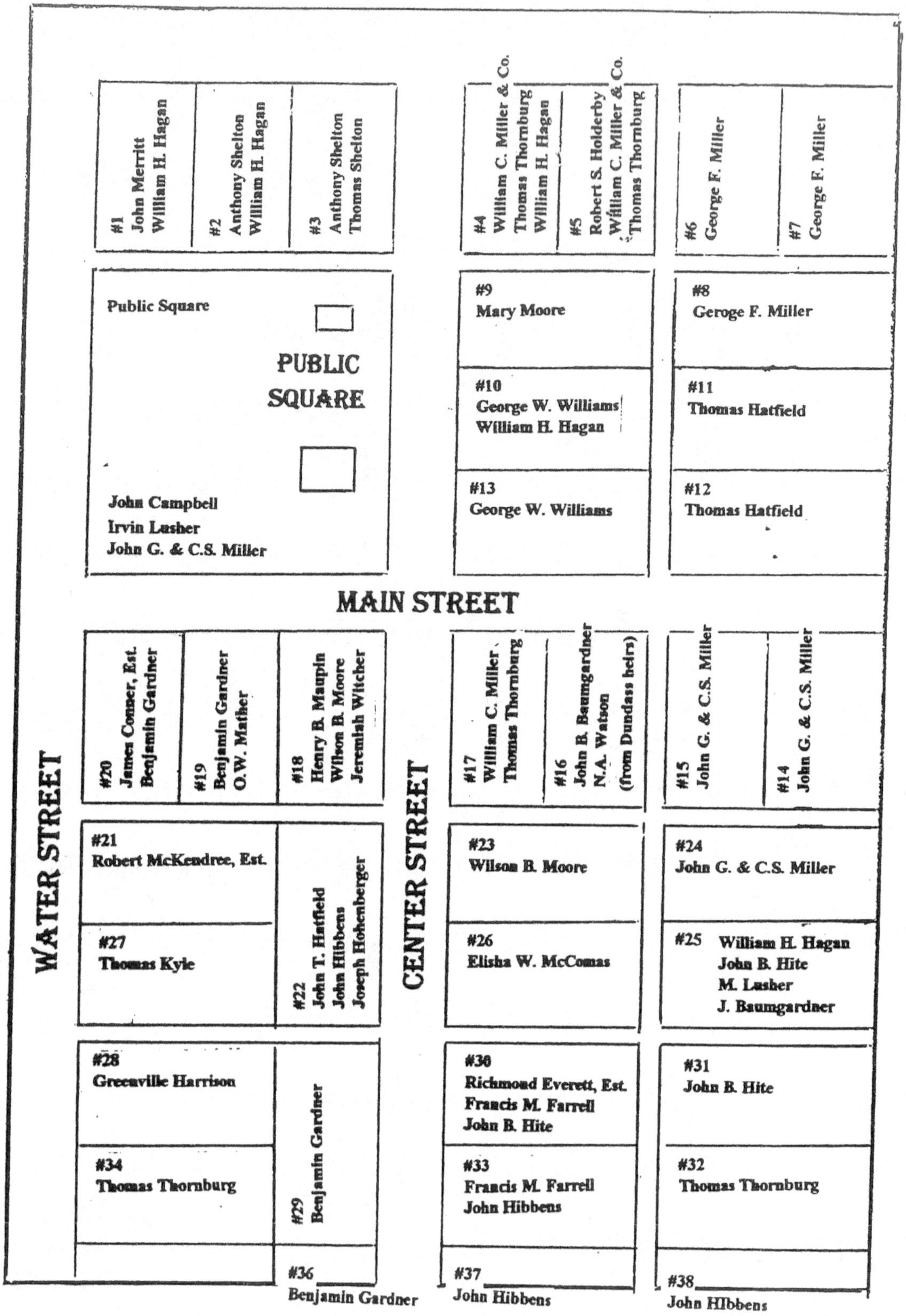

#1 John Merritt William H. Hagan

#2 Anthony Shelton William H. Hagan

#3 Anthony Shelton Thomas Shelton

#4 William C. Miller & Co. Thomas Thornburg William H. Hagan

#5 Robert S. Holderby William C. Miller & Co. Thomas Thornburg

#6 George F. Miller

#7 George F. Miller

Public Square

PUBLIC SQUARE

John Campbell
Irvin Lasher
John G. & C.S. Miller

#9 Mary Moore

#8 Geroge F. Miller

#10 George W. Williams
William H. Hagan

#11 Thomas Hatfield

#13 George W. Williams

#12 Thomas Hatfield

MAIN STREET

#20 James Conner, Est. Benjamin Gardner

#19 Benjamin Gardner O.W. Mather

#18 Henry B. Maupin Wilson B. Moore Jeremiah Witcher

#17 William C. Miller Thomas Thornburg

#16 John B. Baumgardner N.A. Watson (from Dundass heirs)

#15 John G. & C.S. Miller

#14 John G. & C.S. Miller

WATER STREET

CENTER STREET

#21 Robert McKendree, Est.

#27 Thomas Kyle

#22 John T. Hatfield John Hibbens Joseph Hohenberger

#23 Wilson B. Moore

#24 John G. & C.S. Miller

#26 Elisha W. McComas

#25 William H. Hagan
John B. Hite
M. Lasher
J. Baumgardner

#28 Greenville Harrison

#34 Thomas Thornburg

#29 Benjamin Gardner

#30 Richmond Everett, Est.
Francis M. Farrell
John B. Hite

#33 Francis M. Farrell
John Hibbens

#31 John B. Hite

#32 Thomas Thornburg

#36 Benjamin Gardner

#37 John Hibbens

#38 John HIbbens

TOWN OF BARBOURSVILLE 1861

www.ingramcontent.com/pod-product-compliance
Lightning Source LLC
LaVergne TN
LVHW061241100826
845148LV00008B/1000